SERVICE DELIVERY BY BANKS IN RURAL AREAS

(A Comparative Study of Selected Banks in Karimnagar District)

SERVICE DELIVERY BY BANKS IN RURAL AREAS

(A Comparative Study of Selected Banks in Karimnagar District)

BY

E. HARI PRASAD

KALPAZ

First Published, 2018

Published by

Kalpaz Publications
C-30, Satyawati Nagar,
Delhi – 110052
E-mail: kalpaz@hotmail.com
Ph.: 9212142040

Printed at: G. Print Process, Delhi

Cataloging in Publication Data—DK
Courtesy: D.K. Agencies (P) Ltd. <docinfo@dkagencies.com>

Hari Prasad, E., author.
Service Delivery by Commercial Banks: A Study of Rural Customers / by E. Hari Prasad.
pages cm
Includes bibliographical references.
ISBN 9789386397027

1. Banks and banking—Customer services—India—Karimnagar (District) 2. Consumers—India—Karimnagar (District)—Attitudes. I. Title.

LCC HG1616.C87H37 2017 | DDC 332.1068 23

Dedication to my Father

Late Sri Erakachedu Ranga Rao

Contents

Acknowledgements

I express my deep sense of gratitude and indebtedness to my supervisor and guide *Dr Sri. G.V. Bhavani Prasad* garu, professor, University College of Commerce and Management, Kakatiya University, Warangal for his invaluable encouragement, helpful suggestions, moral support and affection. His painless criticisms and suggestions made this work a reality. His priceless and meticulous supervision at each and every phase of work inspired me in innumerable ways.

My special thanks to Dean, Department of Commerce and Business Management, Dr B.R. Ambedkar Open University, Hyderabad and *Dr Y. Kiranmayi* garu Professor and Head, Department of Business Management, Dr B.R. Ambedkar Open University, Hyderabad, *Professor A. Sudhakar* garu Professor Department of Commerce and Business Management and Registrar Dr B.R. Ambedkar Open University, Hyderabad, Dr Anand Pawar, Assistant Professor, Mr Malla Reddy, Associate Professor and Mr Ravindranath Soloman, Assistant Professor Dept. of Commerce, Dr B.R. Ambedkar Open University, Hyderabad for their continuous encouragement and suggestions.

I express my sincere thanks to the officials of Reserve Bank India for providing the chance to work on the area of 'service quality of banks in rural areas'.

My special thanks to chairman and managing director (CMD) of SBH, CMD of HDFC Bank and CMD of DGB for granting their permission to undertake this research work in their banks.

My sincere thanks are due to *Sri Vijaypal Reddy* garu, Regional Manager, SBH Karimnagar Region, *Sri Karunakar Reddy* garu, Regional Manager, Telangana Grameena Bank, Karimnagar Region, and *Sri Madhu Sudhan Hegde* garu, Head, Telangan and AP Region, HDFC Bank for granting permission to collect needed data from their respective bank branches in the Karimnagar district for this study.

My thanks are also due to Mr Gunta Ashok, Manager HDFC bank for his kind cooperation in non-academic matters during the research work.

It is privilege to extend my thanks to branch managers of all the banks who extended their cooperation in collection of needed data from their respected branch customers.

I specially express my deep sense of thanks to Mr M Ratan Jyoth, Chief Librarian, Satavahana University, Karimnagar and other staff of University Library Satavahana University, Karimnagar for their help during the research work.

I specially express my deep sense of thanks to Dr Meesala Appalayya Principal, Ambedkar Institute of Management Sciences, Hyderabad, for his suggestions, help and moral support during the research work.

I will carry in my memory the company of Sri L.K.B.M Sarma, retired lecturer in Political Science from S.R.R. Degree and PG College Karimnagar, for his spiritual guidance and moral support time to time in getting needed strengths and courage and his financial assistance at the time of data collection and continuous support.

I express my deep sense of gratitude to Mr P. Mohan Prasad, Head, Department of Statistics, Vivekananda Degree and PG College, Karimnagar, for his co-operation during this research study.

I am beholden to my mother Laxmi Devi, and express my appreciation to my wife and son and my sister and bother-in-law.

I specially express my deep sense of thanks to my brothers and sisters-in-law for their understanding, patience and active cooperation, constant moral support and inspiration in fulfilling my dream of completing the Ph.D. thesis.

I express my Special thanks to Mrs Mamatha H Rao, my sister, and Mr K. Hanumanth Rao, Principal, Paramitha High School, for his constant support and help at different points of time.

It is my privilege to extend thank to my friends Mr E. Srinivas Raju, software engineer, Mr K. Kumar Swamy, Mr Sunil for their continuous support.

I specially express many thanks to my friendly guru Shri Koredi Narahari and his family for their immense help which they rendered me at the critical time.

I thank to Mr Adithya, my student who extended his cooperation during this research work.

My thanks to Mr Ramakrishna, computer engineer and my student, for his extension prompt cooperation by servicing my computer immediately.

Last, but not the least, I thank all those who have directly or indirectly assisted me for completion of this thesis.

Finally, I would like to pray the **GOD** to give me the strength and drive to make use of the knowledge, I acquired from my teachers and of the insight I gained living in INDIA, to help people in my country and the world at large.

— E. HARI PRASAD

List of Tables

Chapter - 1

Introduction

Introduction to Service

A **service** is the action of doing something for someone or something. It is largely intangible (i.e. not material). A product is tangible (i.e. material) since one can touch it and own it. A service tends to be an experience that is consumed at the point where it is purchased, and cannot be owned since is quickly perishes. A person could go to a café one day and have excellent service, and then return the next day and have a poor experience. Information scientists are often provide services (example advice, or searches), instead of distinct physical products. Marketing experts acknowledge that marketing a service is more difficult than marketing a tangible product. They identify the following characteristic of services:

Right of ownership: Service cannot be owned by the user. The user can merely experience it. For example, an engineer may provide service to air-conditioning, but customer does not own the service, the engineer or his equipment. Customer cannot sell it once it has been consumed, and do not take ownership of it.

Intangible: Service cannot have a real, physical presence as does a product. For example, motor insurance may have a certificate, but the financial service itself cannot be touched i.e. it is intangible.

Inseparable: Service is not separable from the point where it is consumes, and from the provider of the service. For example, it cannot take a live theatre performance home to consume it (a DVD of the same performance would be a product, not a service).

Perishable: Service once effected, it cannot be repeated in exactly the same way. For example, once a 100 meters Olympic final has been run, there will be no other for 4 more years, and even then it will be staged in a different place with many different finalists.

Table 1.1: Characteristics of Services Compared to Goods

Goods	*Services*	*Resulting Implications*
Tangible	Intangible	Services cannot be inventoried. Services cannot be readily displayed. Services cannot be patented.
Standardised	Heterogeneity	Service quality depends on many uncontrollable factors.
Production separate from consumption	Simultaneous production and consumption	Customer participates in and affects the transactions. Decentralisation may be required.
Nonperishable	Perishable	Services cannot be resold or returned.

Variability (or) Heterogeneity: Since the human involvement of service provision means that no two services will be completely identical. For example, servicing customer's car at different intervals might see different levels of customer satisfaction, or speediness of work.

Apart from above features of service, it is important to highlight some behavioural characteristics of service quality that will help to design and monitor services[1].

1. Human Factors and Behavioural Characteristics,
2. Timeliness Characteristics,
3. Service Non-Conformity Characteristics,
4. Facility-Related Characteristics.

Human Factors and Behavioural Characteristics: Service quality is largely influenced by the attitude and behaviour of the provider. Since providers and customers are part of product or service, their behaviour affects the quality of service. To improve the quality of service, the human factors such as eagerness to help, thoughtfulness, complacency and courtesy must be developed through proper training of staff. As far as customer behaviour is concerned, it is beyond the control of company providing the service. The expectations and perceptions of customers' greatly influence the quality of services.

Timely Characteristics: Timeliness characteristics of a service associate with providing service within a specified span of time. Service that is not used during specified time cannot be stored in future. For example, empty beds in a Hospital during certain days of a month cannot be saved for use in the latter month. The factor such as time to order the service, the waiting time before the service is performed; the time to serve and the post-service time are significant for customer satisfaction and service quality improvement.

Service Non-Conformity Characteristics: This characteristic highlights the variation in providing service from a specified performance level i.e. non-conformity of service from its ideal level. For example, number of errors in processing per 100 vouchers by bank staff and the number of data entry errors per 1000 key strokes by a data entry operator, the number of complaints per 100 guests in hotel, represents no-conformity characteristics. For improvement of service quality and customer satisfaction, non-conformities (errors) must be eliminated completely.

Facility-Related Characteristics: Customer satisfaction is also influenced by the physical characteristics of the facilities with a service and its delivery. For example, an uncomfortable bed in a hotel room, unavailability of a swimming pool in a hotel, insufficient leg room in an aircraft, and shabby appearance of a receptionist in hotel or bank and lack of internet facilities in an educational institute deteriorate the service level.

Services Sector Contribution to the Indian Economy

India ranks fifteenth in the services output in the world. It provides employment to around 23 per cent of the total workforce in the country. The various sectors under the Services Sector in India are construction, trade, hotels, transport, restaurant, communication and storage, social and personal services, community, insurance, financing, business services, and real estate.

The services sector in India has the biggest share in the country's GDP accounts for around 54.1 per cent in 2005. The Services Sector contributed only 27.5 per cent to the Indian GDP in 1950-51. Further the Indian Services Sector's share in the country's GDP has increased from 40.69 per cent in 1990-1991 to around 49.3 per cent in 2000 - 01. Further it has increased to 56.8 per cent by the end of the year 2007-08, 54.8 per cent in 2008-09 and in 2009-10 it recorded 55.3 per cent. This shows that the Services Sector in India accounts for over half of the country's GDP. The following Table 1.2 presents the real GDP growth rate during 2004 – 2014.

Table 1.2: India's real GDP statistics at Factor Cost at 1st Dec. 2014

Indicator	*2004*	*2005*	*2006*	*2007*	*2008*	*2009*	*2010*	*2011*	*2012*	*2013*	*2014*
Real GDP growth (per cent growth)	7.97	7.05	9.48	9.57	9.32	6.72	8.59	8.91	6.69	4.74	4.74

Source: Planning Commission, Govt. of India.

Sector-Wise Contribution to GDP in India

The contribution to the country's GDP is very high in numbers. Various sectors falling under the India GDP composition includes food processing, transportation equipment, petroleum, textiles, software, agriculture, mining, machinery, chemicals, steel, cement and many others. Agriculture is the pre-dominant occupation in India, employing more than 50 per cent of the population. The service sector accounts for employing 28.1 per cent while the industrial sector accounts for 17.8 per cent. The details of sector-wise contribution to GDP since 1950 are presented in the Table 1.3.

Table 1.3: Sector - Wise GDP and Employment Shares in India

Year	*Shares in GDP (per cent)*			*Shares in Employment (per cent)*		
	Agriculture	*Industry*	*Service*	*Agriculture*	*Industry*	*Service*
1950-51	59.2	13.3	27.5	NA	NA	NA
1960-61	54.8	16.6	28.6	NA	NA	NA
1970-71	46.3	21.6	32.1	74	11.2	14.8
1980-81	39.2	23.7	36.6	68.1	13.7	18.2
1990-91	32.2	27.2	40.6	63.9	14.9	21.2
2000-01	24	26.7	49.3	60.8	17.1	22.1
2004-05	20.5	27.1	52.1	56.9	17.5	25.6
2005-06	19.7	26.2	54.1	55.7	17.8	26.5
2006-07	20.5	24.4	55.1	54.6	18.1	27.3
2007-08	19.5	23.7	56.8	54.1	17.8	28.1
2008-09	17.0	28.2	54.8	52	14	34
2009-10	16.1	28.6	55.3	NA	NA	NA
2010-11	18.21	26.3	55.6	NA	NA	NA
2011-12	17.86	27.22	54.92	NA	NA	NA
2012-13	17.52	26.21	56.27	49.0	20.0	31.0
2013-14	18.20	24.77	57.03	NA	NA	NA

Source: *Government of India, Economic Survey (2008-09) and Central Statistical Organisation, Handbook of Statistics of Indian Economy (2013-14).*

Financial Sector

Liberalisation, in the nineties led to the emergence of financial services sector, a new sector in the Indian economy. Fast development of information technology has changed financial environment in the country and made financial system as strong. Prior to the financial services sector, commercial banks and other financial institutions were played a dominant role in the economy and they supply to the financial needs of the economy. After the economic liberalisation financial services sector has gained high importance and, at present, this sector termed as an industry.

India has a diversified financial sector undergoing rapid expansion, both in terms of strong growth of existing financial services firms and new entities entering the market. The sector comprises commercial banks, insurance companies, non-banking financial companies, co-operatives, pension funds, mutual funds and other smaller financial entities. The banking regulator (RBI) has allowed new entities such as payments banks to be created recently thereby adding to the types of entities operating in the sector. However, the financial sector in India is predominantly a banking sector with commercial banks accounting for more than 64 per cent of the total assets held by the financial system.

Importance of Financial Sector

The Government of India has introduced several reforms to liberalise, regulate and enhance this industry. The Government and Reserve Bank of India (RBI) have taken various measures to facilitate easy access to finance for Micro, Small and Medium Enterprises (MSMEs). These measures include launching Credit Guarantee Fund Scheme for Micro and Small Enterprises, issuing guideline to banks regarding collateral requirements and setting up a Micro Units Development and Refinance Agency (MUDRA). With a combined push by both government and private sector, India is undoubtedly one of the world's most vibrant capital markets.

The size of banking assets in India reached US$ 1.4 trillion as on August 21, 2015 and is expected to touch US$ 28.5 trillion by FY25. Banks total credit stood at US$ 1 trillion. The Association of Mutual Funds in India (AMFI) data show that assets of the mutual fund industry have hit an all-time high of about ₹ 12.5 trillion (US$ 188 billion) as of August 2015. During April 2014 to February 2015 period, the life insurance industry recorded a new premium income of ₹ 90,579 crore or US$ 13.6 billion. The general insurance industry grew at a rate of 9.3 per cent at ₹ 0.84 trillion (US$ 12.6 billion) in 2014-15 from ₹ 0.77 trillion (US$ 11.6 billion) in 2013-14.

India is the fifteenth largest insurance market in the world in terms of premium volume, and has the potential to grow exponentially in the coming years. Life insurance penetration in India is just 3.9 per cent of GDP, more than doubled from 2000. A fast growing economy, rising income levels and improving life expectancy rates are some of the many favorable factors that are likely to boost growth in the sector in the coming years. The financial services sector has been an important contributor to the country gross domestic product (GDP) accounting for nearly 6 per cent share in 2014-15.

Financial Services

Services such have the financial nature are called as financial services. The term financial services means services provided by banking and non-banking finance companies established under the Reserve Bank of India Act,1934, regulated by the Reserve Bank of India; insurance companies established under the Insurance Regulatory and Development Authority Act,1999, regulated by the Insurance Regulatory and Development Authority, and other entities established under the Securities and Exchange Board of India Act,1992, regulated by the Securities and Exchange Board of India.

Financial services refer to services provided by the finance industry. The finance industry consists of a broad range of organisations that deal with the management of money. These financial services are a part of the financial system and include financial institutions (banks, credit card companies, insurance companies, consumer finance companies, stock brokers, investment funds and some government sponsored enterprises), markets, instruments and services that facilitate the mobility of funds. All these are interrelated.

Functions of Financial Services

1. Financial services assist in mobilising the funds from supply area (household investors) to demand area (business firms, individuals, government etc.).
2. Financial services help in employing the funds effectively.
3. Financial services speed up the economic development of the nation.
4. Financial services provide need-based services.

Classification of Financial Services: Financial services are classified into two categories;

Asset/Fund Based Services	*Non-Fund /Fee Based Financial Services*
1. Lease financing	1. Merchant banking
2. Hire purchase and consumer credit	2. Credit rating
3. Bill discounting	3. Stock broking
4. Venture capital	4. Custodial services
5. Housing finance	5. Loan syndication
6. Insurance services	6. Securitisation
7. Factoring	
8. Forfeiting	
9. Mutual fund	

Players in Indian Financial System: The present financial system include following players;

1. Reserve Bank of India (RBI)
2. Commercial Banks
3. Development Financial Institutions

4. Insurance Companies
5. Public Sector Financial Institutions
6. Mutual Funds
7. Non-Banking Financial Institutions
8. Asset Reconstruction Companies
9. Capital Market Intermediaries
10. Credit Information Companies.

Banking Services

Banking services refer to various ways in which a bank can assist a customer, such as operating accounts, making transfers, paying standing orders, selling foreign currency etc.

Products and Services of Banking Industry: The products of the banking industry broadly include deposit products, credit products and customized banking services. All banks offer the same kind of products with minor variations. The basic differentiation is attained through quality of service and the delivery channels that are adopted.

Products and Services

Deposits	***Credits***	***Other Customised services and Products***
• Term Deposits	• Term Loans	• Guarantee and Advisory Services
• Demand Deposits	• Cash Credits, Overdrafts	• Derivatives and other Treasury Products
• Current Deposits	• Bill Purchased and Discounted	• Investment and Insurance
• Savings Deposits		• Other Services

Importance of Banking Services

Commercial banks are dealers in money at one side and leaders in economic development at another side. They store houses of the country's wealth and also the reservoirs of resources necessary for economic development. They play a vital role in the economic development of a nation. A well-developed banking system is essential for the economic development of a country.

1. Motivate people to save,
2. Channelise household savings into productive capital,
3. Facilitate productive use of surpluses to generate employment and promote economic welfare of the people, and
4. Provides risk-free income to depositors.

Role of Banks in Economic Development

1. **Mobilising Saving for Capital Formation:** The commercial banks mobilise savings from public through network of branch banking and channelise them into productive investments. Thus, they help in the capital formation of a developing country.
2. **Financing Industry:** The commercial banks finance the industrial sector in the form of a short-term, medium-term and long-term loans. In India, the commercial banks undertake short-term and medium-term financing of small scale industries, and also provide hire-purchase finance. They underwrite the shares and debentures of large scale industries.
3. **Financing Trade:** The commercial banks assist in financing both internal and external trade by providing foreign exchange facilities to importers and exporters of goods.
4. **Financing Agriculture:** The commercial banks provide finance directly to farmers, small and marginal farmers and landless agricultural workers, for the modernisation and mechanisation of their farms, for the marketing of their produce, for providing irrigation facilities, for developing land, etc.
5. **Financing Consumer Activities:** The commercial banks advance loans to consumers for the purchase of such items as houses, scooters, fans, refrigerators, etc. and raise the standard of living of the people in developing countries by providing loans for consumptive activities.
6. **Financing Employment Generating Activities:** The commercial banks finance employment generating activities in developing countries. They provide loans to young entrepreneurs, medical and engineering graduates, and other technically trained persons in establishing their own business.
7. **Help in Monetary Policy:** The commercial banks help the economic development of a country by faithfully following the RBI guidelines of monetary policy to control the money supply in the country.
8. **Regional Development:** Banks play an important role in achieving balanced development in different regions of the nation. They transfer surplus capital from the developed regions to the less developed regions, where it is scarce and most demanded. This transfer of funds among regions will transform underdeveloped areas as developed areas.

Service Quality

For services, quality is the dominant element in customers' evolution, the assessment of quality is made during the service delivery process. Each customer contact is referred to as a moment of truth, an opportunity to satisfy or dissatisfy the customer. Customer satisfaction with a service can be defined by comparing perceptions of service received with expectations of service desired. When expectations are exceeded, service is perceived to be of exceptional quality and also to be a pleasant surprise. When expectations are not met, however, service quality is deemed unacceptable. When expectations are confirmed by perceived service quality is satisfactory.

Asubonteng, 1996, defined service quality as "the difference between customers' expectations for service performance prior to the service encounter and their perceptions of the service received". According to (Gefan, D., 2002), service quality is defined as the subjective comparison that customers make between the quality of the service that they want to receive and what they actually get. In other studies, service quality has been defined as the difference between customer's expectations of service provider's performance and their evaluation of the services they received. According to Woodside *et al.,* service quality is represented by answers to the questions (i) is the service delivered to customer what they expected or different from that? (ii) Was the service they received approximately what they expected or better or worse than expected? A majority of studies have sought to find the criteria that contribute to evaluate service quality in the traditional service environment. The traditional service quality can be defined as the overall evaluation of firm's service by comparing the firm's performance with the customer's general expectations of how firms should perform.

Importance of Service Quality

Service quality is considered as the most critical determinant of competitiveness for establishing and sustaining satisfying relationship with customers (Lewis, B.R., 1989). Business firms have recognised the fact that the only one best way to manage the competition is the quality differentiation. Advance technology, customer oriented corporate culture, a well designed service-system and excellent information system are the major factors that decide the superior quality of service of an organisation. Providing excellent service quality and maintaining the high customer satisfaction is the important issue and challenge facing the contemporary service industry (Hung, 2003). Service Quality is an important subject in both public and private sectors, in business and service industries (Zahari, 2008). It is the extent to which a service meets or exceeds customer needs and expectations (Dotchin, 1994).

During the past two decades, service quality has become a major area of attention to practitioners, managers and academicians and researchers because of its strong impact on business performance, lower costs, and return of investment, customer satisfaction, customer loyalty and gaining higher profit. The rapid development and competition of service quality, in both developed and developing countries has made it important for companies to measure and evaluate the quality of service encounters (Brown, 2007).

Service quality has been defined as the degree and direction between customer service expectations and perceptions (Newman, 2001). Perceived service quality is defined as how well a service satisfies the expectations of customers. Service quality has an impact on profitability and costs, as service quality influences customer satisfaction; it impacts customer retention, reduces costs and increases profitability. The important reasons why customers must be given quality service are:

A. Industry has become so competitive that customers now have variety of alternatives. If the customer is lost, it can be extremely difficult to win back the individual.

B. Most customers do not complain when they experience problems. They opt out and take their business elsewhere.

Measuring Service Quality

Banks should provide high quality services to attract customers. Quality of the service is the major concern to customers to decide themselves which bank to use to meet their financial requirements. Prior to the visiting the bank, customers' have certain expectations about the level of service quality and satisfaction they'll get from banks they open an account. Banks should have a habit of estimating these expectations to improve service quality. Thus, it is an essential part of banking business to measure the service quality by considering the customers' opinion.

Expectations of a customer of a particular bank service are influenced by factors such as personal needs, referrals from friends and relatives and past experience with the bank, reputation of the bank etc. In general, the tendency of customers is to compare the service what they 'experience' with what service they 'expect'. If the **experience does not match the expectation**, there arises a gap. Based on this assumption, the service quality model or the 'GAP model' was developed by a group of authors- **Kevin, Kristine and Berry** at Texas and North Carolina in 1985, highlights the main requirements for delivering high service quality. It identifies **five 'gaps'** that cause unsuccessful delivery. Ten determinants (Reliability, Responsiveness, Competence, Access, Courtesy, Communication, Credibility, Security, Understanding the Customer and Tangibles) that may influence the appearance of a gap were described by Parasuraman, Zeithmal and Berry.

Service Quality Gap Model (SERVQUAL)

The gap model (also known as "5 gaps model") of service quality is an important customer-satisfaction framework. In "A conceptual model of service quality and its implications for future research" (*The Journal of Marketing*, 1985), A. Parasuraman, VA Zeithmal and LL Berry identify five major gaps that face organisations seeking to meet customer's expectations of the customer experience. SERVQUAL is one of the tools used in measuring the quality of services. According to Buttle (1996), SERVQUAL is for the measuring and managing the quality of service. Asubeonteng *et al* (1996) also intimated that the model is used to measure the quality of service from the customer's point of view (Parasuraman *et al* 1988), the main aim of SERVQUAL is to have a standard and a reliable tool that can be used to measure the quality of services in different service sectors. Original ten dimensions of SERVQUAL developed by (Parasuraman, 1988) are presented bellow.

Table 1.4: Original Ten SERVQUAL Dimensions

Sl. No.	*Dimension*	*Definition*
1.	Tangibles	Appearance of physical facilities, equipment, personnel and communication materials.
2.	Reliability	Ability to perform the promised service dependably and accurately.
3.	Responsiveness	Willing to help customers and provide prompt service.
4.	Competence	Possession of the required skills and knowledge to perform the service.
5.	Courtesy	Politeness, respect consideration and friendliness of contact personnel.
6.	Credibility	Trustworthiness, believability, honesty of service provider.
7.	Security	Freedom from danger, risk of doubt.
8.	Access	Approachability and ease of contact.
9.	Communication	Keeping customers informed in language they can understand and listening to them.
10.	Understanding the Customer	Making the effort to know customers and their needs.

Source: Zeithmal, Parasuraman and Berry, (1988) ***Delivering Quality Service***, New York, Free Press, pp. 21-22 (Modified).

However, in the 1988 article, these 10 dimensions were reduced to five (Parasuraman, 1988). These are: 1. Tangibles, 2. Reliability, 3. Responsiveness, 4. Assurance and 5. Empathy. Tangibility refers to the physical environment in which the service provider operates. It comprises the physical facilities available, workers, and equipment and communication materials.

Table 1.5: Dimensions of SERVQUAL

Ten Dimension (Original Model)	*Five Dimension (Later Model)*
Tangibles	Tangibles
Reliability	Reliability
Responsiveness	Responsiveness
Competence, Courtesy, Credibility, Security	Assurance
Access Communication, Understanding the customer	Empathy

Source: Zeithmal, Parasuraman and Berry, (1988) ***Delivering Quality Service***, New York, Free Press, p. 26.

Reliability concerns the ability with which the service organisation can deliver the service dependably and accurately. Responsiveness is the preparedness of the service provider to assist customers and render quick and prompt service as possible. Assurance is in connection with knowledge and the courteous attitude of staff and their ability to instill, trust and confidence in customers. Empathy on the other hand, is about the special care and attention given to individual customers when being served.

Table 1.6: Definition of SERVQUAL Dimension

Sl. No.	*Dimension*	*Definition*
1.	Tangibles	Appearance of physical facilities, equipment, personnel and communication materials.
2.	Reliability	Ability to perform the promised service dependably and accurately.
3.	Responsiveness	Willing to help customers and provide prompt service.
4.	Assurance	Knowledge and courtesy of staff and their ability of convey trust and confidence.
5.	Empathy	Caring, individualised attention the firm provides its customers.

Source: Zeithmal, Parasuraman and Berry, (1988) ***Delivering Quality Service***, New York, Free Press, p. 26.

Based on the five service quality dimensions, two sets consists twenty-two statements or questionnaires are developed. The questionnaires are in seven-point Likert scale. One set is about customers expectations (expectation of service quality before using the service) and the other set measures customer perceptions (perceptions of quality after using the service). The difference between the two; perceptions (P) and expectations (E) constitute the service quality gap. According to (Baker, 2007), the service quality gaps are five. These include:

Gap 1: The difference between what customers really expect and what management think (perceptions) of customers expectations. This gap occurs

competence, courtesy, credibility, security, access, communication, understanding, and tangibles. For each determinant, examples of service specific criteria were provided. Additional examination and testing of the SERVQUAL scale, however, has not always been supportive of its author's claims. (Carman, J.M., 1990) and (Babakus, E., 1992) claimed that the five dimensions are not always generic and that they can vary depending on the type of service industry investigated.

Servqual Scale

The foundation for the SERVQUAL scale is the gap model proposed by Parasuraman, Zeithmal and Berry (1985, 1988). With roots in disconfirmation paradigm, the gap model maintains that satisfaction is related to the size and direction of disconfirmation of a person's experience *vis-à-vis* his/her initial expectations. As a gap or difference between customer expectations' and 'perceptions,' service quality is viewed as lying along a continuum ranging from 'ideal quality' to 'totally unacceptable quality,' with some points along the continuum representing satisfactory quality. Parasuraman, Zeithmal and Berry (1988) held that when perceived or experienced service is less than expected service, it implies less than satisfactory service quality. But, when perceived service is greater than expected service, the obvious inference is that service quality is more than satisfactory. Parasuraman, Zeithmal and Berry (1988) posited that while a negative discrepancy between perceptions and expectations — a 'performance-gap' as they call it — causes dissatisfaction, a positive discrepancy leads to consumer delight.

Based on their empirical work, they identified a set of 22 variables/items tapping five different dimensions of service quality construct. Since they operationalised service quality as being a gap between customer's expectations and perceptions of performance on these variables, their service quality measurement scale is comprised of a total of 44 items (22 for expectations and 22 for perceptions). Customers' responses to their expectations and perceptions are obtained on a 7-point Likert scale and are compared to arrive at (P-E) gap scores. The higher (more positive) the perception minus expectation score, the higher is perceived to be the level of service quality. These 22 variables of SERVQUAL scale are presented in Table - 1.7.

Table 1.7: Five Determinants of Service Quality (Zeithmal et al. 1990)

Tangibles - Appearance of physical facilities and personnel
1. Up-to-date appearing equipment
2. Visually appealing physical facilities
3. Well dressed and neat-appearing personnel
4. Visually appealing materials associated with the service

(Contd...)

Reliability - Ability to perform service dependably and accurately	
5.	Doing something by certain times promised
6.	Showing sincere interest in solving problems
7.	Performing the service right the first time
8.	Providing service at the time promised
9.	Insisting on error-free records
Responsiveness - Willingness to help and provide prompt service.	
10.	Telling you exactly when services will be performed.
11.	Giving you prompt service
12.	Willingness to help you
13.	Never being too busy to respond to requests
Assurance - Knowledge and courtesy of staff	
14.	Confidence instilling behaviour
15.	Feeling safe in your transactions
16.	Being consistently courteous
17.	Having the knowledge to answer questions
Empathy - Caring attention the firm provides its customers	
18.	Giving you individualised attention.
19.	Having convenient operating hours.
20.	Giving you personal attention.
21.	Having your best interests at heart.
22.	Understanding your specific needs.

Many criticisms have been levied against the SERVQUAL model. (Teas, R.K., 1993) One of the major shortcomings of the model is that the five service quality dimensions are not universal and cannot be applied in all service industries. They contended that it depends on the context in which the dimensions are applied since the definitions and numbers differ. The results of the study of Babakus amd Boller (1992) on an Electric and Gas Company using SERVQUAL suggested that the dimension of this industry is one and not five. In the same vein, (Crorin, J.J., 2001) conducted an investigation into the banking, pest control and dry cleaning and fast food industries and found that, there was no evidence of the five dimensions. The study of (Wirtz, 2003) in the banking industry did not support the five dimensions. Other studies of (Crorin, J.J., 2001) unveiled 18 service quality attributes at the same time as that of the latter found six dimensions.

Service Performance (SERVPERF) Model

Cronin and Taylor (1992) suggested that the conceptualisation and operationalisation of the SERVQUAL scale is inadequate. This is supported by the fact that various researchers have failed to replicate SERVQUAL's five distinct dimensions (Carman, 1990, Babakus and Boller, 1992, Cronin and Taylor, 1992) and validity (Cronin and Taylor, 1992, Teas 1993).

Cronin and Taylor (1992) reiterated that the perception-expectation gap theory of service quality is supported by little, if any, theoretical and empirical evidence as an appropriate basis for measuring service quality (Carman, 1990). Other arguments against the perception-expectation gap theory come from the notion that expectations are based on experience norms (Woodruff, R.B., 1983). Similarly (Oliver, 1980) suggested that consumers form expectations on the basis of prior experiences with a certain service delivery firm, and that these experiences affect their expectations. Expectations, however, should ideally be formed before any service encounter. In addition, studies on marketing by (Maziz, 1995), (Woodruff *et.al.* 19830), (Boloton, 1991) offered considerable support for the superiority of simple performance-based measures of service quality and suggested using only performance perceptions as a measure of service quality.

Based on their theoretical concerns, Cronin and Taylor (1992) assessed three alternatives to the original SERVQUAL scale. Specifically, they examined the original SERVQUAL scale, an importance-weighted SERVQUAL scale, a performance-based approach to the measurement of service quality called SERVPERF, and a importance-weighted version of the SERVPERF scale in four types of service firms (retail banking, pest control, dry cleaning, and fast food). The results of their oblique rotation analyses suggested that the five-dimensional structure proposed by Parasuraman *et al.* (1988) is not confirmed in any of the four research samples and that all 22 attributes loaded on one single factor. In addition, the stepwise regression analyses affirmed that the unweighted performance-based approach (SERVPERF) is the most appropriate basis for measuring service quality.

In short, arguing that the perception-expectation gap theory of service quality (Parasuraman *et al.,* 1985 and 1988, Zeithmal *et al.,* 1990) was supported by little theoretical and empirical evidence (Carman, 1990). According to Cronin and Taylor (1992), their unweighted performance-based SERVPERF instrument was a better method of measuring service quality. Their SERVPERF scale had a reliability rating ranging from 0.88 to 0.96 (i.e. indicating a high degree of internal consistency), depending on the type of service industry, and exhibited good convergent validity as well as good discriminate validity.

SERVQUAL versus SERVPERF

The SERVQUAL versus SERVPERF debate is ongoing as both groups of researchers have presented further arguments to support their respective perspectives (Parasuraman *et al.,* 1994, Cronin and Taylor, 1994).

The major arguments in favour of SERVQUAL by Parasuraman *et al.*, (1994) are:

1. There was significant theoretical and empirical research to support their perception-expectation gap theory. The writings of (Sasser, 1998) and (Lethinen, 1992) in combination with extensive research by Parasuraman *et al.*, (1985, 1988 and 1991), supported the notion that service quality as perceived by consumers stem from a comparison their expectations from a service provider with their perceptions of actual service delivery. Therefore "Perceived service quality was viewed as the level of discrepancy between consumers' perceptions and expectations."
2. The SERVQUAL instrument is designed to measure perceived service quality at a given point in time (i.e. the attitude level), regardless of the process by which it was formed. To counteract SERVQUAL, however, Cronin and Taylor (1992) cited studies (Bolton and Drew, 1991) that focused on how the perception of service quality was developed (i.e. the formation of attitudes).
3. SERVQUAL's convergent and discriminant validity was as good as SERVPERF's validity. Concerning convergent validity, the virtually identical average pair-wise correlations for SERVPERF (0.689) and SERVQUAL (0.687) with overall service quality does not warrant the conclusion that the former has higher convergent validity than the latter. Concerning discriminant validity, the average pair-wise correlations for SERVPERF with consumer satisfaction and purchase intentions (0.481) is again almost identical for SERVQUAL (0.457).

Finally, Parasuraman *et al.* (1994) argued that while their perceptions-minus-expectations measures may show less predictive power than perceptions only. Their measures do have better diagnostic value. With managers using service quality measurements being more interested in accurately identifying service quality shortfalls, the superior diagnostic value of SERVQUAL more than offsets the loss in predictive power.

The major arguments in favour of SERVPERF by Cronin and Taylor (1994) are:

1. The SERFPERF conceptualisation represents just one of a number of recent challenges to the SERVQUAL conceptualisation of service quality (Carman, 1990, Babakus and Boller, 1992). In addition, emerging literature largely has supported the performance-based paradigm over the disconfirmation-based paradigm. Instead they found that service quality is directly influenced only by perceptions of performance.

2. The disconfirmation-based SERVQUAL instrument is not measuring service quality, but rather it appears at best an operationalisation of only one of the many forms of expectancy-disconfirmation (Boulding *et al.* 1993, Oliver, 1993). Again, it was suggested that performance-based measures better reflect long-term service quality attitudes (Cronin and Taylor, 1992).
3. SERFPERF has greater construct validity when compared to SERVQUAL based on a review of the available literature and the fact that SERFPERF measures also exhibit convergent and discriminate validity. Nowhere in Cronin and Taylor (1992) is there any consideration or comparison of the convergent and discriminate validity of the SERVQUAL scale.

Finally, Cronin and Taylor (1994) asserted that since perceptions-minus-expectations measures seem to have little conceptual and empirical support, the real question that should be asked is whether or not perceptions only measures can adequately measure service quality. Based the emerging literature and their own empirical findings, they insist that the SERVPERF instrument can provide a reliable and valid tool for measuring levels of service quality.

Though SERVQUAL is criticised on a lot of grounds and lot of studies are done comparing between SERVQUAL and SERVPERF, still both the tools are used in different studies on service quality evaluation.

Review of Literature

Numerous studies have been conducted in the banking industry to study service quality using the SERVQUAL model. The following are the some of the summarised most relevant studies reviewed by the eminent researchers at international and national level are presented in the following lines.

International Level

(Dougall, G.h.G. and levesque, 1994) examined the service quality dimensions in Canada retail banking implementing SERVQUAL. The outcome emerged as the specific service quality dimension of interest. They identified two segments reflecting the outcome and process dimensions. The performance segment sought outcome, a financial institution that "got it right the first time" and the convenience segment, sought financial institutions that were conveniently located.

(Lewis, 1994) carried out a work entitled 'Service Quality; Students' assessment of Banks and Building societies' using SERVQUAL and Graphic and Scaling Technique and found that the students were very much satisfied with the banks and building societies, because they performed well in relation to staff role i.e. trustworthiness, appearance and approachability etc. and made loans and overdraft facility decisions fairly and quickly are the main causes for students satisfaction. Another point he highlighted that students were dissatisfied with respect to service delivery; e.g. having product knowledge, defining and explaining the services in right manner, speed and efficiency of dealing with queries etc. Bank opening hours and slow service delivery were the major issues for dissatisfaction.

'Quality in Retail Banking' studied by (Blanchard, 1995) in UK by using 31 questions of SERVQUAL and cleared that 1. Process issues are the most important when customers are evaluating service quality. However, objective issues are more important than subjective whilst those issues are almost as important as soft issues; 2. In the view of the bank's staff, responsiveness and assurance are the most prominent; 3. Bank's staff perception of service using the SERVQUAL gaps indicates that:

1. Relatively little importance was attached to gap 1 (customer expectations and the bank's perceptions of customer expectations).
2. Gap 2 is not considered important since there is no publish set of service standard.
3. With regards to gap 3, the bank fails to value the primary customer contact role sufficiently.
4. In the case of gap 4 the bank fails to communicate effectively to customers (customers are not well informed about services or procedures).

(Levesue, T. and McDougal, 1996) conducted another study in Canada employing SERVQUAL of 17 items to measure Banks' service quality and service features to determine customer satisfaction in retail banking and said that 1. The factor analysis yielded three dimensions; relational, core dimensions and service feature dimension. 2. Service problems and the bank's service recoverability have a high positive correlation with customer satisfaction and intensions to switch.

A comparative study done by (Kangis, 1997) in private and public sector commercial banks in Greece to find out customers' expectations and perceptions by using SERVQUAL (12 dimensions). Quality expectations and perceptions were slightly higher in the private than in the public sector in most of the dimensions measured. There was no difference between customers of both private and public banks with regards to the relative importance attached to each quality attribute. The perception of the profile of Service received was however different between sectors. Customers of the private banks consider the service quality offered by the public sector banks to be inferior to that which clients of the public sector attributed to the private sector. Of the 12 dimensions, they considered public banks rendered inferior services in 11.

Yavas, (1997) in Turkey conducted a customer survey on 'Service Quality in the Banking Sector in and Emerging Economy' adopting SERVQUAL. They designed questionnnaire containing 31 questions (22 SERVQUAL questions plus two questions response and voice plus five questions on complain behaviour plus two commitment questions. They found that 1. Confirmatory factor analysis results reveal six customer satisfaction dimensions (employee competence, reliability, product innovation, value for money, physical and convenience). 2. There is a direct effect of customer satisfaction on the behavioural responses of customers (i.e. when customers assess customer satisfaction to be high, they (i) decide to stay with the existing service provider and (ii) subdue their negative investigative behavioural intentions). 3. There is a positive correlation between customer satisfaction and word-of-mouth. 4. Customer satisfaction is not only industry specific but also country specific.

Lasser, (2000) conducted research in USA and South American countries to analyse the perspectives and satisfaction of customers in Private Banking using SERVQUAL and Technical/Functional Quality Model, and found that the Technical/Functional based model is betther than SRVQUAL-based model to envisaging the customer satisfaction if customers are showing high interest and actively involved in delivery of service. The customer satisfaction mainly influenced by the type of communication between service providers and consumers and quality level of service delivered by the service provider. They concluded that various dimensions of service quality differentially predict the satisfaction of customers against the quality of service.

'Service Quality at Banks and Credit Unions: What Do Their Customers Say', was the study carried out by (Allred, 2000) in USA using SERVQUAL (original 10 dimensions) and explained that 1. Credit Unions are ranked significantly higher than banks in 11 out of 14 service quality dimensions. They are access, courtesy, communication, credibility, security, empathy, tangibles, basic service, fairness, fixing mistakes and guarantees. 2. Both banks credit unions perform poorly in the area of servicing customer needs and relating customers. 3. Half of the respondents have ceased using a financial service provider due to poor service performance. The bank did not offer adequate service.

Anwar, (2003), in Western Brunei, Sumatra in Indonesia tested the marketing orientation of banks manager in the merging economy of Brunei. The study studied the relationship between market orientation and service quality in the banking industry in Western Sumatra, Indonesia reveals that there is a positive relationship between information development, information dissemination and response level toward service quality at confident level of 0.05. The coefficient of those three factors towards service quality is 59.6 per cent.

In UAE (Jabnoun, 2003) performed investigation on measuring perceived service quality in commercial banks in UAE with modified SERVQUAL (5 dimensions with 30 questions). Factor analysis, espoused in the study, was used to test significance of the data. It produced three dimensions i.e. human skills, tangibles and empathy. The difference in significance between the dimensions showed that: the human skills dimensions were the most significant dimension than others, and tangibles and empathy were both equally significant dimensions in measuring the service quality.

Service Quality Measurement in the Banking Sector in South Korea was a research work carried out by, (Cui, 2003), establishing modified SERVQUAL and SERVPERF models. Statistical techniques Confirmatory factor analysis and principal component analysis were used. Using confirmatory factor analysis, the SERVQUAL and SERVPERF are not confirmed, hence could not be used in the South Korea banking setting. It needs adaptations or modifications before can be used. Using principal component analysis, a modified SERVQUAL (SERVQUAL and weighted SERVQUAL) reduced the factors in three components (tangibles, empathy. The third dimension however varies. Weighted SERVQUAL revealed reliability whilst that of SERVQUAL consist items from reliability and responsiveness). Using principal analysis, a modified SERVPERF (SERVPERF and Weighted SERVPERF) reduced the factors in two components tangibles and intangibles.

"The Antecedents of Service Quality and Product quality and their Influence on Bank Reputation: Evidence from the Banking Industry in China's Retail Banking" was the investigation conducted by (Wang, 2003). They discovered that both service quality and product quality have a significant influence on banks' reputation. They found that there is no significant support for the impact of reliability and empathy on overall service quality and there is a significant relationship between reliability and overall product quality. There is a strong influence of tangibles on overall product quality than that of overall service quality.

Duncen, (2004), in Australia evaluated the 'Efficiency, Customer Service and Financial Performance among Australian Financial Institutions'. SERVPERF, DEA (Data Envelop Analysis) input oriented model and four financial performance measures i.e. interest margin, capital adequacy, expense/income ratio and return on assets were used for study purpose and concluded that, there is positive relation between financial performance by return on Assets and Capital Adequacy and Technical Efficiency CRS and a negative relationship between financial performance, as measured by expense/income ratio and interest margin and technical efficiency CRS. 2. Similarly, there is a positive relationship between expense/income ratio and capital adequacy and scale efficiency. 3. Conversely, there is a negative relationship between return on assets and interest margin and scale efficiency. 4. In all models, there exists a positive relationship between customer service quality and the financial performance indicator, and customer service, but there is a negative relationship between customer service and technical efficiency and CRS.

Beerli, (2004) examined the 'model of the customer loyalty in the retail banking market' in Spain implementing SERVPERF. Both satisfaction and switching costs can be regarded as loyalty antecedents. Nevertheless, the influence exerted by satisfaction is far greater than that of switching costs. Satisfaction is antecedent of perceived quality in the retail banking market and not vice versa. In the retail banking market, the degree of elaboration does not exert any moderating influence.

Another study in China inquired in to the measurement of service quality and satisfaction in retail banking by (Zhou, 2004) in the year 2004. The context-dependent SERVPERF dimensions are appropriate predictors of consumer satisfaction. There are significant variations regarding the respective effects of these observed dimensions on satisfaction and that satisfaction leads to different types of behavioural intensions.

Another study in China (Khalifa, 2005) has done a study on measure of service quality adopting SERVQUAL five dimension and two dimensions i.e. value and image. Factor analysis and regression analysis techniques are adopted further analysis. Factor analysis reduces the seven dimensions to four dimensions (personal skills, reliability, values and image). Regressions analysis shows that though all the four factors are significant determinants of quality of service in conventional banks, the most important are values and image. Values and image are however significant in determining the quality of service in Islamic banking.

Chen, (2005) studied the relationship between 'Price, Brand Cues and Banking Customer Value'. They used modified SERVQUAL questionnaire containing 29 questions for this study. They concluded that quality of service is positively related to brand cues. According to them, price cues were negatively affected by the perceived risk. Brand cues indirectly affect customer value through service quality and price cues also indirectly have an effect on customer value through perceived risk.

1. Consumers high on individualism expect power empathy and assurance from service providers.
2. At the national level, Indian consumers attach higher importance to tangibles attributes, whilst Canadian consumers consider service reliability more important.
3. There is no significant difference between India and Canada with regards to overall service quality expectations.

In Greece (Jamal, 2009) investigated the 'Effect of Service Quality Dimensions and Expertise on Loyalty' by using SERVQUAL (22 perceptions questions) + 4 items to measure customer loyalty + adopted a scale to measure expertise to capture the ability to perform product-related tasks successfully, the understanding and the knowledge about attributes and alternatives based on the work of alba and Hutchinson (1987), Cowley (1994) and Mishra *et al.*) and cleared that 1. Reliability, tangibility and empathy positively correlated with customer satisfaction. 2. Customer satisfaction is positively related to loyalty. 3. Expertise is negatively related to loyalty but it positively moderates the link between satisfaction and loyalty.

The research carried out by (Hongxiu Li, 2009) explored the e-service quality dimensions based on a review of the development of e-service quality scales and the SERVQUAL scale. It proposed an 8-dimension scale for measuring e-service quality with rewording and modifying of the SERVQUAL instrument: Website design, reliability, fulfillment, security, responsiveness, personalisation, information and empathy. The study revealed that proposed e-service quality scale presents the dimensions and attributes that were most important to online customer's satisfaction with rewording and modifying of the SERVQUAL scale. Dimension i.e. website design (take the place of tangibles) in SERVQUAL instrument, and become quite important in e-service quality since it is the starting point of online purchase and the access to an organisation.

Raspor, (2010), examined customers' perceptions of service quality in the Croatian hotel industry with an aim to assess the perceived service quality of hotel attributes and to determine the factor structure of service quality perception. The study results indicated that rather high expectations of hotel guests regarding service quality, 'Reliability,' 'empathy and competence of staff,' 'accessibility' and 'tangibles' were the key factors that best explained customers' expectations of hotel service quality.

Zekiri, (2011) carried out the study with the aim to apply the ACSI model in the context of service quality in the Macedonian mobile telecommunication industry in order to describe how customers perceive service quality and whether they are satisfied with services offered by T-Mobile, ONE, and VIP (three mobile telecom players). It was found that the overall service quality perceived by the customers was not satisfactory, that expectations were higher than perceptions. Customers were not satisfied with the service provided by the service providers.

Yildirim, (2012) THY's airlines passengers' expectations and perceptions were found to be close. On the other hand, for other airline firms' passengers' expectations and perceptions had a great gap. With exception of "Empathy" dimension, it was detected that passengers' expectations and perceptions had a significant gap in all other domestic airline firms. The most important dimension in SERVQUAL scale was found to be "Reliability". Both in THY and other domestic airline firms it gave a significant importance to meet the expectations of passengers.

Niveen El Saghier, Service Quality Dimensions and Customers' Satisfactions of Banks in Egypt, 2013, conducted a study and analysed service quality of banking services provided by banks in Egypt. This was an analytical study based mainly on the primary data collected through a scientifically developed questionnaire. The study found that four factors that influence users' evaluation of service quality of banking services. These factors were reliability, responsiveness, empathy and assurance.

The study conducted by (Steenkamp, 2014) in South Africa, revealed that service-quality leadership will become increasingly important, because the world economy is dominated by service industries, and the industrial design and engineering of services will continue to be innovative and new. Services are becoming core business, and service quality a strategic priority.

National Level

Having reviewed the literature on the service quality in the banking industry at international level, an attempt is made to review the past studies in India.

Angure, (1999) in India assessed the service quality in the banking industry installing SERVQUAL and SERVPERF models. They used both conformity and exploratory factory analysis and found that the models are multidimensional and not uni-dimensional in a developing country. Though the five quality dimensions did not hold in India, the most important dimensions that influence the service quality were reliability and responsiveness. SERVQUAL seems to furnish greater diagnostic information about service quality gaps than SERVPERF. Though SERVQUAL and SERVPERF have identical convergent validity, SERVPERF looks like having higher discriminate validity than SERVQUAL.

Debasish, (2002), conducted the comparative study in selected commercial banks in Delhi to analyse the service quality. The study reveals that the foreign banks operating in Delhi provide better service quality (SQ), as compared with the Private sector and the sector banks. Citibank, ICICI Bank and State of India (SBI) were perceived to deliver better services as compared with the other banks in Delhi. Findings reveal that the public sector banks that account for over three-fourth of the banking business in the country have failed to adequately satisfy their customers.

Mukherjee, (2003), in India, studied on the area 'An Empirical Assessment of Comparative Approaches to Service Quality Measurement', using SERVQUAL and Loss Function produced similar results and hence all SERVQUAL dimensions are equally good for service quality measurement.

Ibrahim, (2006) had examined the 'customers' perception of electronic service delivery in retail banking sector' SERVPERF, SERVQUAL, E-SERVQUAL, WEBQUAL and Focus Group Discussions were the instruments used in their study. Exploratory factor analysis reveals six dimensions of electronic service quality. These are the provision of convenient/ accurate electronic banking operations, the accessibility and reliability of service provision, good queue management; service personalisation, the provision of friendly and responsive customer service and the provision of targeted customer service. Further analysis using importance-performance analysis shows that the UK customers' perceptions of their bank actual performance on these revealed that e-SQ dimensions were largely modest.

Khan, "Studies of Some Aspects of Service Quality Evaluation with Specific Relevance to Indian Service Industries", 2007), in India inquired the aspects of service quality evaluation in Indian service industries particular reference technical educational institutions by developing "EDUQUAL" instrument (5 dimensions with 28 questions) considering the expectations and perceptions of customer a back propagation algorithm of neural network was used for the study. For this purpose five dimensions were framed i.e. learning outcomes, responsiveness, physical facilities, personality development and academics. It had been established that P-E gap model is the best suited in Technical Educational System (TES) considering all the important stakeholders. As far as second best model is concerned, it is E-P for alumni and recruiters and E and P for students and parents.

Kumar, (2009) conducted a study using SERVQUAL consisting of six dimensions (five original SERQUAL dimensions plus one - Tangibles, Reliability, Responsiveness, Assurance, and Empathy plus Convenience) and found that in general banks services are of poor quality as customers perceptions are lower than expectations. There is significant difference between four dimensions: (i) Tangibles and Reliability have the lowest gap indicating respondents perceptions are close to expectation and are therefore satisfied, (ii) Both competence and convenience have the largest gaps indicating respondents' banks are not competent and convenient in doing business.

Lenka Usha, (2009) investigated the impact of "Service Quality on Customer Satisfaction and Customer Loyalty in Indian Commercial Banks". They discovered that the improved human, technical and tangible aspects of service quality increase customer satisfaction. Human aspects of service quality were more potent, found to influence customer satisfaction compared to technical and tangible aspects.

Dash, (2009), had conducted the research work tilted "The Effect of Power Distance and Individualism on Service Quality – A Two-Country Individual and national Culture", in Canada and India and discovered that 1. Indian culture is associated with low individualism and high power distance whereas Canadian culture is associated with high individualism and low power distance. 2. In determine banks' service quality by customers, the results indicate that SERVQUAL dimensions have a correlations with Holfstede's power distance and individualism culture dimensions both at the individual and national levels, i.e. Customers low on power distance expects higher importance to tangibles service attributes.

'Influence of Service Quality on Customer Satisfaction of SRVQUAL Model' was another study done by (Ravichandran, 2010) and concluded that 1. Customers are satisfied with the quality of bank's service (all the five dimensions) but in varying degrees. 2. With regards to overall satisfaction of banks' services, responsiveness is the only significant dimension.

Dhandapani, (2010), examined the nature of linkage between service quality and customer loyalty in Indian retail banking. Study used confirmatory factor analysis to identify the service quality dimension. The resulted dimensions are Reliability, Responsiveness, Knowledge and Recovery; and Tangibles. The service quality dimensions lead to customer satisfaction and the customers' satisfaction leads to customer's loyalty. The structural equation model reveals that there is no significant direct linkage between service quality and customers loyalty. At the same time, the service quality has a significant indirect impact on customer's loyalty especially through customer's satisfaction.

Desta, (2011), conducted a study by assessing and measuring the banking service quality perception of the SBI branch customers; and examining the relationship between service quality, customer satisfaction and positive word of mouth and found that the expectations of bank customers were not met and that the largest gap was found in the reliability dimension. This dimension also had the largest influence on customer satisfaction and overall satisfaction of bank customers had a positive effect on their word-of-mouth. The study also suggested that input from staff on what constitutes "service excellence" will be beneficial. The bank need to reassess "what customers expect from the bank" and provide client specific services. It needs to invest on employee training programmes that will provide staff with an understanding of service culture and service excellence particularly at front line levels. Employee training programmes should focus on interpersonal communication and customer care factors in order to be able to meet the customers' need for personalised service.

Study was conducted by (Santhiavally, 2011) to evaluate the service quality of SBI by adopting the SERVQUAL technique developed by A. Parasuraman *et al* (1988) and found that that among five dimensions 'Reliability', 'Responsiveness', 'Empathy' and 'Tangibility' are the major factors responsible for customer satisfaction which stood at 90 per cent regarding the services provided by State Bank of India. Thus, based on the per cent level of customer satisfaction, the State Bank of India has scope to improve the quality of the service rendered to its customers to ensure their loyalty.

Maya Basant Lohani, (2012), examined on service quality in selected banks and measured in five dimensions by using SERVQUAL scale developed by Parasuraman *et al* (1988) and revealed that there exist a small perceptual difference regarding overall service quality with the respective banks. The study found that banks have more concentration on the tangible factor like a computerisation, physical facilities, etc. to attract the customers. The dimensions Reliability, Responsiveness and Assurance are found to be the most vital and strategic determinants of service quality and customer satisfaction for both public and private sector banks. If banks want to sustain customers on a long-term basis, bankers should work towards 100 per cent customer satisfaction that automatically foster customer delight.

Jain, (2012) in their study "Customer Perception on Service Quality in Banking Sector: With Special Reference to Indian Private Banks in Moradabad Region" try to learn and understand the customer perception regarding service quality and to learn and understand the different dimension of service quality in banks. The Sample size used is 100 and the sample universe is Moradabad. The service quality model developed by Zeithmal, Parsuraman and Berry (1988) has been used in the present study. The analysis reveals that among the private sector banks all the dimensions of service quality are equally important.

Rupaa Rathee, (2014) studied the service quality gaps in banks after nationalisation of commercial banks. With the entry of new generation, tech-savvy, private banks the banking sector has become too competitive. Gap analysis was applied to find the gaps between expected and performed service in private banks to find the difference between male and female perception and expectation. This study provided an insight into which attributes of service quality in private bank were most important in providing satisfaction to customers and areas where significant gaps existed. It concluded that the highest gap was found in the dimension of reliability and empathy and suggested that the banks have to reduce this gap giving individual personal attention to understand customer specific needs. The customers trust the public sector banks. These banks have existed in the market for a longer period than the private sector banks. The reliability factor is a positive factor for these banks. Therefore, private banks should position themselves in the market on the basis of this dimension and promote themselves aggressively. It becomes imperative for the private sector banks to train their staff to treat the customers with empathy.

Anand Pawar, (2014), in his study 'Customers' Expectations and Perceptions of Banking Services', analysed service quality with regard to banking services as a case study of IDBI bank by taking five SERVQUAL dimensions such as RATER as an important elements for influencing customers' satisfaction of service quality provided by selected bank. He concluded that reliability and responsiveness are relatively influencing when compared to other dimensions. Hence, suggested that bank should focus relatively more on factors of reliability and responsiveness.

Having reviewed the international and national level studies on the service quality in the banking sector, an attempt has been made to identify the research gap in the previous studies and find need for the study in the following lines.

Research Gap

From the above review, two main points can be made: First, to survive and achieve their mission, banks in India need to be able to compete with other banks and attract their customers (this research focuses on rural customers only) by providing the qualitative service that rural people need. In order to satisfy customers, service quality has to be measured and improved.

Second, SERVQUAL is a well-known measurement scale that has been used to measure service quality worldwide. However, previous studies have recognised that different organisational backgrounds may influence SERVQUAL items and dimensions in urban areas only. Therefore, this research aims, to use the SERVQUAL to study the service quality levels in rural banks and to measure service quality in rural banks. It is hoped that rural banks' managers will be able to use this service quality scale to assess and improve their services and satisfy their customers.

Need for the Study

The real India live in villages and therefore primarily rural in character. Rural Marketing in Indian context assumes greater importance as wind of change is blowing from three angles- firstly, changing rural scene towards development in different spheres owing to success of green revolution, white revolution and grey revolutions and consequent raise in the rural incomes; secondly, changes in market conditions resulted from the transformation of sellers' market into buyers' market consequent to new innovations, modern technology, increased production, increased competition and stagnated urban markets; and lastly the changing government policy towards liberalisation and globalisation of the Indian economy.

- Indian rural market is very vast.73 per cent of population, 56 per cent of income, 64 per cent of expenditure, and 33 per cent of the saving from rural India.

- 41 million Kisan Credit cards have been issued (against 22 million credit-plus-debit cards in urban) with cumulative credit ₹ 997 billion resulting in tremendous liquidity.
- Of the 20 million Rediff mail sign-ups, 60 per cent from small towns. 50 per cent of transactions from these towns are on Rediff online shopping site.
- 42 million rural households are availing banking services in comparison to 27 million urban households.
- Investment in formal savings instruments is 6.6 million households in rural and 6.7 million households in urban.

The above figures reinforce the need to manage of the rural people. Rural financing is a fashionable subject today, though it is far more important for a developing economy like that of India. There is clarion call to explore and not to exploit the rural market. This subject has been unattended by serious academic professionals. The opening up of the domestic economy to external competition and the emergence of purchasing power in the rural areas, business and development professionals call for a better understanding of the concept and the processes of rural financing. This is the time which calls to analyse, rather than just assume what the rural consumers desire, detest, appreciate and expect. Given the importance and contribution of rural economy to total country's economy and GDP, it makes imperative for marketers to have a 360 per cent view of this market. Hence, it is proposed to study the strengths, weaknesses, opportunities and threats (SWOT) of commercial banks in rural areas. This analysis, when probed into the details, is expected to show sufficient light on the existing strengths and weaknesses of the policies of banks in rural areas in strategising their marketing programme and get the best possible results from their truest efforts.

Statement of Problem

Extensive research has been done by eminent scholars, academicians and practitioners on service quality in the banking industry. All these studies have concentrated on urban areas only. No concrete study found out the perceptions of rural customers about the quality of banks' services in India. There is a need for an extensive study on the rural consumers' perceptions on the service quality in banking service offered in rural areas. Hence this research study was undertaken.

Objectives of the Study

The following are the objectives of the study:

1. To examine the growth and development of banking sector in India,
2. To present the profile of selected banks in Karimnagar district,

3. To study the customers' expectations of banking services in the rural context,
4. To analyse the customers' satisfaction on service quality of banks in rural areas.

Methodology and Data Base

The study is primarily a descriptive study of the impact of banking services in the rural areas. One public sector bank, one private sector bank and one rural bank were selected as target banks for the study. SBH from public sector, HDFC from private sector and TGB (earlier DGB) from rural banks for identified as the target banks.

Data Collection

The required data was collected from two sources namely, Primary Data and Secondary Data. Primary data was collected through two structured questionnaires (using SERQUAL questionnaire with 20 variables). While one questionnaire was intended for the bank officials and another one was meant for the bank customers. Secondary data was collected from RBI bulletins, NCAER, IBA, District Statistical Reports, Reports of Institutions and Agencies etc., which are engaged in development of banking sector and other published reports.

Sample Unit

The sample unit consisted of customers of the public sector (SBH), the private sector banks (HDFC) and RRBs (TGB) of rural areas in Karimnagar district of Telangana State. The respondents were farmers, teachers, business peoples and professionals in the age group of 25 – above 60 years.

Reason for Selecting Karimnagar District

Karimnagar district is predominantly an agrarian district. The availability of Lower Manair Dam (LMD) and water resources led to prospective farming due to which the district has become a leading producer of agricultural products. Since the independence rural credit in the form of PACS was the leading provider of finance for the agriculture and allied activities.

The progress in the agriculture piloted the prosperity in the rural Karimnagar which in term showed the way to growth and development of other economic activities such as trade, healthcare, education and business… The district is also endowed with rich mining resources such as coal, limestone and granite. These directed to the booming demand for credit which is mainly providing by commercial banks, regional rural banks (RRBs) apart from the primary agricultural credit societies (PACS).

Hence, the district of Karimnagar is selected as the area of study for the research topic.

Reason for Selecting Mandals

For the present study six mandals i.e. Siricilla, Jagitial, Huzurabad, Jammikunta, Metpally and Sultanabad in Karimnagar district have been selected purposefully. Selected three banks (SBH, TGB and HDFC bank) were located and functioning in these six mandals only. Hence, these mandals were selected for the study.

Sample Size

For the study judgment sampling is used. The following is the sample distribution.

Table 1.8: SAMPLE SIZE

Particulars	*No.*
No. of Mandals Selected for the study (10 per cent of the Total 57 Mandals in the District)	6
No. of Banks Selected (SBH, DGB and HDFC)	3
Target Groups (Farmers, Staff, Business People and SHGs)	4
No. of Respondents from each group	10
Total Sample Size (For SBH & DGB – 6*2*4*10) + (For HDFC – 6*3*10)	**660**
No. of Respondents Responded	**630**
Per cent of Response	**65.45 per cent**

Note: As a private bank *HDFC bank is not offering SHG Scheme.*

Tools of Data Analysis

So, collected data was analyzed with the help of statistical techniques like tables, averages, percentages and bar diagrams. Graphs are presented where necessary. The results are interpreted with the help of percentages in a meaningful manner. Based on the need, the statistical techniques like, factor analysis, paired sample test, multi-variable analysis, correlation, ANOVA, etc., are employed to arrive logical conclusions.

Scope of the Study

The study is restricted to Karimnagar district only. The district is one of the developed districts in Telangana state. So the district is selected purposefully to understand the process of service delivery by selected banks in the rural areas of the district.

Table 1.9: Summary of the Sample Targeted

	Farmers						*Staff*						*Total*
	Siricilla	*Huzurabad*	*Jagitial*	*Metpally*	*Jammikunta*	*Sultanabad*	*Siricilla*	*Huzurabad*	*Jagitial*	*Metpally*	*Jammikunta*	*Sultanabad*	
SBH	10	10	10	10	10	10	10	10	10	10	10	10	120
TGB	10	10	10	10	10	10	10	10	10	10	10	10	120
HDFC	10	10	10	10	10	10	10	10	10	10	10	10	120
	30	30	30	30	30	30	30	30	30	30	30	30	360
	Business People						*SHGs*						*Total*
	Siricilla	*Huzurabad*	*Jagitial*	*Metpally*	*Jammikunta*	*Sultanabad*	*Siricilla*	*Huzurabad*	*Jagitial*	*Metpally*	*Jammikunta*	*Sultanabad*	
SBH	10	10	10	10	10	10	10	10	10	10	10	10	120
TGB	10	10	10	10	10	10	10	10	10	10	10	10	120
HDFC*	10	10	10	10	10	10	0	0	0	0	0	0	60
	30	30	30	30	30	30	20	20	20	20	20	20	300
							TOTAL						**660**

* HDFC bank is not offering SHGs Scheme

Table 1.10: Summary of the Actual Sample Collected

	Farmers						*Staff*						*Total*
	Siricilla	*Huzurabad*	*Jagitial*	*Metpally*	*Jammikunta*	*Sultanabad*	*Siricilla*	*Huzurabad*	*Jagitial*	*Metpally*	*Jammikunta*	*Sultanabad*	
SBH	10	10	10	10	10	10	10	10	10	10	10	10	120
TGB	10	10	10	6	10	10	10	10	10	4	10	10	110
HDFC*	0	2	10	10	10	10	10	10	10	10	10	10	102
Total	20	22	30	26	30	30	30	30	30	24	30	30	332
	Business people						*SHGs*						*Total*
	Siricilla	*Huzurabad*	*Jagitial*	*Metpally*	*Jammikunta*	*Sultanabad*	*Siricilla*	*Huzurabad*	*Jagitial*	*Metpally*	*Jammikunta*	*Sultanabad*	
SBH	10	10	10	10	10	10	10	10	10	10	10	10	120
TGB	10	10	10	10	10	10	10	10	10	8	10	10	118
HDFC	10	10	10	10	10	10	0	0	0	0	0	0	60
Total	30	30	30	30	30	30	20	20	20	18	20	20	298
	TOTAL												**630**

* HDFC bank is not offering SHGs Scheme.

Limitations of the Study

The present study like other research studies is similar and allied lines cannot claim to be a perfect one in all respects. Although every effort was made to conduct the study as rigorously as possible, certain limitations were unavoidable as indicated bellow:

1. Only three banks were selected for deeper analysis. In view of this, it cannot claim to be a comprehensive study concerning all the banks in the sector.
2. Though the analysis of selected banks is for fairly a long period time i.e. five and half years (from June 2010 to Dec. 2015), it does not capture the whole period from their inception.
3. (A) The size of sample respondents is only 630. Hence the findings usually cannot be generalised to the populations or community. (B) This study is limited to only six mandals and does not cover entire mandals in the district.
4. Only five factors of service quality (RATER)* and 20 variables were considered.

   (*R-Reliability, A-Assurance, T-Tangibles, E-Empathy and R-Responsiveness)
5. Required primary data are gathered by interviewing the respondents randomly selected in rural areas. Results reflect opinions of respondents. Data may not be robust enough to explain complex issues.
6. It may not be totally correct to make generalisation on the basis of limited study but its findings and conclusions can be of much generalised to use.

Organisation of the Study

The present study is structured into seven chapters organised to present the study from a basic introduction to findings and conclusions. The following table displays the scheme of Chapterisation of the study:

Table 1.11: Organisation of the Study

Chapter – I	Introduction
Chapter – II	Growth and Development of Banking Sector in India
Chapter – III	Profile of Selected Banks in Karimnagar District
Chapter – IV	Customers' Expectations of Banking Services in Rural Context
Chapter – V	Customers' Satisfaction of Service Quality in Rural Areas
Chapter – VI	Summary of Conclusions, Findings and Suggestions

Chapter – I Introduction

This chapter introduces the study and states the Conceptual Framework, Need for the study, Objectives of the study, Statement of the Problem, Research Methodology, Scope of the study, Limitations of the Study and Scheme of Chapterisation.

Chapter – II Growth and Development of Banking Sector in India

This chapter starts from the meaning, evolution, origin of banking in India, Indian banking system and its growth and classification of banks.

Chapter – III Profile of Selected Banks in Karimnagar District

This chapter deals with the brief profile of the selected banks for the study i.e. public sector bank (SBH), private sector bank (HDFC) and rural bank (TGB).

Chapter – IV Customers' Expectations of Banking Services in Rural Context

This chapter states the demographic profile of the respondents in the selected study area. It includes the analysis of the opinions of the respondents on availability of banking services.

Chapter – V Customers' Satisfaction of Service Quality in Rural Areas

Chapter six deals with the analysis and interpretation of data collected for the study. It includes the analysis of the opinions of the respondents on influencing factors to open an account in the bank, expectations and actual facilities and amenities provided by the banks, service timings, service encounters and evaluation of service quality in rural areas reference to selected public sector banks, private sector banks and regional rural banks. It also includes descriptive and comparative study of selected banks and hypothesis testing.

Chapter – VII Summary of Findings, Suggestions and Conclusions

In this chapter, the introduction, objectives and summary of findings of the research study are presented one by one, based on findings necessary suggestions are offered. It concludes by setting out the study's contribution to knowledge and scope for future research is also stated for the benefit of future researchers.

References

1. Agarwal, J. (2012). Customer Satisfaction in Indian Banking Services (A Study in Aligarh District). *International Journal of Computing and Business Research (IJCBR), 3* (1), 1-14.
2. Allred, A. A. (2000). Service Quality at Banks and Credit Unions: What They Do Their Customers Say. *Managing Service Quality, 10* (1), 52-60.
3. Anand Pawar, I. (2014). Customers' Expectations and Perceptions of Banking Services. *SUMEDHA Journal of Management, 3* (2), 52-65.
4. Angure. (1999). Service Quality in the Banking Industry: An Assessment in Developing Economy. *International Journal of Bank Management, 17* (3), 116-123.
5. Anwar, S. (2003). Testing Marketing orientation of Banks' Manager in the Merging Economy of Brunei, *International Journal of Bank Marketing, 21*, 233-248.
6. Asubonteng, P. M. (1996). SERVQUAL Revisited: A Critical Review of Service Quality. *Journal of Service Marketing, 10* (6), 62-81.
7. Babakus. E., A. G. (1992). An Empirical assessment of SERVQUAL Scale. *Journal of Businesss Research, 24* (3), 253-268.
8. Baker, T. A. (2007). Service Quality Gap and Cusotmers' Satisfaction of Commercial Banks in Malasia. *International Review of Business Research, 3* (4), 327-336.
9. Beerli, A. A. (2004). A Model of Customer Loyalty in Retail Banking Market,. *European Journal of Marketing, 38* (1), 253-275.
10. Blanchard, R. A. (1995). Quality in Retail Banking. *Internaional Journal of Service Industry Management, 5* (4), 5-23.
11. Boloton, R. J. (1991). A Multi Stage Model of Consumers' Assessment of Service Quality and Value. *Journal of Consumer Research, 17* (4), 375-384.
12. Brown, S. (2007). Mandating a Service Revolution for Marketing. *The Service-Dominant Logic of Marketing: Dialog, Debate and Directions*, (pp. 393-405).
13. Carman, J. M. (1990). Consumer Perceptions of Service Quality: An Assessment pf SERVQUAL Dimensions. *Joural of Retailing, 66* (1), 35-55.
14. Chen. (2005). Price, Brand Cues and Banking Customer Value. *International Journal of Bank Management, 23* (3), 273-291.
15. Crorin, J. J., and T. (2001). SERVPERF Versus SERVQUAL: Reconciling Performance -Based and Perceptions - Minus- Expectations Measurements of Service Quality. *Journal of Marketing, 58*, 125-131.
16. Cui, C. L. (2003). Service Quality Management in the Banking Sector in South Korea. *International Journal of Bank Marketing, 21* (4), 191-201.
17. Dash, S. B. (2009). The Effect of Power Distance and Individualism on Service Quality Expectations in Banking: A Two Country Individual and National Cultural Comparison. *International Journal of Bank Marketing, 27* (5), 336-358.
18. Debasish, S. (2002). Cervice Quality in Commercial Banks: A Comparative Analysis of Selected Banks in India. *Indian Journal of Marketing, 1* (1), 3-10.

19. Desta, T. (2011). Perceived Quality of Services Rendered by Commercial Banks: A Case Study of SBI. *International Journal of Research in Commerce and Management, 2* (11), 26-36.
20. Dhandapani, S. (2010). Linkage Between Service Quality and Customers Loyalty in Commercial Banks. *International Journal of Management and Strategy, 1* (1), 1-22.
21. Dotchin, J. O. (1994). Total Quality Management in Services: Understanding and Classifying Services. *International Journal of Quality and Reliability Management, 11* (3), 9-26.
22. Dougall, G.h.G. and levesque, T. (1994). Benefit Segmentation Using Service Quality Dimensions; An Investigation in Retail Banking. *International Journal Bank Marketing, 12* (2), 15-23.
23. Duncen, E. A. (2004). Efficiency, Customers' Service and Financial Performance among Australian Financial Institutions. *The International Journal of Bank Marketing, 22* (5), 319-342.
24. Gefan, D. (2002). Customer Loyalty in e-Commerce. *Journal of Association of Information System, 3* (1), 27-51.
25. Hongxiu Li, R. S. (2009). A Proposed Scale for Measuring E-service Quality. *International Journal of u- and e-Service, Science and Technology, 2* (1), 1-10.
26. Hung, Y. H. (2003). Service Quality Evaluation by Service Quality Performance Matrix. *Total Quality Management and Business Excellence, 14* (1), 79-89.
27. Ibrahim, E. J. (2006). Customers' Perceptions of Electronic Service Delivery in the UK Retail Banking Sector. *International Journal of Bank Marketing, 24* (7), 475-493.
28. Jabnoun, N. a.-t. (2003). Measuring perceived Service Quality At UAE Commercial Banks. *International Journal of Quality and Reliability management, 20* (4), 458-472.
29. Jain, V. (2012). "Customer Perception on Service Quality in Banking Sector"- With Special Reference to Indian Private Banks in Moradabad Region. *International Journal of Research in Finance and Marketing (IJRFM), 2* (2), 597-610.
30. Jamal, A. A. (2009). Investigating the Effects of Service Quality Dimensions and Expertise on Loyalty. *European Journal of Marketing, 43* (3), 398-420.
31. Kangis, P. A. (1997). Private and Public Banks: A Comparison of Customers' Expectations and Perceptions. *International Journal of Bank Marketing, 15* (7), 279-297.
32. Khalifa, A. A. (2005). A Customised Measure of Service Quality in the UAE. *Journal of Managing Service Quality, 15* (14), 374-388.
33. Khan, M. S. (2007). *"Studies of Some Aspects of Service Quality Evaluationwith Specific Relevance to Indian Service Industries"*. Rourkela: A PhD Thesis Submitted to NIT.
34. Khan, M. S. (2007). *Studies on some Aspects of Service Quality Evaluation with Specific Relevance to Indian Service Industires.* PhD Thesis Submitted to NIT Rourkela, India.

35. Kumar. (2009). Determining the Relative Importance of Critical Factors in Delivering Service Quality of Banks An Application Dominance Analysis SERVQUAL Model. *Journal of Managing Service Quality*, *19* (2), 211-228.

36. Lasser. (2000). Service Perspectives and Satisfaction in Private Banking. *Journal of Services Marketing*, *14* (3), 244-271.

37. Lenka Usha, D. S. (2009). Service Quality Customer Satisfaction and Cusotmer Loyalty in Indian Commercial Banks. *The Journal of Entrpreneurship*, *18* (1), 47-64.

38. Lethinen, U. A. (1992). Service Quality: A Study of Quality Dimensions. *International Journal of Marketing*, *56* (4), 19-35.

39. Levesue, T. and McDougal, G. (1996). Determinants of Customers' Satisfaction in Retail Banking. *International Journal of Bank Marketing*, *14* (7), 12-20.

40. Lewis, B. O. (1994). Service Quality: Students' Assessment of Banks and Building Societies. *Internatinal Journal of Bank Marketing*, *12* (4), 3-13.

41. Lewis, B.R. (1989). Quality in Service Sector - A Review. *International Journal of Brand Marketing*, *7* (5), 4-12.

42. Maya Basant Lohani, D. (2012). Assessment of Service Quality in Public and Private Sector Banks of India with Special Reference to Lucknow City. *International Journal of Scientific and Research Publications*, *2* (10), 1-7.

43. Maziz, M. O. (1995). A Comparison of Four Multi Attributes Model in the Prediction of Consumer attributes. *Journal of Consumer Research*, *2* (1), 38-52.

44. Mishra, J. A. (2007). Constituent Dimensions of Customer Satisfaction-A Study of Nationalised and Private Banks. *PRAJAN*, *35* (4), 390-398.

45. Mukherjee, A. A. (2003). A Model of Trust in Online Relationship Banking. *International Journal of Bank Marketing*, *21* (1), 5-15.

46. Newman, K. (2001). Interrogating SERVQUAL: A Critical Assessment of Service Quality Measurement in a High Stree Retail Bank. *International Journal of Bank Marketing*, *19* (3), 126-139.

47. Niveen El Saghier, D. N. Service Quality Dimensions and Customers' Satisfactions of Banks in Egypt. *Proceedings of 20th International Business Research Conference.* Dubai, UAE.

48. Niveen El Saghier, D. N. (2013). Service Quality Dimensions and Customers' Satisfactions of Banks in Egypt. *Proceedings of 20th International Business Research Conference.* Dubai, UAE.

49. Parasuram, A. Z. (1985). A Conceptual Model of Service Quality and its Implications for Future Research. *The Journal of Marekting*, *49*, 41-50.

50. Parasuraman, A. Z. (1988). SERVQUAL: A Multiple - Item Scale for Measuring Customer Perceptions of SErvice Quality. *Journal of Retailing*, *64* (1), 12-35.

51. Rampal, M. S. (2010). *Service marketing - Concepts, Application and Cases.* New Delhi: Galgotia Publishing Company.

52. Raspor, S. M. (2010). Measuring Perceived Service Quality Using SERVQUAL: A Case Study of the Croatian Hotel Industry. *Journal of Management*, *5* (3), 195-209.

53. Ravichandran, K. M. (2010). Influence of Service Quality on Customer Satisfaction: Application of SERVQUAL Model. *International Journal of Business and Management*, *5* (4), 117-124.
54. Rupaa Rathee, D. (2014). To Identify Service quality Gapsin Banking Sector: A Study of Private Banks. *International Journal of Emerging Research in Management & Technology*, *3* (7), 101-106.
55. Santhiavally, D. (2011). Customers' Perception of Service Quality of State Bank of India-a Factor Analysis. *International Journal of Management and Business Studies*, *1* (3), 78-84.
56. Sasser, W. R. (1998). *Management of Service Operations, Text and Cases.* Boston: Allyn 7 Bacon.
57. Singh, S. (Aug. 2004). An Appraisal of Customers Services of Public Sector Banks. *IBA Bulletin*, *XXVI* (8), 33-38.
58. Steenkamp, R. D. (2014). The Exploration of Service Quality and its Measurement for Private Higher Education Institutions. *Southern African Business Review*, *18* (2), 83-107.
59. Sureshchander, G. R. (2002). Customers Perceptions of Service Quality in the Banking Sector of Developing Econom: A Critical Analysis. *International Journal of Bank Marketing*, *21* (5), 233-242.
60. Taylor, S.A., C. (1992). Measuring Service Quality: A Re-examination and Extenstion. *Journal of Marketing*, *56* (3), 55-68.
61. Teas, R.K. (1993). Expectations, Performance Evaluation and Consumers' Perceptions of Quality. *Journal of Marketing, 57* (4), 18-34.
62. Uppal, R. (Jan.-June 2009). Customer Service in Indian Commercial Banks: An Empirical Study. *Asia Pacific Journal of Social Sciences*, *1* (1), 127-141.
63. Vijay, M. (2011). Factors Affecting on Customers' Satisfaction: An Empirical Investigation of ATM Services. *International Journal of Business, Economics and Management Research*, *2* (3), 144-156.
64. Wang, Y. L. (2003). The Antecedents of Service Quality and Product Quality and their Influences on Bank Reputation: Evidence from Banking Industry in China. *Journal of Managing Service Quality*, *13* (1), 72-83.
65. Wirtz, J. (2003). Halo in Customer Satisfaction Measure-The Role of Purpose of Rating, Number of Attributes and Customer Involvement. *International Journal of Service Industry Management*, *14* (1), 96-119.
66. Woodruff. R.B., C. (1983). Modeling Consumer Satisfaction Processess using Experience Based Norms. *Journal of Marketing Research*, *20* (3), 296-304.
67. Woodside, A. F. (1989). Linking Service Quality Customer Satisfaction and Bahavioural Intention. *Journal of Health Care marketing*, *9* (4), 5-17.
68. Yavas. (1997). Service Quality Assessment: A Comparison of Turkish and German Bank Customer, Cross Culture Management. *International Journal of Bank Management*, *14* (2), 161-168.
69. Yildirim, K. A. (2012). The Measurement of Service Quality with Servqual for Different Domestic Airline Firms in Turkey. *Serbian Journal of Management*, *7* (2), 219-230.

70. Zahari, W. Y. (2008). FM-SERVQUAL: A New Approach of Service Quality Measurement Frame Work in Local Authorities. *Journal of Corporate Real Estate, 10* (2), 130-144.

71. Zeithmal, V. P. (1998). The Nature and Determinants of Customer Expectations of Service. *Journal of Academy and Marketing Science, 21* (1), 1-12.

72. Zekiri, B. A. (2011). Measuring Customer Satisfaction with Service Quality Using American Customer Satisfaction Model (ACSI Model). *International Journal of Academic Research in Business and Social Sciences, 1* (3), 232-258.

73. Zhou, L. (2004). A Dimension-Specific Analysis of Performance Only Measurement of Service Quality in China's Retail Banking. *Journal of Services Marketing, 15* (4), 374-388.

Chapter - 2

Growth and Development of Banking Sector in India

Introduction

In the present modern global economy, banking plays an indispensable role. Banking system has been changed dramatically over the past two decades. Banks today offer a wider range of products and services than ever before, and deliver them faster and more efficiently in competitive way. But the central function of banking still remains the same-mobilising the savings in the form of deposits and investments in the economy. But during the last two decades, the following five most powerful forces have shaped the foundation for a forceful and dynamic new environment for banks.

1. **Deregulation:** The exclusion of governmental controls, from banking industry or sector, to allow banks a free and efficient competition among market players.
2. **Securitisation:** Securitisation is the process of converting financial assets into marketable securities.
3. **Financial Innovation:** Financial Innovation is the systematic process of creating and marketing of new types of securities and change in financial instruments, institutions and operating policies that decide the structure of the financial system in the economy.
4. **Advances in Technology:** Technological advancement is the various myriads of technical and organisational elements that impact services management, business management, risk management, and customer relationship management, and offers research to aid the successful implementation of banking operations to satisfy the customers by providing value added services.

5. **Globalisation:** Globalisation is the gradual integration of national economies into the international economy through trade, foreign direct investment (FDI), capital flows, migration, the spread of technology, such that geographical boundaries do not restrict financial transactions.

Concept of Bank

According to Crowther, a bank "*collects money from those who have it to spare or who are saving it out of their incomes, and it lends this money to those who require it*".

Kinley defined the bank as "*an establishment which makes to individuals such advances of money as may be required and safely made, and to which individuals entrust money when not required by them for use*".

In the words of John Paget, "*nobody can be a banker who does not (i) take deposit accounts, (ii) take current accounts, (iii) issue and pay cheques and (iv) collects cheques-crossed and uncrossed for its customers*".

Professor Sayer had given a distinct definition to term bank. According to him a bank as, "*an institution whose debts (bank deposits) are widely accepted in settlement of other peoples' debts to each other*". Another definition, according to him, "*Ordinary banking business consists cash for bank deposits and bank deposits for cash: transferring bank deposits from one person or corporation to another; giving bank deposits in exchange for bills of exchange, government bonds, the secured promises of businessmen to repay and so forth*".

According to section 5(b) of The Banking Regulation Act, 1949 banking as "banking" means "*the accepting, for the purpose of lending or investment, of deposits of money from the public, repayable on demand or otherwise, and withdrawable by cheque, draft, and order or otherwise*". It acts as a medium of exchange and manages the payment system of the nation.

Commercial Banking - Origin

In any economy banks have been playing a pivotal role in the financial system. Though the forms of banking have been changing with the changing needs of the economy, the vital role of banks in the economy is always constant.

Banking in its basic form is an age-old phenomenon and its invention preceded that of coinage when coins made of precious metals like gold and silver emerged as commonly accepted forms of wealth, lending activity at an interest began. This system originated from temples and royal palaces around the 1000 B.C. in Babylon, as the strongest belief of people was keeping their money and valuables at royal houses and gold smiths as safe places. The practicing of depositing personal valuables at these places, which were also functioning as treasuries against a receipt, was perhaps the earliest form of banking.

Revilpout, a French writer clearly mentions about banks and bank notes in Babylon in 600 B.C. Chalden, Egyptian and Phoenician history also records the existence of rudimentary banking in early days. Prof. Marshal in his book "*Money, Credit and Commerce,*" (1923) explained about the activities of money changers in the temples of Olympia and other sacred places in Greece in 2000 B.C. The origin of bank lies in the business of money changing in the ancient period. Another factor that supported the emergence of banks in the early period was the need for borrowing by the monarchical governments from the finance companies to meet the administrative expenses. The first bank in Italy "Bank of Venice" was established in 1157 in the middle ages. It supported the authorities of the State of Venice, who were in financial trouble due to the war. In England, the bankers of Lombardy have taken the initiative to start the modern banking along with their trading activities.

The present day banker has three ancestors; (1) the merchants (2) the goldsmith (3) the money lenders.

1. **The merchants:** The earliest stage in the growth of banking can be traced to the working of merchants. These merchants were traders in commodities. The trading activities were carried on by them from one place to another. It was risky for the traders to carry metallic money with themselves for payment. The traders with high reputation began to issue receipts which were accepted as titles of money. These receipts or letters of transfers also called hundi in into sub-continent were the first mode of payments. The merchant banking thus forms the earliest stage in the evolution of modern banking.
2. **Goldsmiths:** These goldsmiths also called seths in India received gold and gave receipts of gold or money kept with them. These receipts with the passage of time became payable to the bearer on demand. In this way the 'goldsmiths' note, became the fore-runners of the modern bank note.
3. **The money lenders:** The third stage banking system developed when the goldsmiths became the money lenders. The goldsmiths came to know that they could keep a small proportion of the total deposits for meeting the demands of customers for cash and the rest was deposited to their credit. In economic terminology, it can say that they allowed the overdraft facilities to their depositors.

When every money lender/goldsmith issued receipts and most of them allowed the overdraft facilities there was too much confusion in the banking system. The money lenders/goldsmiths, in order to earn profits, could not keep adequate reserves for meeting the demands of the customers for cash.

The failure on the part of the money lenders/goldsmiths to return money caused widespread distress among the people.

The commercial banking has started only after 1640 when the goldsmiths started receiving deposits from the public for safe custody and issued receipts as acknowledgements, which were later used as bearer demand notes.

Crowther also mentions that there are three ancestors of the modern commercial banking- the merchant, the moneylender and the goldsmiths. The merchants of the traders issued documents like 'hundi' to remit the funds, which took the form of cheques or demand drafts in the modern day banking. Moneylenders gave loans while goldsmiths received deposits and created credit. Modern banks give loans and accept deposits and also facilitate issuing of cheques and demand drafts. In short, the evolution of commercial banking is related to the practice of safe keeping of gold and other valuables with merchants/goldsmiths/moneylenders.

Origin of Banking in India

The money economy existed in India since the days of Buddha, but banking in India flourished in the ancient Vedic times. Even in the Rig Veda, there was a mention about indebtedness and the earliest dharma shastras lay down rates of interest and regulations governing debts and mortgages. Reference to money lending business debts and mortgages found in the Manu Smriti too. The literature of the Buddhist period, the Jatakas and archeological discoveries contain evidence of existence of "Sreshthis" or bankers. There was extensive reference in the laws of Manu to money lending and other problems. Trade guilds acted as bankers both for receiving deposits and issuing loans. The larger temples served as bankers and in South India, the village communes occasionally advanced loans to peasants. The emergence of Vaishyas as indigenous bankers and hundi as the earliest form of Indian bill of exchange were two important landmarks in the history of Indian banking. Indigenous bankers played a very important role in lending money for trade and commerce. Every town, big or small had a Seth, a Shroff, or a Chettiar, who performed a number of banking functions.

With the expansion of trade and commerce, the concept of banking gained importance. The handling of banking gradually transcended from individuals to groups and later to companies. With the Industrial Revolution of the eighteenth and nineteenth centuries, it attained a more significant place in the area of lending. Banks in their first primitive beginnings and oater in more developed forms did not enjoy a steady and harmonious growth. Banking emerged and evolved through various phases adapting itself continuously to meet the increasing needs of trade and commerce.

During the Moghul period, the indigenous bankers played a very important role in lending money and financing foreign trade and commerce in India.

During the British rule, the agency houses carried on the banking business. Commercial banking in India began in 1779 with the establishment of the first joint stock bank, named the Bank of Hindustan, by the English Agency in Calcutta. But, this bank failed in 1832. Later the General Bank of India was established in 1786. In fact, real beginning of the modern commercial banking in the country was made with the establishment of the Bank of Calcutta on 2nd June 1806; the bank was redesigned as the Bank of Bengal, three years later, on 2 January 1809. This was the first ever joint-stock bank of the British India, established under the sponsorship of the Government of Bengal. Subsequently the other two being the Bank of Bombay (incorporated on 15 April 1840) and the Bank of Madras, (incorporated on 1 July 1843). All three of which were established under charters from the British East India Company. For many years the Presidency banks acted as quasi-central banks, as did their successors, until when they were amalgamated to form the Imperial Bank of India, on 27 January 1921, which upon India's independence, became the State Bank of India in 1955. The Reserve Bank of India was formed in 1935, by passing Reserve Bank of India Act 1934, which acting as a central bank of India.

Growth of Indian Banking Industry

The first bank in India, though conservative, was established in 1786. From 1786 till today, the journey of Indian Banking System can be segregated into three distinct phases as mentioned below:

- Early phase from 1786 to 1969 Nationalisation of Indian Banks – Phase I.
- Nationalisation of Indian Banks and up to 1991 prior to Indian banking sector Reforms – Phase II.
- New phase of Indian Banking System with the advent of Indian Financial and Banking Sector Reforms after 1991 – Phase III.

Phase – I - Pre-Nationalisation Era (1786 – 1969)

The General Bank of India was set up in the year 1786 followed by Bank of Hindustan and Bengal Bank. The East India Company established Bank of Bengal (1806), Bank of Bombay (1840) and Bank of Madras (1843) as independent units and called them Presidency Banks. These three banks were amalgamated in 1920 and a new bank, the Imperial Bank of India was established on 27th January 1921 which started as private shareholders banks, mostly Europeans shareholders.

In 1865, Allahabad Bank was established and first time exclusively by Indians, Punjab National Bank Ltd. was set up in the year 1894 with headquarters at Lahore. The Swadeshi Movement of 1905 gave a fillip to Indian joint stock banking and several of the present leading banks were established around this time. By 1913, there were 41 Indian banks in the field namely, Bank of India, Central Bank of India, Bank of Baroda, Canara Bank, Indian Bank, and Bank of Mysore etc. Reserve Bank of India, which acts as the Central Bank, was created in 1935 by passing of The Reserves Banks of India Act 1934. During the first phase, the growth was very slow and banks also experienced periodic failures between 1913 and 1948. There were approximately 1100 banks, mostly small. Thus, pre-independence history of Indian commercial banking is by checkered growth. It has long periods of slow-growth intervened by short periods of rapid growth, but followed by great banking crisis.

To streamline the functioning and activities of commercial banks, the Government of India came up with The Banking Companies Act, 1949 which was later changed to Banking Regulation Act 1949 as per amending Act of 1965 (Act No. 23 of 1965). Reserve Bank of India was vested with extensive powers for the supervision of banking in India as the Central Banking Authority.

Phase - II - Post-Nationalisation Era or Pre-Liberalisation Era (Upto 1991)

India marched towards the establishment/expansion of public sector banking through the progressive nationalisation of commercial banks. Government took major steps in this Indian Banking Sector Reform after independence. On 1st July, 1955, it nationalised Imperial Bank of India with extensive banking facilities on a large scale especially in rural and semi-urban areas, and converted into State Bank of India to act as the principal agent of RBI and to handle banking transactions of the Union and State Governments all over the country. Later on in 1959-1960 seven subsidiary banks were also nationalised to form the SBI Group.

The progressive nationalisation of banks had increased the role of public sector banking in the country. On July 19, 1969, the Government of India through passing an Ordinance nationalised the 14 major commercial banks in the country, with deposits of ₹ 50 crores each. Again on 15th April, 1980, six more commercial banks (now five because New Bank of India was merged with Punjab National Bank in September 1993) were nationalised. An extensive banking network has been established after nationalisation, and the banking system in no longer confined to the metropolitan cities and large towns. In terms of number of branches, India's banking system is one of largest in the world. Thus, about 90 per cent of the country's commercial banking system is now in the public sector. In short, nationalisation of banks implied a bold and major economic step in the process of banking reforms in the country.

The following are the steps taken by the Government of India to Regulate Banking Institutions in the Country:

- 1949: Enactment of Banking Regulation Act.

- 1955: Nationalisation of State Bank of India.
- 1959: Nationalisation of SBI subsidiaries.
- 1961: Insurance cover extended to deposits.
- 1969: Nationalisation of 14 major banks.
- 1971: Creation of credit guarantee corporation.
- 1975: Creation of regional rural banks.
- 1980: Nationalisation of six banks with deposits over ₹ 200 crores.

Phase – III – Post-Liberalisation Era (After 1991 – Till Today)

This phase has introduced many more products and facilities in the banking sector in its reforms measure. In 1991, under the chairmanship of M. Narasimham, a committee was set up by his name which worked for the liberalisation of banking practices. On the basis of the recommendations of Narasimham Committee Report, the Government of India announced a number of banking sector reforms during 1992-93 for improving the efficiency and to promote competition in the banking sector to enable it to respond more effectively to the emerging needs of the liberalised Indian economy. The following is the partial list of the banking sector reforms:

- Banks norms were liberalised and banks were given freedom to decide levels of holding of individuals items of inventories and receivables.
- Ceiling on term loans was raised to ₹ 10,000 million for projects involving expansions/modernisation of power generation capacities.
- Capital base of the banks were strengthened by recapitalisation, public equity issues and subordinated debt.
- Prudential norms were introduced and progressively tightened for income recognition, classification of assets, provisioning of bad debts, marking to market of investments.
- Pre-emption of bank resources by the government was reduced sharply.
- New private sector banks were licensed and branch licensing restrictions were relaxed.
- At the same time, several operational reforms were introduced in the realm of credit policy:
- Detailed regulations relating to Maximum Permissible Bank Finance were abolished.
- Consortium regulations were relaxed substantially.
- Credit delivery was shifted away from cash credit to loan method.
- Interest rates were freed on corporate bonds, most bank lending, and bank deposits above one year maturity.

- Introduction of auctions coupled with reduced pre-emption led to more market determined.
- Interest rates for government securities.
- Administered interest rates are now confined mainly to short-term bank deposits, priority sector lending, and deposits of non-banking financial companies.

The liberalisation policy of the Government of India also permitted the entry of private sector into the Indian banking industry. The major differentiating parameter that distinguishes these banks from all the other banks is the quality of service offered to the customer - understanding needs of the customer, pre-empting and providing various configurations of benefits and a wide variety of portfolio of products and services. The popularity of these banks can be gauged by the fact that in a short span of time, these banks have gained considerable customer confidence and consequently have shown impressive growth rates. Today, private banks corner a significant share of the total deposits. Most of the banks in this category are concentrated in the high-growth urban areas in metros (that account for approximately 70 per cent of the total banking business). With efficiency being the major focus, these banks have leveraged on their strengths and competencies viz. Management, operational efficiency and flexibility, superior products positioning and higher employee productivity skills. The private banks with their focused business and service portfolio have a reputation of being niche players in the industry. A strategy that has allowed these private sector banks to concentrate on few reliable high net worth companies and individuals rather than cater to the mass market. These integrated strategies have allowed most of these banks to deliver superlative levels of personalised services.

The Structure of the Banking System

The Indian banking system has the Reserve Bank of India (RBI) as the apex institution for all matters to the banking system. RBI is the 'central bank' of India. It is the banker to all other banks. Following is the classification of banks:

1. ***Non-Scheduled Banks*** – These are banks that are not included in the Second Schedule of the Banking Regulation Act, 1965. It means they do not satisfy the conditions laid by the schedule.
2. ***Scheduled Banks*** - Scheduled banks are banks that are included in the Second Schedule of the Banking Regulation Act, 1965. According to this, a scheduled bank:
   (a) Must have paid-up capital and reserve of not less than Rs 500,000.
   (b) Must have satisfied the RBI that its affairs are not conducted in a manner detrimental to the interest of its deposits.

Scheduled banks are sub-divided as:

(i) **Co-operative Banks**: These are co-operative owned and managed by the state. Co-operative Banks in India are registered under the Co-operative Societies Act. The cooperative bank is also regulated by the RBI. They are governed by the Banking Regulations Act 1949 and Banking Laws (Co-operative Societies) Act, 1965.

Types of Co-operative Banks

There are two types of co-operative banks in India. 1. **Short-term lending oriented Co-operative Banks** are sub-divided into **(a) State Co-operative banks, (b) District Co-operative banks and (c) the Primary Agricultural Co-operative societies.**

2. The **long-term lending oriented Co-operative banks**. In this second category there are land developments banks which function at (a) State level, (b) district level, and (c) village level.

The Co-operative banking structure in India is divided into five main categories:

1. Primary Urban Co-operative Banks.
2. Primary Agricultural Credit Societies.
3. District Central Co-operative Banks.

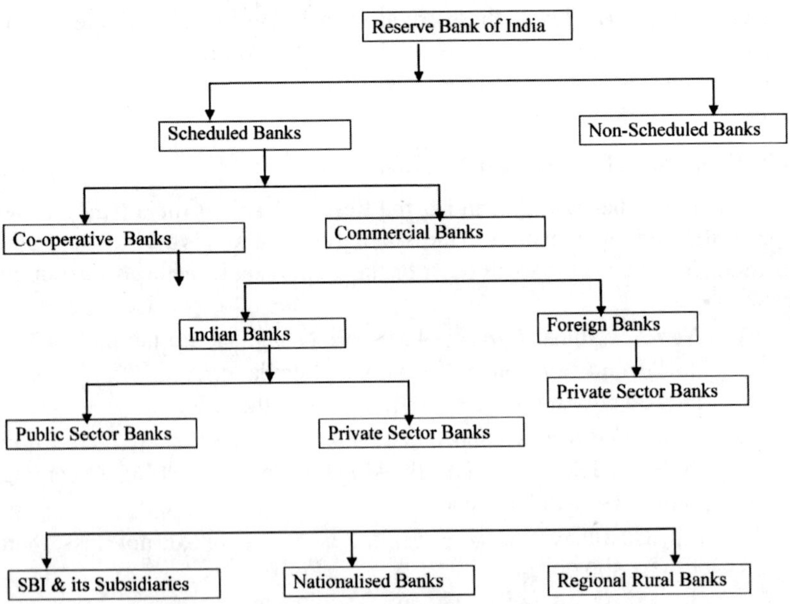

Fig. 2.1: Classifications of Banks.

4. State Co-operative Banks.
5. Land Development Banks.

The co-operative banks have great importance in national development. Without the help of co-operative banks, millions of people in India would be lacking the much needed financial support.

(ii) **Commercial Banks**: These are business entities whose main business is a ccepting deposits and extending loans. Their main objective is profit maximisation and adding shareholder value. Commercial banks are further sub-divided into:

1. **Indian Banks**: These banks are companies registered in India under the Companies Act. Their place of origin is in India.
2. **Foreign Banks**: These are banks that are registered outside India and have originated in a foreign country.

Indian Banks are further sub-divided as Public Sector Banks and Private Sector Banks.

A. Public Sector Banks: Public sector banks further categorised as (a) SBI and its subsidiaries, (b) Nationalised Banks and (c) Regional Rural Banks (RRBs).

(a) **State Bank of India (SBI) and its subsidiaries**: - This group comprises the State Bank of India and its seven subsidiaries (**at present five**) viz. State Bank of Patiala, State Bank of Hyderabad, State Bank of Travancore, State Bank of Bikaner and Jaipur, (State Bank of Saurashtra merged on 13th August 2008 and State Bank of Indore merged in April 2010 with SBI).

(b) **Other Nationalised Banks**: This group consists of private sector banks that were nationalised. The Government of India nationalised 14 banks in 1969 and another six banks in the year 1980. In the year 1993, the government merged New Bank of India with Punjab National Bank. It was the only merger between nationalised banks and resulted in the reduction of the number of nationalised banks from 20 to 19.

(c) **Regional Rural Banks**: These were established by the RBI in 1975. These were established to operate exclusively in rural areas to provide credit and other facilities to small and marginal farmers, agricultural labourers, artisans and small entrepreneurs.

B. Private Sector Banks: Private sector Banks are again classified into (a) Old Private Sector Banks and (b) New Private Sector Banks.

(i) Old Private Sector Banks: The banks that were established by the privy states, community organisations or by group professionals for

Table 2.1: Statistics of Commercial Banks in India

Year	No. of Banks			No. of Bank Offices					Deposits of SCBs (₹ Crores)	Advances of SCBs (₹ Crores)	CD Ratio	Advances to Priority Sector of SCBs (₹ Crores)	Investment of SCBs (₹ Crores)
	SCBs (RRBs)	Non-SCBs	Total	Rural	Semi-Urban	Urban	Metro-Politan	Total					
2001	295 (195)	5	300	32,585 (48.00)	14,843 (22.00)	11,193 (16.00)	9,316 (14.00)	67,937 (100.00)	9,89,141	5,29,271	53.5	1,82,255	3,67,184
2002	293 (195)	4	297	32,503 (48.00)	14,962 (22.00)	11,328 (16.00)	9,402 (14.00)	68,195 (100.00)	11,31,188	6,09,053	53.8	1,77,718	4,37,482
2003	288 (195)	4	292	32,283 (47.00)	15,135 (22 per cent)	11,566 (17.00)	9,516 (14.00)	68,500 (100.00)	13,11,761	7,46,423	56.9	2,18,251	5,47,546
2004	286 (195)	4	290	32,227 (47.00)	15,288 (22.00)	11,806 (17.00)	9,750 (14.00)	69,170 (100.00)	15,04,416	8,40,785	56.1	2,76,621	6,77,588
2005	285 (195)	4	289	30,790 (44.00)	15,325 (22.00)	12,419 (18.00)	11,839 (16.00)	70,373 (100.00)	17,00,198	11,00,428	64.9	3,70,603	7,39,154
2006	218 (133)	4	222	30,436 (42.00)	15,811 (22.00)	13,034 (18.00)	14,204 (20.00)	71,685 (100.00)	21,09,049	15,07,077	72.5	5,12,790	7,17,454
2007	179 (96)	4	183	30,575 (41.00)	16,620 (22.00)	14,049 (19.00)	13,102 (18.00)	74,346 (100.00)	26,11,934	19,31,190	73.9	6,55,317	7,91,516
2008	170 (91)	4	174	31,105 (40.00)	17,897 (23.00)	15,530 (20.00)	14,134 (18.00)	78,666 (100.00)	31,96,940	23,61,913	73.9	7,81,476	9,71,714
2009	166 (86)	4	170	31,699 (39.00)	19,082 (23.00)	16614 (20.00)	15,013 (18.00)	82,408 (100.00)	38,34,110	27,75,549	72.4	9,08,929	11,66,410
2010	163 (82)	4	167	32,528 (37.00)	20,771 (24.00)	18,171 (20.00)	16,298 (19.00)	87,768 (100.00)	44,92,826	32,44,788	72.2	10,91,574	13,84,753
2011	162 (82)	4	171	33,602 (36.10)	23,048 (24.76)	19,156 (20.58)	17,274 (18.56)	93,080 (100.00)	52,07,969	39,42,082	75.7	13,15,861	15,01,619
2012	169 (82)	4	173	35,364 (36.81)	25,076 (26.10)	18,541 (19.30)	17,078 (17.78)	96,059 (100.00)	59,09,082	46,11,82	78.0	14,90,900	17,37,270
2013	153 (64)	4	157	38,451 ((36.74)	27,822 (26.59)	20,127 (19.23)	18,247 (17.44)	1,04,647 (100.00)	69,34,280	53,93,158	77.8	18,18,000	26,13,100
2014	146 (57)	4	150	43,641 (37.74)	30,926 (26.70)	21,783 (18.81)	19,472 (16.81)	1,15,822 (100.00)	79,13,443	61,39,045	77.6	21,54,900	28,82,900
CAGR (per cent)								**3.88**	**16.01**	**19.13**		**19.30**	**15.86**

Source: RBI Reports of 2014.

the cause of economic betterment in their area of operations. Initially, their operations were concentrated in a few regional areas. However, their branches slowly spread throughout the nation as grew.

(ii) New Private Sector Banks: These banks were started as profit oriented companies after the RBI opened the banking sector to the Private Sector. These banks are mostly technology driven and better managed than other banks.

The data in the Table 2.1 presents the statistics of commercial banks in India from 2001 – 2014. Total no. of bank branches increased from 67,937 in 2001 to 1,15,822 in 2014 recording as annual average growth rate of 3.88 per cent. Out of the total branches (1,15,822) 43,641 indicating 37.74 per cent of the total were in rural, 30,926 branches in semi-urban area, 21783 were in urban and 19,472 were in metropolitan cities. Deposits of the all scheduled commercial banks (SCBs) were raised to ₹ 79,13,443 crores in 2014 from ₹ 9,89,141 crores in 2001 showing an average annual growth rate of 16.01 per cent. Advances of all SCBs in 2001 ₹ 5,29,271 crores were raised to ₹ 61,39,045 crores recording CAGR of 19.13 per cent. CD ration of all SCBs in India stood at 77.60 per cent in 2014 against 53.5 per cent in 2001. Advances to priority sector and investment recorded a CAGR of 19.30 per cent and 15.86 per cent during the 2001 to 2014 respectively.

Table 2.2: Branches and ATMs of Scheduled Commercial Banks as of end December, 2014

Sector	*Bank Type*	*No. of Banks*	*No. of Branches*	*ATMs*		
				On-Site	*Off-Site*	*Total*
Public Sector Banks	State Bank of India	6	13661	28926	22827	51753
	Nationalised Banks	19	33627	38606	22265	60871
	Other Public Sector Banks (IDBI + Mahila Bank)	2	-	-	-	-
Private Sector Banks	Old Private Sector Banks	13	4511	4761	4624	9385
	New Private Sector Banks	8	1685	12546	26839	39385
	Foreign Banks	43	242	295	854	1149
	Total	**91**	**53726**	**85134**	**77409**	**162543**

Source: RBI Reports.

As of end of the December 2014, India has 91 scheduled commercial banks (SCBs) – 27 public sector banks (that is with the Government of India holding a stake), 21 private banks (these do not have government stake; they may be publicly listed and traded on stock exchanges) and 43 foreign banks. They have a combined network of over **53,726** branches and **162,543** ATMs. According to a report by ICRA Limited, a rating agency, **the public sector banks** hold over **75 per cent** of total assets of the banking industry, with the **private** and **foreign banks** holding **18.2 per cent** and **6.5 per cent** respectively.

Rural Banking

Two sectors i.e. agriculture and rural sector are playing an essential role in country's overall economic development in terms of income and employment generation and poverty alleviation. For this reason, a great significance has been afforded to developing suitable institutionalisation and mechanism for accommodating needed financial assistance to these sectors.

To viaduct the gap in the flow of credit to the rural poor, Indian government upholded separate banking institution called Regional Rural Banks (RRBs), on the recommendations of Narsimham Committee, passing the RRBs Act of 1976. The RRBs have been occupied a special place in the multi-agency approach adopted to provide agricultural and rural credit in India. These banks are state-sponsored, regionally-based and rural-oriented. Besides the RRBs, commercial and co-operative banks have been furnishing to the credit requirements of the rural India.

Setting up of Regional Rural Banks (RRBs) in the mid-seventies was a major initiative in this direction. The RRBs are specialised rural financial institutions for developing the rural economy by providing credit to small and marginal farmers, agricultural labourers, artisans and small entrepreneurs. Besides the RRBs, commercial and co-operative banks have been catering to the credit requirements of the rural sector.

While the commercial banks, with their focus on profitability had certain limitations in accelerating agricultural credit, the cooperative banks efforts were also hampered by several financial weaknesses. Though over the years the RRBs have been able to expand their outreach and business and meet the credit requirements of the poor, several weaknesses have emerged, eroding their profitability and viability. The recent focus of the Government of India on doubling the flow of credit to the agricultural sector has warranted a re-look at the relative roles of co-operative banks, RRBs and commercial banks. As the very objective of setting up RRBs was to extend adequate credit to the rural borrowers and particularly the economically weaker sections, owing to their rural orientation, there is a growing realisation that RRBs could be used as an effective vehicle for credit delivery in the rural areas. There is, therefore a need to devise ways and means to improve the health and viability of RRBs so as to reposition them in the credit delivery mechanism in India.

The changed prominence on agricultural and rural development by the Government of India would lead to an enhancing demand for innovative financial services in the rural areas. The present structure of rural credit may not be able to meet the requirement and cater to the same. Being specialised financial institution for rural, RRBs would be called upon to play a greater role in providing such services due to their rural character and feel. RRBs have to take over a larger share of credit disbursements calling for much larger resource mobilisation, as also greater efforts for their institutional strengthening.

Rural banking in India started since the establishment of banking sector in India. Rural Banks in those days mainly focused upon the agro sector. Now, Regional Rural Banks in India penetrated every corner of the country and extended a helping hand in the growth process of the country.

An Overview of RRBs

The Government of India promoted Regional Rural Banks (RRBs) through the RRBs Act of 1976 to bridge the gap in the flow of credit to the rural poor. Despite the various measures taken by the Government and the Reserve Bank through social control and the nationalisation of 14 major commercial banks, a large proportion of the rural poor remained outside the banking fold. A Working Group was appointed in 1975 under the Chairmanship of M. Narsimham, to explore the possibilities of evolving an alternative rural credit agency to benefit the rural poor. The group recommended formation of a new set of regionally oriented rural banks which would combine the local feel and familiarity of rural problems characteristic of cooperatives and the professionalism and large resource base of commercial banks. Following the recommendation, RRBs were set up in 1975.

The RRBs have a special place in the multi-agency approach adopted to provide agricultural and rural credit in India. These banks are state-sponsored, regionally based and rural-oriented. The RRBs were established "with a view to developing the rural economy by providing, for the purpose of development of agriculture, trade, commerce, industry and other productive activities in the rural areas, credit and other facilities, particularly to small and marginal farmers, agricultural labourers, artisans and small entrepreneurs, and for matters connected therewith and incidental thereto" (RRBs Act,1976). Their equity is held by the Central Government, concerned State Government and Sponsor bank in the proportion of 50:15:35.

The first five RRBs were set up in five States in Haryana, West Bengal, Rajasthan, with one each and two in Uttar Pradesh, which were sponsored by different commercial banks. These banks covered 11 districts of these five states. The first five Regional Rural Banks are as follows:

1. Prathama Bank,
2. Gorakhpur Kshetriya Gramin Bank in Uttar Pradesh,
3. Haryana Krishi Gramin Bank in Haryana,
4. Gour Gramin Bank in West Bengal,
5. Jaipur-Nagpur Anchalik Gramin Bank, Rajasthan.

RRBs have played a key role in rural institutional financing in terms of geographical coverage, clientele outreach, business volume as also contribution to development of the rural economy. A remarkable feature of their performance over the past three decades has been the massive expansion of their retail network in rural areas from the modest beginning of five RRBs with 17 branches covering 12 districts in December 1975.

As on 31st March, 2014, 57 RRBs operated with a network of 19,082 branches (17,861 branches during previous year) covering 642 districts. seventy five per cent of the branches of the RRBs were in the rural areas. As on 31st March, 2013 the rural branches of RRBs formed 38 per cent of the total rural branch network in the country (excluding cooperatives).

RRBs, with their wide outreach in rural India, region-centric banking activities and close relationship with the local authorities and population, were expected to cater to the credit requirements of the rural areas and provide necessary banking infrastructure. Though the RRBs have been able to mobilise small savings of the rural sector, they have been relatively less successful in enhancing the flow of credit to the targeted rural poor.

References

Books

1. *An Overview of Banking.* (2006). Hyderabad: ICFAI University Press.
2. *Banking Services Operations.* (2006). Hyderabad: ICFAI University Press.
3. Desai, V. (2001). *The Indian Financial System and Development.* Bangalore: Himalaya Publishers.
4. Gordon, M. A. (2001). *Banking and Financial Systems* (1st ed.). Hyderabad: Himalaya Publishing House.
5. Mishra, S. S. (2005). *Indian Banking System.* New Delhi: Mahamaya Publishing House.
6. *Money and Banking.* (2005). Hyderabad: ICFAI University Press.
7. Paul, S. M. (2000). *Banking and Financial Services.* Hyderabad: Kalyani Publishers.
8. Puri, M. A. (2009). *Indian Economy* (27th ed.). New Delhi: Himalaya Publishing House.
9. *Rural Banking and Micro Finance.* (2006). Hyderabad: ICFAI University Press.
10. Sarkar, P.N., V. A. (1999). *Banking Law and Practice* (18th ed.). New Delhi: Sultan Chand and Sons.
11. Sundaram, R. D. (2010). *Indian Economy* (61th ed.). New Delhi: S. Chand.

Journals

1. Indian Journal of Marketing
2. Indian Journal of Finance

3. Indian Journal of Management
4. International Journal of Finance and Banking Studies [IJFBS]
5. International Journal of Banking
6. Journal of Finance and Banking Management

Websites

1. www.nabard.org
2. www.rbi.org.in

Chapter – 3

Profile of Selected Banks in Karimnagar District

Introduction

Having discussed the growth and development of banking sector in India in the above chapter an attempt was made to study of brief profile of the selected banks in the Karimnagar district. This chapter consists two major parts A and B. The part-A deals with the profile of the selected banks (SBH, TGB and HDFC banks) and the part – B explains the brief profile of Karimnaar district.

A. Profile of Selected Banks

3.1 State Bank of Hyderabad: State Bank of Hyderabad (SBH) is a nationalised bank in India, with headquarters at Hyderabad, Telangana State. It is one of the five associate banks of State Bank of India and is one of the scheduled banks. It was founded in 1941 as Hyderabad State Bank. Since 1956 it has been a subsidiary of State Bank of India and now is State Bank's largest associate bank. The Bank's head office is situated at Gunfoundry Area, in Hyderabad, SBH has over 1,500 branches and about 12,800 employees. Assets are in excess of Rupees 767 billion as on March 2014.

The bank has performed well in the past decades, winning several awards for its banking practices. Smt Arundhati Bhattacharya is the current Chairman and Sri Santanu Mukherjee is the current Managing Director. It is the chief banker of Telangana State.

Evolution of the SBH Bank

The bank originated as the central bank of the erstwhile Nizam state under the name, **Hyderabad State Bank**. It was established on 8 August 1941 under the Hyderabad State Bank Act, during the reign of the last Nizam of Hyderabad, Mir Osman Ali Khan. The bank managed the Osmania Sicca, the currency of Hyderabad state, which covered the present-day Telangana, Hyderabad-Karnataka of Karnatak and Marathwada of Maharashtra. (At the time a number of the princely states had their own currencies.) The bank also carried out commercial banking. The bank opened its first branch at Gunfoundry, Hyderabad on 5 April, 1942. The Imperial Bank of India, which had established a branch in Hyderabad in 1868 and another in Secunderabad in 1906, provided officers and clerical employees in the initial stages, and later the trained were provided for training new recruits. The first Secretary of Hyderabad State Bank was Muhammad Saleh Akbar Hydari, son of Sir Akbar Hydari. After Partition, on 17 September 1948 the Indian Army conducted Operation Polo, which resulted in the annexation of Hyderabad to India. By 1950, the bank had some 50 branches, including branches in parts of the then Hyderabad State that would later be transferred to other states.

In 1953, the bank absorbed, by merger, the **Mercantile Bank of Hyderabad**, which Raja Pannalal Pitti had founded in 1935. (Other accounts gave year of funding as 1946 and that of merger as 1952). In the same year, the Bank started conducting government and Treasury business as agent for the Reserve Bank of India. In 1956, the Reserve Bank of India took over the bank as its first subsidiary and renamed it State Bank of Hyderabad. That same year saw the break-up of Hyderabad State. Aurangabad, Beed, Parbhani, Nanded,and Osmanabad merged with Maharashtra state. Gulbarga, Bidar, Raichur, and parts of Osmanabad were attached to Karnataka state. The remaining districts formed Telangana. After the trifurcation, the branches of Hyderabad State Bank continued to conduct government transactions in their new states as well.

The Subsidiary Banks Act was passed in 1959, so on 1 October 1959 it and the other banks of the princely states became subsidiaries of SBI.

Performance of SBH Bank

Branch Expansion

The total branch network expanded from 929 in FY 2005 to 1,694 as at March 2014. The population-wise breakup is as under. The Table 3.1 furnishes the details of branch network of SBH. According to the table, over the course of 10 years period, the total branch network grew an average of 6.19 per cent. The highest growth rate was recorded in the semi-urban area with an average growth rate of 6.49 per cent annually. In this area bank established 544 branches by the end of March 2014. Following this, metropolitan area stood at second with an average growth rate of 6.25 per cent.

Table 3.1: Population-Wise Share of Bank Branches - SBH

Sl. No.	*Year*	*Rural*	*Semi-urban*	*Urban*	*Metropolitan*	*Total*
1	2005	286	290	197	156	929
2	2006	287	293	204	160	944
3	2007	280	298	211	176	965
4	2008	284	308	224	185	1001
5	2009	287	312	237	195	1031
6	2010	317	376	277	215	1185
7	2011	256	438	286	235	1215
8	2012	424	468	321	262	1475
9	2013	472	495	330	261	1558
10	2014	513	544	356	281	1694
CAGR		**6.02**	**6.49**	**6.10**	**6.25**	**6.19**

Source: Compiled from various Annual Reports of State Bank of Hyderabad.

SBH established a total of 513 branches in rural area by the end of March 2014 from 286 branches in 2005. It is clear that SBH bank had given much priority to semi-urban and rural areas in establishing its bank branches.

Deposits and Advances of the Bank

Table 3.2: Deposits and Advances of SBH Bank (₹ Crores)

Sl. No.	*Year*	*Deposits*	*Advances*	*CD Ratio*	*Net NPA (per cent)*
1	2005	28929.52	15599.74	53.92	0.61
2	2006	34024.60	20863.02	61.32	0.36
3	2007	41502.67	28109.25	67.73	0.22
4	2008	50108.30	35848.75	71.54	0.16
5	2009	62448.91	43676.17	69.94	0.38
6	2010	72970.72	53040.07	72.69	0.55
7	2011	88627.87	64720.31	73.02	0.87
8	2012	98731.91	77052.31	78.12	1.30
9	2013	117270.00	92171.00	78.60	1.61
10	2014	120868.00	98886.00	81.81	3.12
CAGR		**15.37**	**20.28**	**4.26**	**17.13**

Source: Compiled from various Annual Reports of State Bank of Hyderabad.

The data in the above table shows the deposits accepted, Advances given, CD Ratio and Percentage of net NPAs to Net Advances of SBH bank over the period of 10 years from 2005 to 2014. The Compounded Annual Growth Rate for the period of 10 years from 2005 to 2013-14 for Deposits shows that the Deposits of the bank grew from ₹ 28929.52 crores in 2005 to ₹ 120868.00

recording an average of 15.37 per cent growth rate annually. Advances of the bank reached to ₹ 98886.00 crores in 2014 from ₹ 15599.74 crores in 2005 showing average growth rate of 20.28 per cent. The CD ratio raised from 53.92 per cent in 2005 to 81.81 per cent in 2014 registering 4.26 per cent growth rate. The percentage of CAGR relating to the Net NPAs to Net Advances has registered a growth rate of 17.13 per cent for the 10 years period indicating high growth in the NPAs.

Profitability of SBH Bank

Profit can be defined as, in simple terms, as excess of income over expenditure. In order for a business to become self-sustaining and capable of attracting investment, it must generate profits. Otherwise, it will eventually become insolvent. Without profit, a business would stagnate and risk on losing its market share to other competitors. Profits and losses are indications showing whether the business is doing the right things or not. It is how the people in the marketplace tell a business what is needed and wanted, what should be eliminated, what should be expanded, what needs to be improved, etc. Profits and losses constitute an important feedback that improves economic efficiency. Profits also enable the business to grow. If what the business is doing good, then the business needs to grow so that it can do more good. If business does not make profits, then there's something wrong with what business is doing, and such they deserve to go out of business.

It is fact that the absolute figures may not always exhibit the true profitability. Therefore along with Net Profit, the Return on Assets, Earning per Share and Profit per Employee are considered for analysis of the profitability.

Table 3.3: Profitability of the Bank - SBH

Sl. No.	*Year*	*Net Profit (₹ In Crores)*	*Return on Assets (per cent)*	*Earnings per Share (₹)*	*Profit per Employee (₹ In Lakhs)*
1	2005	250.90	0.72	1454.49	1.91
2	2006	427.04	1.13	2475.59	3.26
3	2007	505.50	1.15	2930.43	3.92
4	2008	556.99	1.00	3228.92	4.35
5	2009	615.81	0.91	3569.91	4.90
6	2010	822.71	1.03	4766.66	5.58
7	2011	1166.24	1.22	5620.38	7.58
8	2012	1298.27	1.15	6256.71	8.63
9	2013	1250.22	0.99	6025.00	8.29
10	2014	1019.51	0.70	4913.00	6.10
CAGR		**15.05**	**-0.28**	**12.94**	**12.31**

Source: Compiled from various Annual Reports of State Bank of Hyderabad.

The table shows that State Bank of Hyderabad has registered an increase of Net Profit at a Compounded Annual Growth Rate of 15.05 per cent. The CAGR for Return on Assets has registered a negative growth rate of 0.28 per cent indicating actual decrease in the RoAs and Earnings per Share (EPS) at 12.94 per cent and Profit per Employee at a rate of 12.31 per cent. With the above table it is clear that the profitability of the State Bank of Hyderabad may be said, is good and is growing at a healthy rate.

Priority Sector Lending

Priority Sector Lending primarily consists of lending to Agriculture, Small Scale Industries, Small Business and Other Priority Sectors like small road and water transport operators, Retail trade, loans to professional and self employed persons, Housing loans etc. The details of priority sector lending by SBH are presented in the following table.

The Compounded Annual Growth rate for the period 2005 to 2014 for the total Priority Sector Lending (PSL) is calculated as 20.62 per cent, for Agricultural Advances it is 23.11 per cent, for advances to MSMEs (Micro, Small and Medium Enterprises) Units it is 28.07 per cent, and for Advances to Other Priority Sectors the Compounded Annual Growth Rate is 12.73 per cent. The bank had fulfilled the norm of RBI i.e. 40 per cent of total lending to priority sector.

Table 3.4: Priority Sector Lending by State Bank Hyderabad (₹ in crores)

Sl. No.	*Year*	*Agri-cultural*	*MSMEs*	*Others*	*Total*	*Per cent of Total Advances*	*RBI Norm*
1.	2005	2113.42	1237.56	3037.74	6388.72	40.65	40 per cent of total lending
2.	2006	2879.35	1445.57	4065.95	8390.87	40.14	
3.	2007	3873.00	1659.00	5783.00	11315.00	40.31	
4.	2008	5289.74	2391.00	5188.26	12869.00	45.40	
5.	2009	7049.53	2909.92	5229.55	15189.00	42.14	
6.	2010	8580.18	4318.22	5249.74	18148.14	41.16	
7.	2011	10675.02	5642.00	7322.45	23639.47	44.31	
8.	2012	12908.51	6779.60	7399.64	27087.75	41.40	
9.	2013	14511.00	11932.38	NA	NA		
10.	2014	16905.00	14686.00	10069.67	41660.67	42.13	
CAGR		**23.11**	**28.07**	**12.73**	**20.62**		

Source: Compiled from various Annual Reports of State Bank of Hyderabad.

The CAGR for the Advances to Agriculture and MSMEs surpassed the CAGR for the Total Priority Sector Advances furnishes that the bank had given much priority to business people of small enterprises and agricultural farmers in lendings.

It can be inferred, from the above table, that there is a consistent increase in the advances to the Agriculture, MSMEs and Other Priority Sectors.

Products and Services of SBH

SBH offers a basket of myriad deposit products catering to all age groups. SBH is *inter alia,* into rural finance, especially credit to agriculture and allied activities. Loans for self help groups, Tractor loans and loans for horticulture development are part of prioritized activities. In the retail segment the bank is very active in financing housing and education apart from financing two wheelers and cars. The bank has focused on financing the SME sector in a big way over the last two years. The bank has several pioneering loan products like Laghu Udyami credit card, SME Credit Plus, SME Smart Score and Kanya Vivah Suvidha scheme to help Indian households to perform their daughters' marriages. The bank has its fair share of business in financing India's manufacturing sector especially the small and medium enterprises. Almost 50 per cent of the bank's credit is extended to commercial and industrial projects. Through its network of specialised branches the bank has good exposure in financing infrastructure projects such as airports, seaports, roads, power etc. The bank has financed large number of industrial export activities in sectors like diamonds, textiles, pharmaceuticals, steel etc. Among the new Initiatives, SBH has implemented technology driven initiatives such as Core Banking Solutions (CBS), Internet Banking, Any Branch Banking, Real Time Gross Settlement (RTGS), and NEFT (National Electronic Funds Transfer). Business Process Reengineering (BPR) initiatives focus on improving the quality of customer service, reducing turnaround time for sanction and disbursement of loans with several centralised processing centres launched in the last one year in both retail and small enterprise segments.

Other Services

- Debit Card Loyalty
- Online Shopping
- ASBA (Application Supported by Blocked Amount) Facility
- Secure Card Transactions
- Railway Booking

All the branches of the Bank are totally networked under Core Banking Solutions, offering a wide range of products to its customers. All the customers of the Bank have access to the latest technologies like Internet Banking, ATMs etc. The Bank has pan India presence and operates through more than 1600 Bank branches.

Telangana Grameena Bank

Brief History of TGB

The Telangana Grameena Bank-TGB (formerly known as Deccan Grameena Bank – TGB) was established by amalgamating four RRBs sponsored by State Bank of Hyderabad, viz. (1) Sri Saraswathi Grameena Bank, Adilabad (2) Sri Satavahana Grameena Bank, Karimnagar (3) Sri Rama Grameena Bank, Nizamabad and (4) Golconda Grameena Bank, Ranga Reddy (Hyderabad) with an aggregate network of 300 branches. The Area of operation of the Bank covers the districts of Adilabad, Karimnagar, Nizamabad, Hyderabad and Ranga Reddy districts of Telangana state. The authorised share capital of the Bank is ₹ 5 crores. The paid-up capital is ₹ 4 crores which is contributed by Government of India, Sponsor Bank i.e. State Bank of Hyderabad and Government of Telangana in the ratio of 50: 35: 15 respectively.

Performance of TGB

TGB is growing with consistent performance from branch level to Regional level. During the year 2012-13, the bank introduced new products i.e., Deccan Haritha and Deccan Shakti in term deposit segment with a view to enlarge small investor base, the focus of the bank has been spread across many areas in business development. The most significant of them are structural adjustments in deposits portfolio for sustainable business growth. The vision of the bank is to be the premier RRB in the state providing technologically advanced, committed and quality service in all spheres of banking and be the most trusted bank for rural development.

The mission of the bank with "Providing transparent and efficient Banking Services at a reasonable cost at the doorsteps of our customers by ensuring 100 per cent Financial Inclusion, empowerment of rural customers, promotion Self Help Group (SHG) movement with special emphasis on women and earn continuous profits by having a healthy business mix, thus, becoming a leading Bank in our area of operation". This paper throws light in the various aspects of TGB such as branch-wise development, TGB financial Performance, classification of assets Recovery, Profitability etc.

Branch Network

TGB has given emphasis for opening of branches in rural unbanked areas as per the Government of India policy. During the year 2013-14 the bank has opened 31 new branches against the target of 27 branches under MoU and reached 300 mark. Year-wise branch details are furnished in the following table.

Table 3.5: Development of Branches of TGB During 2004-05 to 2013-14

Area	*2004-05*	*2005-06*	*2006-07*	*2007-08*	*2008-09*	*2009-10*	*2010-11*	*2011-12*	*2012-13*	*2013-14*
(i) Rural	138 (83.64)	138 (83.13)	138 (83.13)	142 (82.08)	149 (74.50)	155 (72.09)	160 (70.80)	168 (69.14)	186 (69.14)	209 (69.67)
(ii) Semi Urban	17 (10.30)	17 (10.24)	17 (10.24)	19 (10.98)	30 (15.00)	35 (16.28)	36 (15.93)	42 (17.28)	50 (18.60)	52 (17.33)
(iii) Urban	10 (6.06)	11 (6.63)	11 (6.63)	12 (6.94)	21 (10.50)	25 (11.63)	30 (13.27)	33 (13.58)	20 (7.43)	26 (8.67)
(iv) Metropolitan	-	-	-	-	-	-	-	-	13 (4.83)	13 (4.33)
Total	**165 (100.00)**	**166 (100.00)**	**166 (100.00)**	**173 (100.00)**	**200 (100.00)**	**215 (100.00)**	**226 (100.00)**	**243 (100.00)**	**269 (100.00)**	**300 (100.00)**

The Table 3.5 contains the development of the branches during the years 2004-05 to 2013-14. The performance indicator shows the branches' development in rural, semi-urban, urban areas in five districts of Telangana State.

On examination of data presented in the above table the most of the branches are clearly placed at rural areas with 83.64 per cent (138) in the year 2004-05 and maximum reached to 209 branches in the financial year 2013 - 14. Thirteen branches were started in the metropolitan areas in the financial year 2012-2013. With the above data, it is said that TGB has less focus on semi-urban and urban in areas because it is Under RRB.

From the financial years 2007-08 to 2013 -14 the bank zooming on branch expansion and slowly increased, by the end of the 2013-14 (300) during the period under study. It may be concluded from the analysis that TGB will expand its branches all over the rural areas in Telangana State to assist the farmers, rural artisans and small business people to meet their financial needs.

Deposits and Advances of the Bank

The data in the above table shows the deposits accepted, Advances given, CD Ratio and Percentage of net NPAs to Net Advances of SBH bank over the period of 10 years from 2005 to 2014. The Compounded Annual Growth Rate for the period of 10 years from 2005 to 2013-14 for Deposits shows that the Deposits of the bank grew from ₹ 932.14 crores in 2005 to ₹ 4155.43 crores recording an average of 16.12 per cent growth rate annually. Advances of the bank reached to ₹ 3531.10 crores in 2014 from ₹ 599.14 crores in 2005 showing average growth rate of 20.24 per cent.

Table 3.6: Deposits and Advances of the Bank - TGB

(₹ In Crores)

Sl. No.	*Year*	*Deposits*	*Advances*	*CD Ratio*	*Net NPA (per cent)*
1.	2005	932.14	559.14	59.98	4.73
2.	2006	1011.44	605.93	59.91	4.75
3.	2007	1261.75	750.49	59.48	1.64
4.	2008	1444.18	1001.41	69.34	0
5.	2009	1790.43	1296.38	72.41	0
6.	2010	2261.05	1610.78	71.24	0
7.	2011	2600.94	1966.16	75.59	0
8.	2012	2920.67	2362.37	80.88	1.70
9.	2013	3444.92	2775.46	80.57	0.86
10.	2014	4155.43	3531.10	84.98	0.42
CAGR (per cent)		**16.12**	**20.24**	**3.55**	**-21.51**

Source: Compiled from various Annual Reports of TGB.

The CD ratio raised from 59.98 per cent in 2005 to 84.98 per cent in 2014 registering 3.55 per cent growth rate. The percentage of CAGR relating to the Net NPAs to Net Advances has registered a negative growth rate of 21.51 per cent for the 10 years period indicating high decline in the NPAs.

Profitability of TGB

Table 3.7: Profitability of the Bank - TGB

Sl. No.	*Year*	*Net Profit (₹ in Crores)*	*Return on Assets (per cent)*	*Profit per Employee (₹ in Lackhs)*
1.	2005	15.40	3.46	3.47
2.	2006	17.45	3.87	2.99
3.	2007	10.00	7.58	2.92
4.	2008	10.00	7.97	3.54
5.	2009	39.88	8.67	4.42
6.	2010	54.90	7.94	5.08
7.	2011	45.10	8.47	5.32
8.	2012	36.24	8.64	5.17
9.	2013	49.28	8.90	6.31
10.	2014	63.62	9.00	6.72
CAGR		**15.24**	**10.03**	**6.83**

The above table shows that Telangana Grameena Bank has registered an increase of Net Profit at a Compounded Annual Growth Rate of 15.24 per cent. The CAGR for Return on Assets has registered a growth rate of 10.03 per cent and Profit per Employee at a rate of 6.83 per cent. With the above table it is clear that the profitability of the Telangana Grameena Bank may be said, is good and is growing at a healthy growth rate.

Priority Sector Lending

According to the data in the Table 3.8, the Compounded Annual Growth Rate (CAGR) for the period 2005 to 2014 for the total Priority Sector Lending (PSL) is calculated as 22.27 per cent, for Farm-Sector (Agricultural and Allied to Agricultural Advances), it is 25.56 per cent, for advances to Non-Farm Sector, MSMEs (Micro, Small and Medium Enterprises) Units and others, it is 13.09 per cent.

Table 3.8: Priority Sector Lending by TGB (₹ In Crores)

Sl. No.	*Year*	*Farm-Sector*	*Non-Farm Sector*	*Total*	*Per cent of Total Advances*
1.	2005	241.38	135.79	377.17	67.46
2.	2006	258..00	151.50	409.50	66.00
3.	2007	295.59	224.94	520.54	69.36
4.	2008	532.02	156.58	688.59	68.76
5.	2009	760.93	156.05	916.98	70.73
6.	2010	1006.95	263.13	1270.08	78.84
7.	2011	1249.89	294.69	1544.58	78.56
8.	2012	1517.70	340.03	1857.73	78.64
9.	2013	1802.93	359.24	2162.17	77.90
10.	2014	2351.31	464.50	2815.81	65.76
CAGR		**25.56**	**13.09**	**22.27**	

Source: Compiled from various Annual Reports of TGB.

The CAGR for the Farm-Sector Advances surpassed the CAGR for the Total Priority Sector Advances and indicating that TGB had given much priority to the agriculture and allied activities in lending.

Products and Services of TGB

Table 3.9: Products and Services of TGB

1.	**Deposits**	Savings Bank Account	**2.**	**Loans and Advances**	Agricultural
		Basic Savings Bank Account			Industry
		Current Account			Trade
		Fixed Deposit			Self-Employment
		Short Term Deposit			Personal
		Special Term Deposit			Education
		Sri Rama Raksha Tax Saver Fixed Deposit Scheme			Housing
		Recurring Deposit			Other Facilities
		Deccan Lakpati scheme	**3.**	**Services**	NEFT
		Tax Implications			Non Home Transactions
		"DECCAN AKSHAYA"			SMS ALERTS
		TGB SARAL RD			Safety Lockers
		TGB VISVAS 666 days scheme			

New Schemes

The bank is going to launch new schemes like Deccan Kranti, Deccan Star, Deccan Akshaya, Deccan Double Dhamaka, Deccan Saral RD and Deccan Viswas to suit the requirements of different clientele of the bank.

HDFC Bank

Evolution of HDFC Bank

The Housing Development Finance Corporation Limited (HDFC) was amongst the first to receive an 'in principle' approval from the Reserve Bank of India (RBI) to set up a bank in the private sector, as part of RBI's liberalisation of the Indian Banking Industry in 1994. The bank was incorporated in August 1994 in the name of 'HDFC Bank Limited', with its registered office in Mumbai, India. HDFC Bank commenced operations as a Scheduled Commercial Bank in January 1995.

Performance of HDFC Bank

HDFC is India's premier housing finance company and enjoys an impeccable track record in India as well as in international markets. Since its inception in 1977, the Corporation has maintained a consistent and healthy growth in its operations to remain the market leader in mortgages. Its outstanding loan portfolio covers well over a million dwelling units. HDFC has developed a significant expertise in retail mortgage loans to different market segments and also has a large corporate client base for its housing related credit facilities. With its experience in the financial markets, strong market reputation, large shareholder base and unique consumer franchise, HDFC was ideally positioned to promote a bank in the Indian environment.

Branch Expansion of HDFC Bank

Today, HDFC Bank is a 'one stop shop' financial services provider. By focusing on understanding its customers' needs, they have created a comprehensive range of world class products. Its emphasis on operational excellence allows presenting the right product to the right person at the right time. It is committed to execute the business strategy while ensuring the highest levels of ethical standards, professional integrity, corporate governance and regulatory compliance. Its financial performance in the yester years has been commendable despite an economic slowdown. The normal basis for growth, which is to gain market share of 3-5 per cent with the banking system growing at roughly three times the real GDP, is intact. HDFC Bank's competitive strength lies in the way used technology to deliver service that is relevant, world class and timely. For instance, Hindi mobile app, Hindi SMS Banking and a Toll free number to carry out basic banking activities have allowed reaching out more to people, and have received great response, particularly in rural and semi-urban areas.

Table 3.10: Expansion of Bank Branches - HDFC

Sl. No.	*Year*	*Rural*	*Semi-urban*	*Urban*	*Metropolitan*	*Total*
1	2005	NA	NA	NA	NA	467
2	2006	NA	NA	NA	NA	535
3	2007	NA	NA	NA	NA	684
4	2008	NA	NA	NA	NA	761
5	2009	NA	NA	NA	NA	1412
6	2010	NA	NA	NA	NA	1725
7	2011	NA	NA	NA	NA	1986
8	2012	NA	NA	NA	NA	2544
9	2013	NA	NA	NA	NA	3062
10	2014	NA	NA	NA	NA	3403
CAGR						**21.97**

Source: Compiled from various Annual Reports of HDFC Bank.

HDFC bank is one among the largest private sector new generation commercial banks in the country, with a distribution network comprising 3,403 branches on 31st March 2014 recording an average growth rate of 21.97 per cent. The Bank recognised that the rural population in India remains under banked and underserved, and faced with limited choices when it comes to financial services. So, bank is putting much concentration on rural area by establishing its branches in rural to mobilise the rural resources.

Deposits and Advances of the Bank

The bank's focus has been to go deeper into the rural hinterland and provide full range of customised banking services across savings, loans and payment and investment products in all branches.

The data in the Table 3.11 shows the deposits accepted, Advances given, CD Ratio and Percentage of net NPAs to Net Advances of HDFC bank over the period of 10 years from 2005 to 2014. The Compounded Annual Growth Rate for the period of 10 years from 2005 to 2013-14 for Deposits shows that the Deposits of the bank grew from ₹ 36354.25 crores in 2005 to ₹ 367337.48 recording an average of 26.02 per cent growth rate annually.

Table 3.11: Deposits and Advances of HDFC Bank

(₹ In Crores)

Sl. No.	Year	Deposits	Advances	CD Ratio	Net NPA (per cent)
1.	2005	36354.25	25566.30	70.33	0.24
2.	2006	55796.82	35061.26	62.84	0.44
3.	2007	68297.94	46944.78	68.74	0.43
4.	2008	100768.60	63426.89	62.94	0.47
5.	2009	142811.58	98883.00	69.24	0.63
6.	2010	167404.44	125831.00	75.17	0.31
7.	2011	208586.41	159983.00	76.70	0.19
8.	2012	246706.45	195420.00	79.21	0.18
9.	2013	296246.98	239720.64	80.92	0.20
10.	2014	367337.48	303000.27	82.49	0.28
CAGR		**26.02**	**28.05**	**1.61**	**1.55**

Source: Compiled from various Annual Reports of HDFC Bank.

Advances of the bank reached to ₹ 303000.27 crores in 2014 from ₹ 25566.30 crores in 2005 showing average growth rate of 28.05 per cent. The CD ratio raised from 70.33 per cent in 2005 to 82.49 per cent in 2014 registering continuous growth rate indicating an average of 1.16 per cent annually. The percentage of CAGR relating to the Net NPAs to Net Advances has registered a growth rate of 1.55 per cent for the 10 years period indicating very low growth in the NPAs.

Profitability of HDFC Bank

The Table 3.12 shows that HDFC bank has registered an increase of Net Profit at a Compounded Annual Growth Rate of 28.97 per cent. The CAGR for Return on Assets has registered a growth rate of 3.13 per and Earnings per Share (EPS) at 12.94 per cent and Profit per Employee at a rate of 12.31 per cent.

Table 3.12: Profitability of the Bank - HDFC

Sl. No.	Year	Net Profit (₹ In Crores)	Return on Assets (per cent)	Earnings per Share (₹)	Profit per Employee (₹ In Lakhs)
1.	2005	666.00	1.47	4.58	8.80
2.	2006	871.00	1.38	5.58	7.39
3.	2007	1141.00	1.33	7.26	6.13
4.	2008	1590.00	1.32	9.24	4.97

(Contd...)

5.	2009	2245.00	1.28	10.57	4.18
6.	2010	2948.70	1.53	13.51	5.98
7.	2011	3926.40	1.58	17.00	7.37
8.	2012	5167.07	1.77	22.11	8.00
9.	2013	6726.28	1.90	28.49	10.00
10.	2014	8478.38	2.00	35.47	12.00
CAGR		**28.97**	**3.13**	**22.72**	**3.15**

Source: Compiled from various Annual Reports.

With the above table it is clear that the profitability of HDFC Bank may be said, is good and is growing at a healthy rate.

Priority Sector Lending

Table 3.13: Priority Sector Lending by HDFC Bank

Sl. No.	*Year*	*Agricultural*	*MSMEs*	*Others*	*Total PSL Lending*	*Total Advances*	*Per cent of Total Advances*
1	2005	NA	NA	NA	5616.62	25566.30	21.97
2	2006	NA	NA	NA	10864.53	35061.26	30.99
3	2007	NA	NA	NA	17683.07	46944.78	37.67
4	2008	NA	NA	NA	17426.29	63426.89	27.47
5	2009	NA	NA	NA	29781.59	98883.00	30.12
6	2010	NA	NA	NA	44157.57	125831.00	35.09
7	2011	NA	NA	NA	54781.22	159983.00	34.24
8	2012	NA	NA	NA	63863.00	195420.00	32.68
9	2013	NA	NA	NA	76743.03	239720.64	32.01
10	2014	NA	NA	NA	89612.87	303000.27	29.58
CAGR					**31.91**		

Source: Compiled from various Annual Reports of HDFC Bank.

Note: The sector-wise details of the priority sector lending were not available.

The Compounded Annual Growth rate for the period 2005 to 2014 for the total Priority Sector Lending (PSL) is calculated as 31.91 per cent. The sector-wise details of the priority sector lending were not available. It is to note that the bank had not met the RBI norm of 40 per cent of the total advances to the priority sector in any year under study.

Products and Services

The Bank caters to a wide range of banking services covering commercial and investment banking on the wholesale side and transactional/branch banking on the retail side. The Bank serves customers through three key business segments which comprise mainly of:

1. Wholesale Banking
2. Retail Banking
3. Treasury

Wholesale Banking

With superior product delivery, service levels and strong customer orientation, bank made significant inroads into the banking consortia of a number of leading Indian corporate including multinationals, companies from the domestic business houses and prime public sector companies and are recognised as a leading provider of cash management and transactional banking solutions to corporate customers, mutual funds, stock exchange members and banks.

Table 3.14: Wholesale Banking Products/Services

Commercial Banking	Working Capital, Term Loans, Bill / Invoice discounting, Forex & Derivatives, Wholesale, Deposits, Letters of Credit, Guarantees
Transactional Banking	Cash Management, Custodial Services, Clearing Bank to Public Issues
Investment Banking	Debt Capital Markets, Equity Capital Markets, Project Finance, M&A and Advisory

Retail Banking

Retail banking business provides customers with a full range of financial products and banking services, giving them a one-stop window for all their banking requirements. The products are backed by world class service and delivered to customers through growing branch network, as well as through alternative delivery channels like ATMs, Phone Banking, Net Banking and Mobile Banking.

Table 3.15: Retail Banking Products/Services

Loan Products	Auto Loans, Personal Loans, Home Loans, Vehicle Finance, Agri and Tractor Loans, Credit cards, Loans against Gold/ Securities, Construction Equipment Finance, Education Loans, SHG Loans, Kisan Gold Card
Deposit Products	Savings Accounts, Current Accounts, Fixed/Recurring Deposits, Corporate Salary Accounts
Other Services	Depository Accounts, Mutual Fund Sales, Private Banking, Insurance Sales (Life, General), NRI Services, Bill Payment Services, POS Terminals, Debit Cards, Foreign Exchange Services, Broking (HDFC Securities Ltd)

Treasury

With the liberalisation of the financial markets in India, corporate need more sophisticated risk management information, advice and product structures. Along with such services, fine pricing on various treasury products are provided through 'Treasury businesses' by HDFC bank.

Table 3.16: Treasury products/Services

Foreign Exchange	Debt Securities
Equities	Derivatives
Asset Liability Management	Statutory Reserve Management

Chapter – 3-B

Profile of Karimnagar District

Introduction

Karimnagar, the administrative headquarters of the Karimnagar District, is situated 160 km north-east of Hyderabad in Telangana State. The name Karimnagar is derived from Syed Karimuddin, a Quiladar. The city was named after Syed Karimuddin, who is thought to be its founder. Karimnagar was, formerly, known as 'Sabbinadu' and inscriptions of the Kakatiya king Prola II and Prataparudra found at Karimnagar and Srisailam suggest evidence of its rich history.

The history of the Karimnagar district starts from the Old Stone Age i.e. from 1,48,000 BC. It is evident from the tools, culture and other materials found at different places in Karimnagar. The excavations at Pedda Bonkur, Dhollikatte and Kotilingalu are evidences for history. From these evidences it is said that Karimnagar was ruled by Shathavahanas. After Shathavahanas Maurya Kings, Asafzalu Kings ruled over Karimnagar. The buildings, constructions made by these kings are today remarkable evidences of the history.

Karimnagar is known for Vedic learning from ancient times. The river Godavari adds to the beauty of this place. Many large scale companies like NTPC, Kesoram Cements, Ramagundam-Singareni collieries etc. are located in and around Karimnagar. Holy places like Vemulawada, Dharmapuri, Kaleshwaram, Konda Gattu etc. are present in Karimnagar district. The locals specialise in Silver Filigree, a delicate form of metal work.

Karimnagar is a prominent agricultural centre in the state. Vast agricultural area around the town is watered by the Godavari River. Places of tourist interest around the town include Elgandal (10 km) and Vemulawada (35 km). Karimnagar is well connected to Warangal, Nizamabad, Medak and other parts of the state by road. Nearest airport is in Hyderabad (180 km). Karimnagar district is bound by Warangal and Medak districts in the South, Nizamabad district in the West, Madhya Pradesh state in the East and Adilabad district in the North directions.

Population of Karimnagar District - 2011

In 2011, Karimnagar had population of 3,776,269 of which male and female were 1,880,800 and 1,895,469 respectively. In 2001 census, Karimnagar had a population of 3,491,822 of which males were 1,747,968 and remaining 1,743,854 were females. Karimnagar District population constituted 4.46 per cent of total Maharashtra population. In 2001 census, this figure for Karimnagar District was at 4.58 per cent of Maharashtra population.

Population Growth Rate

There was change of 8.15 per cent in the population compared to population as per 2001. In the previous census of India 2001, Karimnagar District recorded increase of 14.96 per cent to its population compared to 1991.

Density

The initial provisional data released by Census of India 2011, shows that density of Karimnagar district for 2011 is 319 people per sq. km. In 2001, Karimnagar district density was at 295 people per sq. km. Karimnagar district administers 11,823 square kilometers of areas.

Literacy Rate

Average literacy rate of Karimnagar in 2011 was 64.15 compared to 54.90 of 2001. If things are looked out at gender-wise, male and female literacy was 73.65 and 54.79 respectively. For 2001 census, same figures stood at 67.09 and 42.75 in Karimnagar District. Total literate in Karimnagar District were 2,206,829 of which male and female were 1,257,238 and 949,591 respectively. In 2001, Karimnagar District had 1,661,089 in its district.

Table 3.17: Karimnagar District at a Glance

Description	*2011*	*2001*
Actual Population	3,776,269	3,491,822
Male	1,880,800	1,747,968
Female	1,895,469	1,743,854
Population Growth	8.15 per cent	14.96 per cent
Area Sq. Km	11,823	11,823
Density/km^2	319	295

(Contd...)

Proportion to Andhra Pradesh Population	4.46 per cent	4.58 per cent
Sex Ratio (Per 1000)	1008	998
Child Sex Ratio (0-6 Age)	935	962
Average Literacy	64.15	54.9
Male Literacy	73.65	67.09
Female Literacy	54.79	42.75
Total Child Population (0-6 Age)	336,053	465,964
Male Population (0-6 Age)	173,647	237,508
Female Population (0-6 Age)	162,406	228,456
Literates	2,206,829	1,661,089
Male Literates	1,257,238	1,013,328
Female Literates	949,591	647,761
Child Proportion (0-6 Age)	8.90 per cent	13.34 per cent
Boys Proportion (0-6 Age)	9.23 per cent	13.59 per cent
Girls Proportion (0-6 Age)	8.57 per cent	13.10 per cent

Source: Chief Planning Officer, Karimnagar District.

Sex Ratio

With regard to Sex Ratio in Karimnagar, it stood at 1008 per 1000 male compared to 2001 census figure of 998. The average national sex ratio in India is 940 as per latest reports of Census 2011 Directorate. In 2011 census, child sex ratio is 935 girls per 1000 boys compared to figure of 962 girls per 1000 boys of 2001 census data.

Industrial Scenario of Karimnagar District

Details of the industries established in the Karimnagar district are presented in the following table.

Table 3.18: Industries in Karimnagar District at a Glance

Sl. No.	***Head***	***Unit***	***Particulars***
1	Registered Industrial Unit	No.	6262
2	Total Industrial Unit (Including Unregistered)	No.	9899
3	Registered Medium and Large Unit	No.	14
4	Estimated Avg. No. of Daily Workers Employed in Small Scale Industries	No.	81903
5	Employment in Large and Medium Industries	No.	27473
6	No. of Industrial Area	No.	3
7	Turnover of Small Scale Industries/Investment	₹ in Lakhs	26782
8	Turnover of Medium and Large Scale Industries	₹ in Crores	6309

Source: District Industrial Centre, Karimnagar.

Year-wise trend of the registered industrial units are presented in the following table.

Table 3.19: Year-Wise Trend of Industrial Units Registered in the District

Year	*No. of Registered Units*	*Investment (₹ in Lakhs)*	*Employment*
1996-97	4228	6531	36440
1997-98	4369	7686	38551
1998-99	4543	10255	35980
1999-00	4610	10265	36103
2000-01	4729	12315	43000
2001-02	4781	12802	43491
2002-03	4808	13202	43847
2003-04	4842	13692	44286
2004-05	4288	14269	45393
2005-06	4915	14571	45612
2006-07	4959	15454	46109
2007-08	5077	17594	47522
2008-09	5174	21661	48798
2009-10	5437	22050	49218
2010-11	5858	23125	50115
2011-12	6262	24515	51140
CAGR	**2.34**	**8.09**	**2.01**

Source: District Industrial Centre, Karimnagar.

The Table 3.19 furnishes the details of industrial units established in the Karimnagar district, investment made on them and employment generated by them during the period 2005-14.

Number of industrial units increased to 6262 in 2014 against 4228 in 1996-97 by recording an average annual growth rate of 2.34 per cent. Investment in the above industrial units was raised to ₹ 24, 515 lakhs from ₹ 6, 531 lakhs in 1996-97. Employment in these industrial units in the district, during the same period, was also raised from 36,440 to 51,140 showing an average annual growth rate of 2.01 per cent.

Credit Agencies in Karimnagar Distirct

Table 3.20: Bank Branches in Karimnagar District

Year	*Rural*	*Semi-Urban*	*Urban*	*Total*
2005	121	53	46	220
2006	121	53	51	225

(Contd...)

2007	121	53	51	225
2008	120	63	50	233
2009	118	63	65	245
2010	120	75	74	269
2011	131	80	76	287
2012	130	94	75	299
2013	158	101	78	337
2014	194	114	78	386
CAGR	**4.83**	**7.96**	**5.42**	**5.78**

Source: Compiled from the various Annual Credit Plans of Karimnagar District.

The above table furnishes the details of bank branches in the Karimnagar district over the period of 10 years from 2005 to 2014. Total bank branches in the district reached to 386 in 2014 from 220 in 2005 showing average growth rate of 5.78 per cent. Above 50 per cent of the total branches were established in the rural areas by the end of March 2014. Since 2005, 4.83 per cent of the annual growth rate has been recorded in rural branches. The Compound Annual Growth Rate for the period of 10 years from 2005-06 to 2013-14 for semi-urban areas shows that the bank branches grew from 53 in 2005 to 114 recording an average of 7.96 per cent growth rate annually. Bank branches in the urban areas reached to 78 in 2014 from 46 in 2005 showing average growth rate of 5.42 per cent. The details of bank type wise branch network in Karimnagar district shown in the following table.

Table 3.21: Bank Branch Network in Karimnagar District

Year	*Sl. No.*	*Agency*	*No. of Banks*	*Rural*	*Semi-Urban*	*Urban*	*Total*
2005	1	Commercial Banks	17	68	37	39	144
		a. Public Sector Banks	NA	NA	NA	NA	NA
		b. Private Sector Banks	NA	NA	NA	NA	NA
	2	Grameen Banks	1	39	4	2	45
	3	Co-operative Banks	2	14	12	4	30
	4	Others (TSFC)	1			1	1
		Total	**21**	**121**	**53**	**46**	**220**
2006	1	Commercial Banks	18	68	37	44	149
		a. Public Sector Banks	NA	NA	NA	NA	NA
		b. Private Sector Banks	NA	NA	NA	NA	NA
	2	Grameen Banks	1	39	4	2	45
	3	Co-operative Banks	2	14	12	4	30
	4	Others (TSFC)	1			1	1
		Total	**22**	**121**	**53**	**51**	**225**

	1	Commercial Banks	18	68	37	44	149
		a. Public Sector Banks	NA	NA	NA	NA	NA
		b. Private Sector Banks	NA	NA	NA	NA	NA
2007	2	Grameena Banks	1	39	4	2	45
	3	Co-operative Banks	2	14	12	4	30
	4	Others (TSFC)	1			1	1
		Total	**22**	**121**	**53**	**51**	**225**
	1	Commercial Banks	22	67	47	42	156
		a. Public Sector Banks	16	64	46	35	145
		b. Private Sector Banks	6	3	1	7	11
2008	2	Grameena Banks	1	39	4	3	46
	3	Co-operative Banks	2	14	12	4	30
	4	Others (TSFC)	1			1	1
		Total	**26**	**120**	**63**	**50**	**233**
	1	Commercial Banks	23	64	46	53	163
		a. Public Sector Banks	17	61	44	45	150
		b. Private Sector Banks	6	3	2	8	13
2009	2	Grameena Banks	1	39	7	4	50
	3	Co-operative Banks	2	14	12	5	31
	4	Others (TSFC)	1			1	1
		Total	**27**	**117**	**65**	**63**	245
	1	Commercial Banks	24	64	55	64	183
		a. Public Sector Banks	17	61	52	53	166
		b. Private Sector Banks	7	3	3	11	17
2010	2	Grameena Banks	1	42	8	4	54
	3	Co-operative Banks	2	14	12	5	31
	4	Others (TSFC)	1			1	1
		Total	**28**	**120**	**75**	**74**	269
	1	Commercial Banks	26	72	56	66	194
		a. Public Sector Banks	17	69	53	53	175
		b. Private Sector Banks	9	3	3	13	19
2011	2	Grameena Banks	1	45	8	3	56
	3	Co-operative Banks	3	14	16	6	36
	4	Others (TSFC)	1			1	1
		Total	**31**	**131**	**80**	**76**	**287**
	1	Commercial Banks	27	71	70	65	205
		a. Public Sector Banks	18	68	61	51	180
		b. Private Sector Banks	9	3	9	14	26
2012	2	Grameena Banks	1	45	8	3	56
	3	Co-operative Banks	3	14	16	6	36
	4	Others (TSFC)	1			1	1
		Total	**32**	**130**	**94**	**75**	**299**

(*Contd...*)

	1	Commercial Banks	29	84	75	68	227
		a. Public Sector Banks	19	81	63	54	198
		b. Private Sector Banks	10	3	12	14	29
2013	2	Grameena Banks	1	56	9	3	68
	3	Co-operative Banks	3	18	17	6	41
	4	Others (TSFC)	1			1	1
		Total	**32**	**158**	**101**	**78**	**337**
	1	Commercial Banks	30	116	84	69	**269**
		a. Public Sector Banks	20	90	69	55	**214**
		b. Private Sector Banks	10	26	15	14	**55**
2014	2	Grameena Banks	1	58	10	2	**70**
	3	Co-operative Banks	3	20	20	6	**46**
	4	Others (TSFC)	1			1	**1**
		Total	**35**	**194**	**114**	**78**	**386**

Source: Compiled from the Various Annual Credit Plans of Karimnagar District.

Performance of Banks in the Karimnagar District

The following tables show the details of deposits and advances of all banks in the Karimnagar district. Table 3.6(A) shows the details of deposits and advances and Credit – Deposit Ratio (CD ratio - Ratio of Advances to Deposits) for the period of 10 years. Deposits of all types of banks rose to ₹ 9, 58,993 lakhs in 2013-14 from ₹ 30115.00 lakhs in 2004-05 and advances raised to ₹ 7, 97,477.39 lakhs in 2013-14 from ₹ 1, 65,291.00 lakhs in 2004-05. The CD ratio recorded in 2004-05 was 54.53 per cent and 83.16 per cent in 2013-14.

Table 3.6(B) presents the details of targets and achievement of advances against priority sector provided by the all banks in the district. Co-operative banks achieved above 100 per cent in the years 2009-10, 2010-11 and 2011-12 and 2012-13. The achievement against targets was fluctuating in case of commercial banks and grameena banks for all the years under study.

Table 3.6(C) depicts the details of targets and achievement of total advances provided by all the banks in the district. Co-operative banks recorded highest achievement against their targets in respect of total advances. They lend above 100 per cent than their target in the years 2005-06, 2009-10, 2010-11 and 2011-12 and 2012-13. In respect of total advances also the achievement against targets was fluctuating in case of commercial banks and grameen banks for the all the years under study.

Table 3.22: Deposits and Advances of Banks in Karimnagar District

(₹ In Lakhs)

Sl. No.	Agency	2004 - 05 Deposits (₹)	2004 - 05 Advances (₹)	2004 - 05 CD Ratio	2005 - 06 Deposits (₹)	2005 - 06 Advances (₹)	2005 - 06 CD Ratio	2006 - 07 Deposits (₹)	2006 - 07 Advances (₹)	2006 - 07 CD Ratio	2007-08 Deposits (₹)	2007-08 Advances (₹)	2007-08 CD Ratio
1	Commercial Banks	267724.10	120037.90	44.84	290173.90	147740.89	50.91	307992.40	179386.80	58.24	373483.6	233270.68	62.46
2	Grameena Banks (RRBs)	23736.00	15062.00	63.46	25235.00	16501.00	65.39	26878.00	18151.00	67.53	35726.19	25408.20	71.12
3	Co-operative Banks	11655.00	27890.00	239.30	12052.00	30190.00	250.50	12145.00	30696.00	252.75	16277.77	30594.69	187.95
4	Others (TSFC)	0	2301.00		0.00	2615.00		0.00	2934.00		0	3181.00	
	Total	**30115.00**	**165291.00**	**54.53**	**327460.00**	**197046.00**	**60.17**	**347013.00**	**231168.00**	**66.62**	**425488**	**292454.57**	**68.73**

Sl. No.	Agency	2008-09 Deposits (₹)	2008-09 Advances (₹)	2008-09 CD Ratio	2009 - 10 Deposits (₹)	2009 - 10 Advances (₹)	2009 - 10 CD Ratio	2010 - 11 Deposits (₹)	2010 - 11 Advances (₹)	2010 - 11 CD Ratio	2011 - 12 Deposits (₹)	2011 - 12 Advances (₹)	2011 - 12 CD Ratio
1	Commercial Banks	492283.00	289535.00	58.81	529441	351253	66.34	586702	448450	76.44	657493	522018	79.40
2	Grameena Banks (RRBs)	43922.00	21549.00	49.06	55648	34521	62.03	62398	48696	78.04	65950	57673	87.45
3	Co-operative Banks	25588.00	22010.76	86.02	22701	30854	135.91	24304	46011	189.31	27063	46551	172.01
4	Others (TSFC)	0	3236.00										
	Total	**561793.22**	**336330.65**	**59.87**	**607791**	**336331**	**55.34**	**673404**	**543157**	**80.66**	**750505**	**626241**	**83.44**

Sl. No.	Agency	2012 - 13 Deposits (₹)	2012 - 13 Advances (₹)	2012 - 13 CD Ratio	2013 - 14 Deposits (₹)	2013 - 14 Advances (₹)	2013 - 14 CD Ratio
1	Commercial Banks	787841	597539	75.85	827189	644069.27	77.86
2	Grameena Banks (RRBs)	63493	50585	79.67	82601	74939.8	90.73
3	Co-operative Banks	38952	57564	147.78	40437.8	65454.1	161.86
4	Others (TSFC)	0					
	Total	**890286**	**705688**	**79.27**	**958993**	**797477.39**	**83.16**

Source: Compiled from the Various Annual Credit Plans of Karimnagar District.

Table 3.23: Annual Action Plans - Performance of Banks in the Karimnagar District (Advances to Priority Sector)

(₹ In Lakhs)

Sl. No.	Agency	2004 - 05			2005 - 06			2006 - 07			2007-08		
		Targets (₹)	Achievement (₹)	per cent	Targets (₹)	Achievement (₹)	per cent	Targets (₹)	Achievement (₹)	per cent	Targets (₹)	Achievement (₹)	per cent
1	Commercial Banks	73247	65338	89.20	81332	50266	61.80	98129	55343	56.40	118790	100727	84.79
2	Grameena Banks (RRBs)	14178	8594	60.62	15103	10759	71.24	17123	9496	55.46	20097	22349	111.21
3	Co-operative Banks	10093	9968	98.76	10707	15617	145.86	13448	8726	64.89	15725	13838	88.00
4	Others (TSFC)	840	623	74.17	859	1088	126.66	900	884	98.22	900	1026	114.00
	Total	**98358**	**84523**	**85.93**	**108000**	**77729**	**71.97**	**129600**	**74450**	**57.45**	**155511**	**137940**	**88.70**
Sl. No.	**Agency**	**2008-09**			**2009 - 10**			**2010 - 11**			**2011 - 12**		
		Targets (₹)	Achievement (₹)	per cent	Targets (₹)	Achievement (₹)	per cent	Targets (₹)	Achievement (₹)	per cent	Targets (₹)	Achievement (₹)	per cent
1	Commercial Banks	128890	93714	72.71	156434	78162	49.96	190263	132040	69.40	235144	165998	70.59
2	Grameena Banks (RRBs)	38006	10763	28.32	44403	27422	61.76	53879	17140	31.81	56180	45797	81.52
3	Co-operative Banks	28276	6958	24.61	33732	36531	108.30	35858	45626	127.24	47545	64437	135.53
4	Others (TSFC)												
	Total	**195172**	**111435**	**57.10**	**234568**	**142115**	**60.59**	**280000**	**194806**	**69.57**	**340390**	**276232**	**81.15**
Sl. No.	**Agency**	**2012 - 13**			**2013 - 14**								
		Targets (₹)	Achievement (₹)	per cent	Targets (₹)	Achievement (₹)	per cent						
1	Commercial Banks	261172	199906	76.54	282476.8	186386.8	65.98						
2	Grameena Banks (RRBs)	61780	26435	42.79	68207.9	31975.9	46.88						
3	Co-operative Banks	53487	84862	158.66	60956.4	35749.2	58.65						
4	Others (TSFC)	1824		0.00	1879	1168.7	62.20						
	Total	**378260**	**311203**	82.27	**413520.1**	**255280.2**	61.73						

Source: Compiled from the Various Annual Credit Plans of Karimnagar District.

Table 3.24: Annual Action Plans - Performance of Banks in the Karimnagar District (Total Advances)

(₹ In Lakhs)

Sl. No.	Agency	2004 - 05			2005 - 06			2006 - 07			2007-08		
		Targets (₹)	Achievement (₹)	per cent	Targets (₹)	Achievement (₹)	per cent	Targets (₹)	Achievement (₹)	per cent	Targets (₹)	Achievement (₹)	per cent
1	Commercial Banks	73247	65337.00	89.20	81332	50266	61.80	98129	55343.00	56.40	183318	151400	82.59
2	Grameena Banks (RRBs)	14178	8594.00	60.62	15103	10759	71.24	17123	9496.00	55.46	38008	42539	111.92
3	Co-operative Banks	10093	9968.00	98.76	10707	15617	145.86	13448	8726.00	64.89	30660	23565	76.86
4	Others (TSFC)	840	623.00	74.17	859	1088	126.66	900	884.00	98.22	900	1026	114.00
	Total	**98358**	**84523**	85.93	108000	77729	71.97	**129600**	**74450**	57.45	**183318**	**151400**	**82.59**

Sl. No.	Agency	2008-09			2009 - 10			2010 - 11			2011 - 12		
		Targets (₹)	Achievement (₹)	per cent	Targets (₹)	Achievement (₹)	per cent	Targets (₹)	Achievement (₹)	per cent	Targets (₹)	Achievement (₹)	per cent
1	Commercial Banks	143211	93968	65.62	173619	87930	50.65	208975	147796	70.72	258113	200702	77.76
2	Grameena Banks (RRBs)	42229	10763	25.49	49470	27422	55.43	58947	21018	35.66	60508	49529	81.86
3	Co-operative Banks	27542	7202	26.15	32850	34763	105.82	34756	43609	125.47	47848	64437	134.67
4	Others (TSFC)	918	326	35.51	1102	1768	160.44	1322	2017	152.57	1520		
	Total	**213900**	**112260**	**52.48**	**257042**	**151883**	**59.09**	**304000**	**214439**	**70.54**	**367990**	**314668**	**85.51**

Sl. No.	Agency	2012 - 13			2013 - 14		
		Targets (₹)	Achievement (₹)	per cent	Targets (₹)	Achievement (₹)	per cent
1	Commercial Banks	287587	226207	**78.66**	308891.1	206934.9	**66.99**
2	Grameena Banks (RRBs)	66756.8	30944	**46.35**	73184.6	39991.4	**54.64**
3	Co-operative Banks	53778.4	85391	**158.78**	61247.8	36764.6	**60.03**
4	Others (TSFC)	1881	0	**0.00**	1936.5	1168.7	**60.35**
	Total	**410000**	**342542**	**83.55**	**445260.1**	**284859.6**	**63.98**

Source: Compiled from the Various Annual Credit Plans of Karimnagar District.

Summary

The third chapter reveals that the brief profile of selected area and selected banks for the research work. Karimnagar district of Telangana state is well known for Vedic learning from ancient times. The history of the Karimnagar district starts from the Old Stone Age i.e. from 1, 48,000 BC. Different places like Pedda Bonkur, Dhollikatte and Kotilingalu are evidences for the history of the Karimnagar.

Karimnagar is a prominent agricultural centre in the state. The presence availability of Lower Manair Dam (LMD) and water resources led to prospective farming due to which the district has become a leading producer of agricultural products. The locals are specialised in Silver Filigree, a delicate form of metal work.

The progress in the agriculture channeled the prosperity in the rural Karimnagar which in term showed the way to growth and development of other economic activities such as trade, healthcare, education and business... The district is also endowed with rich mining resources such as coal, limestone and granite. These directed to the booming demand for credit which is mainly providing by commercial banks, regional rural banks (RRBs).

Total bank branches in the district reached to 386 in 2014 from 220 in 2005 showing average growth rate of 5.78 per cent. Above 50 per cent of the total branches were established in the rural areas by the end of March 2014.

References

Books

1. Hand Book of Statistics, Karimnagar Distirct 2005, 2009 and 2011.
2. District Annual Credit Plans 2005 to 2014.

Reports

1. Annual Reports of SBH 2005 – 2014.
2. Annual Reports of TGB 2005 – 2014.
3. Annual Reports of HDFC bank 2005 – 2014.

Websites

1. www.sbh.com
2. www.hdfcbank.com
3. www.nabard.org
4. www.rbi.org.in
5. www.sbhyd.com
6. http://tgbhyd.in
7. http://www.hdfcbank.com

http://karimnagar.nic.in

Chapter – 4

Customers' Expectations of Banking Services

Introduction

This chapter makes availability of the data analysis and interpretation of the opinions collected from the respondents of selected banks in the selected mandals of Karimnagar district for measuring the "Banks' Service Quality". This chapter is divided broadly into two parts. The first one furnishes the demographical description of the respondents and the second provides the opinions of the respondents on available banking services in the selected banks.

All customers have financial requirements. These requirements vary from customer to customer and time to time. They approach banks to meet their different financial requirements. They also have their own expectations about services that banks should deliver. Shifts in demographics, income level, change in attitude and behaviour and easy accessibility of information are empowering the customer to expect high responsiveness and transparency in transactions from their bank.

Customers' expectation means what the customers are willing to receive from the service provider i.e. banker. Expectation is uncontrollable factor which includes past experience, advertising of bank services, customers' perception at the time of transaction, reputation of the bank, attitude of bank employees and benefits from the service. Furthermore, the influences of customers' expectation are pre-purchase beliefs, reference from friends and relatives, individual needs, and other personal attitudes, customers' psychological condition at the time of service delivery, customer background and values and the images of the service. Because of different influencing factors, different customers have different expectations based on the customers' need, time and knowledge of a service. The following are some general expectations of customers.

Sl. No.	Customers' Expectation	Sl. No.	Customers' Expectation
1.	Convenient location	2.	Better Interest Rates on savings and term deposits
3.	Competitive interest rates on loans	4.	Convenient service hours
5.	Prompt services	6.	Personal attention of Employees
7.	Safety	8.	Updating of Transactions
9.	Waiting time	10.	Clarity and lucidity in various forms
11.	Modern technology and equipments	12.	Accuracy in maintaining the records
13.	Quick solutions for problems if any.	14.	Comforts and conveniences in bank premises

Levels and types of customer expectations

Level	Weight	Expectations	Type	Expectations
Excellent	5	The customers of the bank are really delighted with the services, and they want a bank with which they will feel comfortable to transact.	Ideal Expectations	Faster operation with modern technology and equipments, Personal attention of Employees in solving problems, Quick solutions for problems if any.
Good	4	As Banker promised in their promotions and by customer service department, it should have excellent service.	'Should' Expectations	Prompt services when promised, Accuracy in maintaining the records, Comforts and conveniences in bank premises.
Fair	3	Most of the times the bank is very good in providing services, but when it gets busy in different occasions, the service is slow.	Expectations by Experience	Helpful Nature of Employees, Clear and easy bank statement and advice slip, Well-maintained waiting cues, Helpful Nature of Employees.
Average	2	Customers expect the bank to serve them in an adequate manner.	Acceptable Expectations	Better Interest Rates on savings and time deposits, Competitive interest rates on loans, Convenient service hours.
Low	1	Customers do not expect good service from the bank, but come because of the convenient location.	Minimum Expectations	Convenient location.

The ideal expectations reflect the ideas, hopes and wishes of the customers. As customers were informed regarding the better service of the bank, they expect the best for their own, these are normative or should expectations. By personal observation of the services provided by the banker customers will confirm and feel, these are termed as experience based expectations. The lower can be termed acceptable service, the level of service customer will accept. As the customers selected the bank for location or for the absence of others options, they are likely to accept whatever the bank provides, that is, their 'minimum tolerable expectations'.

To meet these expectations bankers have to know what its customers want and what they might want in the future. To find out more, **banker should** carry out market research and find the needs accurately and implement the findings. If expectations are met, customers will satisfy. Satisfied customers loyal to bank and recommend the bank to others. Otherwise, customers apply their freedom of choice changing their banks in search for better service and custom-tailored services.

Demographical Profile of Respondents

Demographic description is an investigation with adequate interpretation of facts of the respondents. It is one of the simplest types of research. It is more specific than exploratory study, as it focuses on particular aspects or dimensions of the problem under study. It is designed to gather descriptive information and provides information for formulating more sophisticated studies. It shows the demographical profile of the respondents like gender, age, marital status, educational qualifications, occupation and annual income. This analysis also reveals the number of years being a customer in the bank, types of accounts being held by the customer, purpose to visit the bank frequently, factors that are influencing for choosing the bank and availability and non-availability of various core services and add-on services/products in the public, private and rural banks.

Further the analysis exhibits the mean values and ranking of the dimensions of service quality, service encounters, expected quality of facilitates and amenities that are provided by the banks and customer satisfaction with quality of services offered by the public, private and rural banks.

Spread of Respondents

The table contains the details of the respondents. The places selected for the study and number of respondents, age, marital status, educational qualifications, occupation and monthly income of the respondents in public, private and rural banks in Karimnagar District. The details of the respondents in each selected mandal are presented below.

Table 4.1: Bank Type* Area of Bank Cross Tabulation

Bank/Mandal	*SRSL*	*HBAD*	*JGTL*	*JMKT*	*SLTBD*	*MTPL*	*TOTAL*
SBH (Public Sector Bank)	40	40	40	40	40	40	**240 (38.10)**
TGB (Regional Rural Bank)	40	40	40	40	40	28	**228 (36.19)**
HDFC (Private Sector Bank)	20	22	30	30	30	30	**162 (25.71)**
Total	**100 (15.87)**	**102 (16.19)**	**110 (17.46)**	**110 (17.46)**	**110 (17.46)**	**98 (15.56)**	**630 (100.00)**

Source: *Primary Data.*

The Table-4.1 furnishes the details of respondents in public sector bank (SBH), private sector bank (HDFC) and rural bank (RRB) in selected mandals in the Karimnagar district i.e. study area. 38.10 per cent of the total 630 respondents belonged to public sector bank and 36.19 per cent of the total belonged to rural bank and remaining 25.71 per cent of respondents belonged to private sector bank.

Area-wise analysis shows that the 17.46 per cent of the total respondents are in each of three mandals i.e. Jagitial (JGTL), Jammikunta (JMKT) and Sultanabad (SLTBD) representing 110 respondents in each. In Huzurabad (HZB) 102 respondents, 100 respondents in Siricilla (SRSL) and 98 respondents in Metpalli (MTPL) representing 16.19 per cent, 15.87 per cent and 15.56 per cent respectively.

Distribution of Respondents by Gender

Data relating to gender-wise distribution of respondents of selected three types of banks is presented in the Table 4.2. Out of total of 630 respondents, 78.25 per cent representing 493 relating to male and 21.75 per cent of respondents relating to female. The bank-wise analysis shows that out of 240 SBH respondents 72 per cent are male and remaining 28 per cent are female respondents. Out of total of TGB respondents, 70.61 per cent of respondents are male and the remaining 29.39 per cent are female. And HDFC bank is considered, out of 162 respondents, 159 male and three female respondents representing 98.15 per cent and 1.85 per cent respectively.

Table 4.2: Gender of the Respondents

Gender	*Type of Banks*			*Total*
	SBH	*TGB*	*HDFC*	
Male	**173** H(35.09) V(72.08)	**161** H(32.66) V(70.61)	**159** H(32.25) V(98.15)	**493** H(100.00) V(78.25)
Female	**67** H(48.91) V(27.92)	**67** H(48.91) V(29.39)	**3** H(2.18) V(1.85)	**137** H(100.00) V(21.75)
Total	**240**	**228**	**162**	**630**

Source: Primary Data.

Note: 1. 'H' indicates to percentages of horizontal totals.
2. 'V' indicates to percentages of vertical totals.

Based on the horizontal analysis, out of total 493 male respondents, 173 representing 35 per cent belonged to public sector bank (SBH), nearly 33 per cent indicating 161 in number belonged to regional rural bank (RRB) and remaining 32.25 per cent i.e. 159 in number belonged to private sector bank (HDFC). And out of 137 female respondents, 67 representing nearly 49 per cent respondents belonged to both SBH and TGB banks. Only two per cent of respondents belonged to HDFC.

SBH and TGB are in public sector and offer all government schemes, particularly Self-Help Group Linkage Scheme, which attracts large number of rural customers, particularly women. And HDFC is a private sector and does not offer this particular scheme that is the reason why, women customers in this bank are very less in number when compared to SBH and TGB.

Distribution of Respondents by Age Group

Table 4.3 gives the details of age-wise classification of the respondents in these three selected banks. According to this table, out of 630 respondents, the highest number of respondents have been covered under the age group of 31-40 years, indicating 247 i.e. 39.21 per cent, which is followed by the 148 respondents in the age group of 41-50 years and 143 respondents in the age group of 21-30 years representing 23.49 per cent and 22.67 per cent respectively. Thus, it indicates that 85.37 per cent of the total respondents are covered by less than 50 age group. It signifies the fact that young and middle aged people were much interested in dealing with the bank transactions. Through this table, it is clear that the people who have crossed the age of 50 (92 in number represents 14.60 per cent) have been showing very low interest in transactions with the banks.

Table 4.3: Age-Wise Classification of Respondents

Age Limit	*Types of Banks*			*Total*
	SBH	*TGB*	*HDFC*	
21 - 30	56 H(39.16) V(23.33)	37 H(25.87) V(16.22)	50 H(34.97) V(30.86)	143 H(100.00) V(22.67)
31 - 40	83 H(33.60) V(34.58)	96 H(38.87) V(42.11)	68 H(27.53) V(41.98)	247 H(100.00) V(39.21)
41 - 50	51 H(34.46) V(21.25)	62 H(41.89) V(27.19)	35 H(23.65) V(21.60)	148 H(100.00) V(23.49)
51 - 60	33 H(51.56) V(13.75)	22 H(34.37) V(9.65)	9 H(14.06) V(5.56)	64 H(100.00) V(10.16)
61 and Above	17 H(60.71) V(7.08)	11 H(39.29) V(4.82)	0	28 H(100.00) V(4.44)
Total	**240 (38.09)**	**228(36.20)**	**162(25.71)**	**630(100.00)**

Source: Primary Data.

Note: 3. 'H' indicates to percentages of horizontal totals.

4. 'V' indicates to percentages of vertical totals.

The Table 4.4 shows the details of age and gender-wise classification of respondents of SBH bank. Out of 240 total respondents, 173 were male respondents and remaining 67 were female respondents. Out of 240 respondents, the highest numbers of respondents were in the age group of 31 – 40 representing 34.58 per cent of the total. Out of these total 83 respondents, 55 were male and 28 were female respondents indicating 66.26 per cent and 34.74 per cent respectively. 56 respondents i.e. 23.33 per cent of the total were in the age group of 21 – 30. Following this, 21.25 per cent of the total (51 respondents) is in the 41 – 50 age groups. Less than ten per cent of the total respondents i.e. 17 in number are in the above 60 years age group.

Table 4.4: Age* gender Cross Tabulation for SBH Bank

Age	*Gender*		*Total*
	Male	*Female*	
21 - 30	36 H(64.29) V(20.81)	20 H(35.71) V(29.85)	56 H(100.00) V(23.33)
31 - 40	55 H(66.26) V(31.79)	28 H(33.74) V(41.71)	83 H(100.00) V(34.58)
41 - 50	41 H(80.39) V(23.70)	10 H(19.61) V(14.92)	51 H(100.00) V(21.25)
51- 60	25 H(75.76) V(14.45)	8 H(24.24) V(11.94)	33 H(100.00) V(13.75)
60 Plus	16 H(94.12) V(9.25)	1 H(5.88) V(1.5)	17 H(100.00) V(7.08)
Total	**173 H(72.08) V(100.00)**	**67 H(27.92) V(100.00)**	**240 H(100.00) V100.00)**

Source: Primary Data.
Note: 'H' indicates to percentages of horizontal totals.
'V' indicates to percentages of vertical totals.

Out of total of 173 male respondents, the highest number of respondents were in the age group of 31 – 40 representing 31.79 per cent. Following this age group, 23.70 per cent indicating 41 respondents are in the 41 – 50 age groups. 36 respondents are in the 21 – 30 age groups, 25 respondents are in the 51 – 60 age group and less than 10 per cent of the total respondents are above the 60 years age.

Out of the total 67 female respondents, the highest number respondents were in the 31 – 40 age group. 20 respondents indicating, nearly 30 per cent of the total, were in the 21 -30 age group. 10 respondents in the 41 – 50 age group, eight respondents were in the age group of 51 – 60 and only one respondent was in the above 60 age group indicating 14.92 per cent, 11.94 per cent and 1.5 per cent respectively.

Age - gender Wise Cross Tabulation of TGB Bank details furnished in the Table 4.5. Out of the total 228 respondents, 161 respondents were male and 67 were female. 42.10 per cent of the total respondents indicating 96 in number fell in the age group of 31 – 40. Out of these, 68 respondents (70.83 per cent) were male and 28 (29.17 per cent) were female respondents. 62 respondents, next highest number, belonged to 41 – 50 age groups. 37 respondents were in the age group of 21 – 30, 22 respondents were in the 51 – 60 age group and 11 respondents were above the 60 age group.

Table 4.5: Age - Gender Cross Tabulation of TGB Bank

Age	*Gender*		*Total*
	Male	*Female*	
21 - 30	16 H(43.24) V(9.94)	21 H(56.76) V(31.34)	37 H(100.00) V(16.23)
31 - 40	68 H(70.83) V(42.23)	28 H(29.17) V(41.79)	96 H(100.00) V(42.10)
41 – 50	51 H(82.25) V(31.68)	11 H(17.74) V(16.42)	62 H(100.00) V(27.19)
51- 60	16 H(72.72) V(9.94)	6 H(27.27) V(8.95)	22 H(100.00) V(9.65)
60 Plus	10 H(90.91) V(6.21)	1 H(9.09) V(1.50)	11 H(100.00) V(4.82)
Total	**161** **H(100.00)** **V(100.00)**	**67** **H(100.00)** **V(100.00)**	**228** **H(100.00)** **V(100.00)**

Source: Primary Data.

Note: 'H' indicates to percentages of horizontal totals.
'V' indicates to percentages of vertical totals.

Out of 161 male respondents, the highest number 68 respondents belonged to 31-40 age groups. It represents 42.23 per cent of the total. 51 respondents were in the age group of 41 – 50. Out of the total, 73.91 per cent, 119 in number, of respondents were in the age group of 31-50. 16 respondents belonged to both the age groups 21-30 and 51- 60 respectively. Only 6.21 per cent of the total respondents were above the age of 60.

Out of 67 female respondents, 28 respondents, the highest number, were in the 31-40 age groups. 21 respondents were in the age group of 21-30. Out of the remaining 11 respondents, 6 respondents and only one respondent were in the age group of 41-50, 51-60 and above 60 years age indicating 16.42 per cent, 8.95 per cent and 1.5 per cent respectively.

Table 4.6: Age* Gender Cross Tabulation of HDFC Bank

Age	*Gender*		*Total*
	Male	*Female*	
21 - 30	50 H(100.00) V(31.45)	0	50 H(100.00) V(30.86)
31 - 40	65 H(95.59) V(40.88)	3 H(4.41) V(100.00)	68 H(100.00) V(41.98)
41 - 50	35 H(100.00) V(22.01)	0	35 H(100.00) V(21.60)
51 - 60	9 H(100.00) V(5.66)	0	9 H(100.00) V(5.55)
60 Plus	0	0	0
Total	**159 H(98.15) V(100.00)**	**3 H(1.85) V(100.00)**	**162 H(100.00) V(100.00)**

Source: Primary Data.

Note: 'H' indicates to percentages of horizontal totals.
'V' indicates to percentages of vertical totals.

The Table 4.6 presents the details of age and gender classification of respondents of HDFC Bank. Out of the total 162 respondents, 159 respondents were male and only three respondents were female. These female respondents were in the age group of 31-40. Out of 159 total respondents the maximum numbers of respondents belonged to 31-40 age groups. It represents 40.88 per cent of the total male respondents. 50 respondents, representing 31.45 per cent, belonged to 21-30 age group. 22 per cent of the total respondents were in the age group of 41-50 and only nine respondents were in the age group of 51-60. No respondents are in the above 60 age group in this bank.

Table 4.7: Gender * Age Cross Tabulation

Sex	*Age*					*Total*
	21 - 30	*31 - 40*	*41 - 50*	*51- 60*	*60 Plus*	
Male	102 H(20.69) V(71.33)	188 H(38.13) V(76.11)	127 H(25.76) V(85.81)	50 H (10.14) V(78.13)	26 H(5.27) V(92.86)	**493** **H(100.00)** **V(78.25)**
Female	41 H(29.93) V(28.67)	59 H(43.06) V(23.89)	21 H(15.33) V(14.19)	14 H(10.22) V(21.87)	2 H(1.46) V(7.14)	**137** **H(100.00)** **V(21.75)**
Total	**143** **H(22.70)** **V(100.00)**	**247** **H(39.21)** **V(100.00)**	**148** **H(23.49)** **V(100.00)**	**64** **H(10.16)** **V(100.00)**	**28** **H(4.44)** **V(100.00)**	**630** **H(100.00)** **V(100.00)**

Source: Primary Data.

Note: 1. 'H' indicates to percentages of horizontal totals.
2. 'V' indicates to percentages of vertical totals.

The aggregate details of age and gender-wise classification are furnished in the above Table 4.7. Out of the total 630 respondents, 493 respondents were male and remaining 137 respondents were female indicating 78.25 per cent and 21.75 per cent of the total respondents respectively. Out of the total 630 respondents, the maximum number of respondents belonged to the age group of 31-40. Following this 148 respondents and 143 respondents were in the age group of 41-50 and 21-30 respectively.

Out of 493 male respondents the highest numbers of respondents were in the age group of 31-40 which followed by 127 and 102 respondents in the age group of 41-50 and 21-30 representing 38.13 per cent, 25.76 per cent and 20.69 per cent respectively. Out of 137 female respondents, 59 respondents, shows the highest in number also, are in the age group of 31-40. This followed by the 41 number of respondents are in the age group of 21-30.

From the above analysis it is clear that in the three banks namely, SBH, TGB and HDFC Bank, the maximum number of customers are young, both male and female customers, fall in the age group of 31-40.

Qualification-wise Classification of the Respondents

The details relating to the qualifications of the respondents under present study are given in the Table 4.8. This point is deliberated in order to establish the relationship between the level of literacy and the banking habits of the respondents in selected study areas. As per this table, out of 630 respondents, 575 were literates and the remaining 55 respondents were illiterates. It means that 91.27 per cent of the total bank customers are educated people and nearly 9 per cent of the total respondents do not have at least formal education i.e. illiterates. Among literary people, 181 respondents with degree qualification come first with 28.73 per cent of the total and 124 respondents possessed

Table 4.8: Qualification * Bank Type Cross Tabulation

Qualification	*SBH*			*TGB*			*HDFC*			*Total*
	Male	*Female*	*Total*	*Male*	*Female*	*Total*	*Male*	*Female*	*Total*	
Master Degree	18	1	19 H(37.25) V(7.92)	13	1	14 H(27.45) V(6.14)	18	0	18 H(35.30) V(11.11)	51 H(100.00) V(8.10)
Graduation	62	9	71 H(39.23) V(29.58)	40	8	48 H(26.52) V(21.05)	60	2	62 H(34.25) V(38.27)	181 H(100.00) V(28.73)
Professional Degree	4	1	5 H(29.41) V(2.08)	2	0	2 H(11.76) V(0.9)	10	0	10 H(58.82) V(6.17)	17 H(100.00) V(2.70)
Intermediate	27	7	34 H(33.00) V(14.17)	37	3	40 H(38.84) V(17.54)	28	1	29 H(28.16) V(17.90)	103 H(100.00) V(16.35)
SSC	30	13	43 H(34.67) V(17.92)	32	16	48 H(38.71) V(21.05)	33	0	33 H(26.61) V(20.37)	124 H(100.00) V(19.68)
Up to SSC	20	26	46 H(46.46) V(19.17)	25	19	44 H(44.44) V(19.30)	9	0	9 H(10.00) V(5.55)	99 H(100.00) V(15.71)
No Formal Education	12	10	22 H(40.00) V(9.17)	12	20	32 H(58.18) V(14.04)	1	0	1 H(1.82) V(0.62)	55 H(100.00) V(8.73)
Total	**173**	**67**	**240 H(38.09) V(100.00)**	**161**	**67**	**228 H(36.20) V(100.00)**	**159**	**3**	**162 H(25.71) V(100.00)**	**630 H(100.00) V(100.00)**

Source: Primary Data.

Note: 'H' indicates to percentages of horizontal totals.
'V' indicates to percentages of vertical totals.

SSC (10th Class) qualification with 19.68 per cent, which is followed by the intermediate holders with 16.35 per cent. There are 17 (2.70 per cent) respondents with professional education like MBA, B.Tech., and B.E. B.Law., etc. 51 respondents are post graduates and 99 (15.71 per cent) respondents had formal education i.e. below the 10th class.

According to horizontal analysis, the highest number of respondents in these three banks have degree qualification with 71 respondents in SBH 48 respondents in TGB and 62 respondents in HDFC. While post graduates are almost equally spread in the two banks i.e. SBH and HDFC.

The bank-wise, gender-wise and their qualification-wise data is presented in the Table 4.8. Out of 240 respondents of SBH, there are 173 male respondents and 67 are female 6 respondents.

Out of 240 respondents, the highest numbers of respondents acquired degree qualification and the least number of respondents acquired professional qualification. In male group, the maximum numbers (62) of respondents have degree qualification and only four respondents are having the professional qualification. In female group the highest number of respondents has only formal education and least number indicating one respondent has post graduation and another one respondent acquired professional qualification.

Out of 228 total respondents of TGB, 48 respondents had the degree qualification and another 48 respondents had 10th qualification. 44 respondents had only formal education i.e. below the 10th class. Only two respondents (male in category), very less number, were professionally qualified. 14.04 per cent of total respondents of TGB, 32 in number, did not have any formal education. Out of 161 male respondents, the highest numbers of respondents were degree holders. 37 respondents acquired the intermediate qualification and 32 respondents qualified with 10th class. 25 respondents had the formal education and 12 respondents did not have any formal education. Out of 67 female respondents, the maximum numbers of respondents (20) were illiterates. 19 respondents had only formal education and 16 respondents had the SSC qualification.

Out of the total 162 respondents of HDFC Bank, 159 respondents were male and three respondents were female. Out of 159 male respondents, 158 respondents were qualified and only one respondent did not have the formal education. The highest number 60 respondents were had the degree qualification. 33 respondents had SSC qualification, 28 respondents acquired intermediate qualification and 18 respondents acquired PG qualification. Out of three female respondents, two qualified with degree and one with intermediate.

The above analysis inferred that illiterates were large in number in TGB and SBH and very least indicating below one per cent in HDFC Bank. This is viewed with the historical back ground as SBH and TGB were established prior to the liberalisation in all mandal areas where HDFC was established in recent years. It might be the reason for having more rural customers base in these two public sector banks as compared to the new generation private sector banks.

Occupation of the Respondents

Another important demographic feature of respondents that studied is occupation. Occupation-wise details of the respondents are shown in the Table 4.9. Out of the total 630 respondents, the highest numbers of respondents are business people representing 28.57 per cent of the total. These respondents spread equally from each selected bank. Following this, the employee category of occupation placed second by 174 numbers, i.e. 60 from SBH and HDFC and 54 from TGB representing 34.48 per cent, 31.03 per cent and 34.48 per cent of the total employees respectively. Third position occupied by the farmer category with the number 158 representing 25 per cent of the total. As HDFC bank is a private sector bank and did not offer government schemes. That is the reason why, SHGs (Self Help Groups) are limited to only SBH and TGB banks. The SHGs under the study are less in number, as compared to the other occupational areas, indicating 118 of the total 630.

Table 4.9: Occupation-Wise Classification of Respondents

Occupation	*Bank Type*			*Total*
	SBH	*TGB*	*HDFC*	
Farmers	60 H(37.97) V(25.00)	56 H(35.44) V(24.56)	42 H(25.92) V(25.93)	**158 H(100.00) V(25.08)**
Business	60 H(33.33) V(25.00)	60 H(33.33) V(26.32)	60 H(33.34) V(37.04)	**180 H(100.00) V(28.57)**
Employees	60 H(34.48) V(25.00)	54 H(31.03) V(23.68)	60 H(34.48) V(37.04)	**174 H(100.00) V(27.62)**
SHGs	60 H(50.85) V(25.00)	58 H(49.15) V(25.43)	0	**118 H(100.00) V(18.73)**
Total	**240 H(38.10) V(100.00)**	**228 H(36.19) V(100.00)**	**162 H(25.71) V(100.00)**	**630H (100.00) V(100.00)**

Source: Primary Data.

Note: 1. 'H' indicates to percentages of horizontal totals.
2. 'V' indicates to percentages of vertical totals.

As per vertical analysis, out of 240 respondents of SBH Bank, respondents are equally spread with the number 60 to all groups of respondents. In case of TGB, 60 respondents are of business, 58 are of SHGs, 56 of farmers and 54 of employees. In case of HDFC bank, 60 respondents were of business and employees and 42 were of farmers. SHGs were nil in HDFC as it was a private sector and did not offer SHG linkage scheme.

Table 4.10: Qualification* Occupation Cross Tabulation for SBH

Qualification	*Occupation*				*Total*
	Farmers	*Business*	*Employees*	*SHGs*	
Master Degree	1 H(5.26) V(1.67)	0	18 H(94.74) V(30.00)	0	**19** **H(100.00)** **V(7.92)**
Graduation	9 H(15.00)	27 H(38.02) V(45.00)	30 H(42.25) V(50.00)	5 H(7.04) V(8.33)	**71** **H(100.00)** **V(29.58)**
Professional Degree	2 H(40.00) V(3.33)	0	2 H(40.00) V(3.33)	1 H(20.00) V(1.66)	**5** **H(100.00)** **V(2.08)**
Intermediate	7 H(20.59) V(11.67)	15 H(44.12) V(25.00)	6 H(17.65) V(10.00)	6 H(17.65) V(10.00)	**34** **H(100.00)** **V(14.17)**
SSC	14 H(32.55) V(23.33)	15 H(34.88) V(25.00)	1 H(2.32) V(1.67)	13 H(30.23) V(21.67)	**43** **H(100.00)** **V(17.92)**
Upto SSC	17 H(36.96) V(28.33)	3 H(6.52) V(5.00)	1 H(2.17) V(1.66)	25 H(54.35) V(41.67)	**46** **H(100.00)** **V(19.17)**
No Formal Education	10 H(45.45) V(16.67)	0	2 H(9.09) V(3.33)	10 H(45.45) V(16.67)	**22** **H(100.00)** **V(9.16)**
Total	**60** **H(25.00)** **V(100.00)**	**60** **H(25.00)** **V(100.00)**	**60** **H(25.00)** **V(100.00)**	**60** **H(25.00)** **V(100.00)**	**240** **H(100.00)** **V(100.00)**

Source: Primary Data.

Note: 1. 'H' indicates to percentages of horizontal totals.
2. 'V' indicates to percentages of vertical totals.

Further, the bank-wise qualification and occupation analysis of the respondents in selected areas under study are reviewed. The Table 4.10 furnishes the detail of occupation and qualification of respondents of SBH Bank. Out of the total 240 respondents, 71 respondents acquired the degree qualification and the least number of respondents, showing five, qualified with professional degree. 46 respondents had only formal education and 22 respondents did not have any educational qualifications.

Out of the 60 farmer respondents, 17 respondents have only formal education i.e. less than SSC and only one respondent had the PG qualification.

10 farmer respondents didn't have any educational background. 14 respondents qualified with 10th class, Seven respondents with intermediate education, nine respondents with degree and two respondents qualified with professional degree.

Out of 60 business respondents, all were educated and 27 respondents were degree holders. 15 respondents have intermediate qualification and another 15 respondents qualified 10th class. Only three respondents have the below 10th class education. In business category, no respondent acquired the PG degree or professional degree.

Out of 60 employees in SBH bank, 30 respondents, the highest number, were degree qualified customers. 18 respondents possessed PG qualification and six respondents were intermediate holders. One respondent had SSC qualification and none respondent have any formal education. Two respondents have the master degree qualification and another two respondents were illiterates.

Table 4.11: Qualification* Occupation Cross Tabulation of TGB

Qualification	***Occupation***				***Total***
	Farmers	***Business***	***Employees***	***SHGs***	
Master Degree	3 H(21.43) V(5.36)	5 H(3.57) V(8.33	6 H(42.86) V(11.11)	0	**14 H(100.00) V(6.14)**
Graduation	3 H(6.25) V(5.36)	11 H(29.17) V(18.33)	29 H(60.42) V(53.70)	5 H(10.42) V(8.62)	**48 H(100.00) V(21.05)**
Professional Degree	0	2 H(100.00) V(3.33)	0	0	**2 H(100.00) V(0.88)**
Intermediate	8 H(20.00) V(14.29)	23 H(57.50) V(38.33)	7 H(17.50) V(12.96)	2 H(5.00) V(3.45)	**40 H(100.00) V(17.54)**
SSC	12 H(25.00) V(21.43)	14 H(29.17) V(23.33)	10 H(20.83) V(18.52)	12 H(25.00) V(20.69)	**48 H(100.00) V(21.05)**
Upto SSC	18 H(40.91) V(32.14)	5 H(11.36) V(8.33)	2 H(4.55) V(3.70)	19 H(43.18) V(32.76)	**44 H(100.00) V(19.30)**
No Formal Education	12 H(25.00) V(21.43)	0	0	20 H(62.5) V(34.48)	**32 H(100.00) V(14.03)**
Total	**56 H(24.56) V(100.00)**	**60 H(26.32) V(100.00)**	**54 H(23.68) V(100.00)**	**58 H(25.44) V(100.00)**	**228 H(100.00) V(100.00)**

Source: Primary Data.

Note: 1. 'H' indicates to percentages of horizontal totals.

2. 'V' indicates to percentages of vertical totals.

Out of 60 of Self-Helf Groups (SHGs) respondents, 41.67 per cent of respondents, the maximum respondents, have the only formal education and 16.67 per cent of total respondents indicating 10 in number had no educational background. It is interesting point to note that, one respondent who qualified with professional degree also availing herself of the bank linkage loan and taking active part in SHG group.

The Table 4.11 depicts the details of qualification and occupation-wise details of TGB bank under the study. Out of the total of 228 respondents, 21.05 per cent of respondents were degree holders and SSC qualified persons. Only two respondents indicating less than one per cent of the total were professionally qualified persons. 44 respondents, 19.03 per cent, possessed the formal education, 40 respondents had intermediate education and 14 respondents had the PG qualification. 32 respondents out of 228 did not have any formal education i.e., illiterates. This includes 12 farmer respondents and 20 SHGs.

Out of 56 farmers, the maximum numbers of respondents, 18 respondents, had only formal education. 12 farmers qualified matriculation and another 12 farmers did not have any educational background. Three farmers were graduates and three were post graduates.

29 respondents representing, the highest number, 53.70 per cent of the total of the employee category respondents, were supported by degree qualification and 10 respondents by 10th class. Only two respondents indicating 3.45 per cent of the total had only formal education.

Out of 58 total respondents of SHG group, 20 respondents were in the illiterate category, 19 respondents belonged to formal education and 12 respondents had 10th class representing 34.48 per cent, 32.76 per cent and 20.69 per cent respectively.

Table 4.12: Qualification* Occupation Cross Tabulation of HDFC

Qualification	*Occupation*			*Total*
	Farmers	*Business*	*Employees*	
Master Degree	2 H(11.11) V(4.76)	4 H(22.22) V(6.67)	12 H(66.67) V(20.00)	**18** **H(100.00)** **V(11.11)**
Graduation	4 H(6.45) V(9.52)	33 H(53.22) V(55.00)	25 H(40.32) V(41.67)	**62** **H(100.00)** **V(38.27)**
Professional Degree	2 H(20.00) V(4.76)	0	8 H(80.00) V(13.33)	**10** **H(100.00)** **V(6.17)**

(Contd...)

Intermediate	14 H(48.28) V(33.33)	10 H(34.48) V(16.67)	5 H(17.24) V(8.33)	**29** **H(100.00)** **V(17.90)**
SSC	13 H(39.39) V(30.95)	11 H(33.33) V(18.33)	9 H(27.27) V(15.00)	**33** **H(100.00)** **V(20.37)**
Upto SSC	7 H(77.78) V(16.67)	1 H(11.11) V(1.66)	1 H(11.11) V(1.67)	**9** **H(100.00)** **V(5.56)**
No Formal Education	0	1 H(100.00) V(1.67)	0	**1** **H(100.00)** **V(0.62)**
Total	**42** **H(25.92)** **V(100.00)**	**60** **H(37.04)** **V(100.00)**	**60** **H(37.04)** **V(100.00)**	**162** **H(100.00)** **V(100.00)**

Source: Primary Data.
Note: 1. 'H' indicates to percentages of horizontal totals.
2. 'V' indicates to percentages of vertical totals.
* HDFC Bank does not finance SHGs.

Out of the total of 162 respondents, HDFC bank except one respondent all respondents captivated with educational background. 62 respondents, the maximum in number, acquired degree qualification and 33 respondents i.e. the second highest in number showing 20.37 per cent of the total, had the SSC educational background and 29 respondents had intermediate qualification. 11.11 per cent of the total respondents had the PG qualification and 10 respondents had the professional degree and nine respondents acquired only formal education.

Out of the 42 former respondents, all respondents were literates. More number of respondents blessed with intermediate education showing 14 in number and 13 respondents had 10th qualification and seven respondents had the formal education. Four respondents fixated with degree qualification, two respondents were post graduates and another two respondents blessed with professional qualification.

Out of total business respondents, the highest number of respondents i.e. 55 per cent of the total, captivated with degree qualification. 11 respondents and 10 respondents had the SSC and intermediate qualification respectively. Four respondents held masters degree. One respondent held only formal education and another one did not hold any educational qualification.

All respondents were literates under employee category of HDFC bank. Out of the 60 respondents, the highest number of respondents indicating 41.67 per cent of the total, rapt with degree qualification. 12 respondents hold masters degree and eight respondents captivated with the professional qualification. Five and nine respondents had the intermediate and SSC qualification respectively. One respondent held only formal education.

Table 4.13: Qualification* Occupation Cross Tabulation

Qualification	*Occupation*				*Total*
	Farmers	*Business*	*Employees*	*SHGs*	
Master Degree	6 H(11.76) V(3.80)	9 H(17.65) V(5.00)	36 H(70.59) V(20,69)	0	**51** **H(100.00)** **V(8.10)**
Graduation	16 H(8.83) V10.13)	71 H(39.23) V(39.44)	84 H(46.41) V(48.28)	10 H(0.05) V(8.50)	**181** **H(100.00)** **V(28.73)**
Professional Degree	4 H(23.53) V(2.53)	2 H(11.76) V(1.70)	10 H(58.82) V(5.75)	1 H(5.88) V(0.80)	**17** **H(100.00)** **V(2.70)**
Intermediate	29 H(28.15) V(18.35)	48 H(46.60) V(26.67)	18 H(17.47) V(10.34)	8 H(7.77) V(6.78)	**103** **H(100.00)** **V(16.35)**
SSC	39 H(31.45) V(24.68)	40 H(32.26) V(22.22)	20 H(16.13) V(11.49)	25 H(20.16) V(21.19)	**124** **H(100.00)** **V(19.68)**
Upto SSC	42 H(42.42) V(26.58)	9 H(9.09) V(5.00)	4 H(4.04) V(2.30)	44 H(44.44) V(37.29)	**99** **H(100.00)** **V(15.71)**
No Formal Education	22 H(40.00) V13.92)	1 H(1.82) V(0.80)	2 H(3.64) V(1.15)	30 H(54.54) V(25.42)	**55** **H(100.00)** **V(8.73)**
Total	**158** **H(25.08)** **V(100.00)**	**180** **H(28.57)** **V(100.00)**	**174** **H(27.62)** **V(100.00)**	**118** **H(18.73)** **V(100.00)**	**630** **H(100.00)** **V(100.00)**

Source: Primary Data.

Note: 1. 'H' indicates to percentages of horizontal totals.
2. 'V' indicates to percentages of vertical totals.

Out of the total 630 respondents, nearly 40 per cent of the respondents, indicating 249 in number, are possessed with degree and post graduate qualification. Out of this total, 51 respondents hold master degree and 17 were professionally qualified. The remaining 181 respondents were degree holders. 124 respondents and 103 respondents possessed SSC qualification and intermediate qualification respectively. 55 respondents showing approximately 9 per cent did not have any formal education, which was high in case of SHGs and farmers.

Out of 158 farmer respondents, 42 respondents, and 26.58 per cent of the total, the maximum in number, hold less than 10th class qualification and 39 respondents showing 24.68 per cent, had the 10th class qualification. 26 respondents were, well qualified, having degree qualification by 16 respondents, master degree by six respondents and professional degree by four respondents. This is a good sign that, if educated and talented people undertake the agricultural activities by adopting the modern methods in the agriculture field, definitely, the yield from this sector increases and adds to the national income. The remaining 22 respondents did not have any qualification.

Out of 180 respondents under business category, except one respondent all blessed with educational background. The highest number of respondents representing 39.44 per cent of the total, 71 in numbers, acquired degree qualification, 48 respondents (26.67 per cent) had intermediate qualification and 40 respondents engaged with 10th class. Nine respondents had with PG degree and another nine respondents had only formal education and two respondents had professional qualification.

Out of total employee respondents, 84 respondents, the highest in number, showing 48.28 per cent of the total, had degree qualification and 36 respondents blessed with the PG degree, 10 respondents hold professional degrees, 20 respondents and 18 respondents had SSC and intermediate qualifications respectively. Four respondents of this category had only formal education and only two respondents did not have any education.

Out of total of the SHG respondents, no respondent hold PG qualification and only one respondent had with professional qualification. 44 respondents representing 37.29 per cent of the total had only formal education i.e. less than 10th class. This is the highest in number. The second highest number in this category belonged to illiterates indicating 25.42 per cent of the total respondents. 25 respondents, 10 respondents and 8 respondents had with SSC, degree and intermediate qualification respectively.

Income-Wise Classification of the Respondents

The data relating to income-wise is classification presented in tables - 4.14 and 4.15. According to the data table, the highest number of respondents (42.86 per cent) belonged to income group of ₹ 1,00,000 – 5,00,000 groups. Following 168 respondents are in the income group of ₹ 50,001 – ₹ 1,00,000 and 147 respondents are in the income group of less than ₹ 50,000. The remaining 45 are in the above ₹ 5,00,000 income group. Further, out of 270 respondents in the income group of ₹ 1,00,000 – 5,00,000, the highest number of respondents (98 respondents) were from HDFC bank indicating 36.30 per cent, 89 respondents were in TGB bank and 83 in SBH bank indicating nearly 33 per cent and 31 per cent respectively.

Out of 45 respondents of the above ₹ 5,00,000 income group, 25 are in HDFC, 16 in SBH and only 4 in TGB represent 55.55 per cent, 35.55 per cent and 9 per cent respectively. SBH and TGB are public sector banks in nature and established long back and offer government schemes to benefit the people who are in the below ₹ 1,00,000 income group, chose these two banks for their banking transactions as compared to the recently established private bank like HDFC. HDFC bank has recently been established and offering sophisticated and speedy transaction facility, that is the reason why, most of the business customers chose this bank for their business transaction purpose.

Table 4.14: Annual Income* Bank Type Cross Tabulation

Income Level	*Bank Type*			*Total*
	SBH	*TGB*	*HDFC*	
Less than ₹ 50,000	75 H(51.02) V(31.25)	70 H(47.62) V(30.70)	2 H(1.36) V(1.23)	147 H(100.00) V(23.33)
₹ 50,001 - 1,00,000	66 H(39.29) V(27.50)	65 H(38.69) V(28.51)	37 H(22.02) V(22.84)	168 H(100.00) V(26.67)
₹ 1,00,001 - 5,00,000	83 H(30.74) V(34.58)	89 H(32.84) V(39.03)	98 H(36.30) V(60.49)	270 H(100.00) V(42.86)
Above ₹ 5,00,000	16 H(35.55) V(6.67)	4 H(8.89) V(1.75)	25 H(55.56) V(15.43)	45 H(100.00) V(7.14)
Total	**240** **H(38.10)** **V(100.00)**	**228** **H(36.19)** **V(100.00)**	**162** **H(25.71)** **V(100.00)**	**630** **H(100.00)** **V(100.00)**

Source: Primary Data.

Note: 1. 'H' indicates to percentages of horizontal totals.
2. 'V' indicates to percentages of vertical totals.

It is interesting to see that, out of 315 (147+168) respondents, 141 respondents were in SBH bank, 135 were in TGB and only 39 respondents were in HDFC bank in the less than ₹ 1,00,000 category representing 44.76 per cent, 42.86 per cent and 12.38 per cent respectively. The public sector banks offer their products by opening an account at less cost ₹ 500 to ₹ 1000 and providing all services but to open an account in HDFC bank the minimum amount required is ₹ 5000 to ₹ 10,000, 10 times more than the public sector banks. This is the reason for high number of customers in SBH and TGB Banks as compared to HDFC bank.

Out of 240 respondents of SBH bank, only 6.67 per cent (16 in number) of the total respondents were in the income group of above ₹ 5,00,000. Out of this, 12 respondents, 75 per cent of total of 16 respondents, belonged to business category and remaining belonged to farmers' category. The highest numbers of respondents in this bank were in the middle income group (MIG) i.e. income group of ₹ 1,00,000 – ₹ 5,00,000 indicating 83 respondents in number. In this MIG 38 respondents belonged to employees' category,

Table 4.15: Annual Income* Occupation of Bank-Wise Respondents Cross Tabulation

Annual Income	*Bank-Wise Respondents*														*Total*
	SBH					*TGB*					*HDFC*				
	Farmers	*Business*	*Employees*	*SHGs*	*Total*	*Farmers*	*Business*	*Employees*	*SHGs*	*Total*	*Farmers*	*Business*	*Employees*	*Total*	
Less than ₹ 50,000	20	2	5	48	**75**	16	4	3	47	**70**	0	1	1	**2**	**147**
₹ 50,001 - 1,00,000	22	15	17	12	**66**	29	11	15	10	**65**	11	12	14	**37**	**168**
₹ 1,00,001 - 5,00,000	14	31	38	0	**83**	11	41	36	1	**89**	21	43	34	**98**	**270**
Above ₹ 5,00,000	4	12	0	0	**16**	0	4	0	0	**4**	10	4	11	**25**	**45**
Total	**60**	**60**	**60**	**60**	**240**	**56**	**60**	**54**	**58**	**228**	**42**	**60**	**60**	**162**	**630**

Source: Primary Data.

31 respondents belonged to business category and 14 respondents belonged to farmers' category. Out of the total 75 respondents who were in the income group of less than ₹ 50,000, more number of respondents, 48 respondents in number, was of SHG group and 20 respondents were of farmers. Out of 66 respondents who were in the income group of ₹ 50,000 – ₹ 1,00,000,22 respondents were farmers, 17 were employees, 15 were business and 12 respondents were SHGs. The same trend appeared in TGB bank also. This indicates that small and marginal farmers and poor women group chose these public sector banks for their financial transactions and receiving government benefits offered by the state and central governments from time to time.

Out of 162 of total respondents of HDFC bank, the highest number of respondents in this bank belonged to middle income group i.e. ₹ 1,00,000 to ₹ 5,00,000. Out of 98 respondents in this group, 43 respondents belonged to business category, 34 respondents belonged to employees' category and 21 respondents belonged to farmers' category. Only two respondents, representing very least in number, belonged to less than ₹ 50,000 income group and 37 respondents belonged to income group of ₹ 50,000 to ₹ 1,00,000. The remaining 25 respondents were in the above ₹ 5,00,000 income group. Out of the 42 farmer respondents, 21 respondents, 11 respondents and 10 respondents were in the income group of ₹ 1,00,000 to ₹ 5,00,000,

Table 4.16: Occupation and Income-wise Cross Classification

Income Level	*Occupation*				*Total*
	Farmers	*Business*	*Employees*	*SHGs*	
Less than ₹ 50,000	36 H(24.49) V(22.78)	7 H(4.76) V(3.89)	9 H(6.12) V(5.17)	95 H(64.63) V(80.51)	147 H(100.00) V(23.33)
₹ 50,001 - 1,00,000	62 H(36.90) V(39.24)	38 H(22.62) V(21.11)	46 H(27.38) V(26.64)	22 H(13.09) V(18.64)	168 H(100.00) V(26.67)
₹ 1,00,001 - 5,00,000	46 H(17.04) V(29.11)	115 H(42.59) V(63.89)	108 H(40.00) V(62.07)	1 H(0.37) V(0.85)	270 H(100.00) V(42.86)
Above ₹ 5,00,000	14 H(31.11) V(8.86)	20 H(44.44) V(11.11)	11 H(24.44) V(6.32)	0	45 H(100.00) V(7.14
Total	**158 H(25.08) V(100.00)**	**180 H(28.57) V(100.00)**	**174 H(27.62) V(100.00)**	**118 H(18.73) V(100.00)**	**630 H(100.00) V(100.00)**

Source: Primary Data.

Note:

1. 'H' indicates to percentages of horizontal totals.
2. 'V' indicates to percentages of vertical totals.

₹ 50,001 to ₹ 1,00,000 and above the ₹ 5,00,000 respectively. Out of the total 60 business respondents, 43 respondents were in the middle income group, 13 respondents were below the one lakh income group and four respondents were above ₹ 5,00,000 income group. Out of 60 employee category respondents, 34 employees were in the income range between ₹ 1,00,000 to ₹ 5,00,000, 15 respondents were below the rupees one lakh income and 11 respondents were above rupees five lakh income.

The details of occupation-wise and income-wise data presented in the table 4-16. Out of the total 630 respondents from all selected banks, the highest number of respondents belonged to business category. 174 respondents belonged to employees' category, 158 respondents representing 25.08 per cent of the total belonged to farmers' category, and 18.73 per cent of the total belonged to SHGs. Only public sector banks (SBH and TGB) offer the self help group linkage loans to the poor, women respondents in this category related to these two banks. That is the reason why, total respondents under SHG category were less in number.

Out of the 158 farmer respondents, 98 respondents (nearly 62 per cent) were in the lower income group i.e., below the income of rupees one lakh. Below 10 per cent of the total respondents, in this category, were belonged to ₹ above five lakhs.

Out of 180 business respondents, nearly 64 per cent of respondents belonged to middle income group and 45 respondents belonged to below the income of ₹ 1,00,000. 20 respondents, indicating 11.11 per cent of the total, were above ₹ 5 lakh income group.

Total of 118 employees respondents, the highest number of respondents i.e. 108 in number were in the income class of ₹ 1,00,000 to ₹ 5,00,000 and the least number of respondents in the income class of below ₹ 50,000. 46 respondents and 11 respondents belonged ₹ 50,001- 1,00,000 and above ₹ 5,00,000 income class respectively.

In the category of SHG respondents, except one respondent (belonged to rupees one lakh to rupees five lakh) all respondents were in the income of below the one lakh.

Marital Status of the Respondents

Another most important social feature of the respondents is marital status is presented in the Table 4.17. As per table, it was found that 597 respondents out of 630, representing 94.76 per cent, were married and remaining 5.27 per cent respondents were unmarried. Out of married respondents 77.39 per cent of respondents were male respondents and remaining 22.61 respondents were women respondents.

Table 4.17: Gender Wise Marital Status of the Respondents

Status	*Male*	*Female*	*Total*
Married	462 H(77.39) V(93.71)	135 H(22.61) V(98.54)	**597** **H(100.00)** **V(94.76)**
Single	31 H(93.94) V(6.29)	2 H(6.06) V(1.46)	**33** **H(100.00)** **V(5.24)**
Total	**493** **H(78.25)** **V(100.00)**	**137** **H(21.75)** **V(100.00)**	**630** **H(100.00)** **V(100.00)**

Source: Primary Data.

Note:

1. 'H' indicates to percentages of horizontal totals.
2. 'V' indicates to percentages of vertical totals.

Out of the total 630 respondents, 493 respondents belonged to male category and 137 respondents were female respondents representing 78.25 per cent and 21.75 per cent respectively. 462 respondents out of total male respondents were married and 6.29 per cent indicating 31 in number were unmarried respondents. Out of 137 women respondents, only two respondents were unmarried and remaining 135 were married.

It has been found that married people are large in numbers that have banking habits. To meet the present money requirements and to satisfy the future financial commitments, it is necessary to open an account in a financial

Table 4.18: Gender Wise Marital Status of the Respondents of SBH

Status	*Male*	*Female*	*Total*
Married	163 H(71.18) V(94.22)	66 H(28.82) V(98.50)	**229** **H(100.00)** **V(95.42)**
Single	10 H(90.90) V(5.78)	1 H(9.10) V(1.50)	**11** **H(100.00)** **V(4.58)**
Total	**173** **H(72.08)** **V(100.00)**	**67** **H(27.92)** **V(100.00)**	**240** **H(100.00)** **V(100.00)**

Source: Primary Data.

Note:

1. 'H' indicates to percentages of horizontal totals.
2. 'V' indicates to percentages of vertical totals.

institution is mandatory. This necessity is very high in case married people which indicate their present and future responsibility towards their family.

The Table 4.18 shows that, out of 240 SBH respondents 229 i.e., 95.42 per cent of the total, were married and remaining 11 respondents were unmarried. Out of the total of married 229 respondents, 71.18 per cent i.e. 163 respondents were male respondents and 66 were female respondents. Only one respondent, out of 11 unmarried respondents, was female and rest 10 respondents were male respondents.

Out of the 173 male respondents, 94.22 per cent, 163 respondents were married and 10 respondents were unmarried. Only one respondent out of 67 female respondents was unmarried and remaining 66 were married.

The details of gender and marital status of the respondents of TGB were present in the Table 4.19. Out of total 228 of TGB 220 were married and

Table 4.19: Gender Wise Marital Status of the Respondents of TGB

Status	*Male*	*Female*	*Total*
Married	154 H(70.00) V(95.65)	66 H(30.00) V(98.50)	**220** **H(100.00)** **V(96.50)**
Single	7 H(87.50) V(4.45)	1 H(12.50) V(1.50)	**8** **H(100.00)** **V(3.50)**
Total	**161** **H(70.61)** **V(100.00)**	**67** **H(29.39)** **V(100.00)**	**228** **H(100.00)** **V(100.00)**

Source: Primary Data.

Note:

1. 'H' indicates to percentages of horizontal totals.
2. 'V' indicates to percentages of vertical totals.

remaining 8 were unmarried respondents. 154 respondents, out of 220 married respondents i.e. 70 per cent, were male respondents and 66 respondents representing, 30 per cent of the total, were female respondents.

Out of 161 male respondents, 95.65 per cent of the respondents indicating 154 in number were married and remaining seven respondents were unmarried. 66 respondents, out of the total of female respondents, were married and one female respondent was unmarried.

Table 4.20: Gender Wise Marital Status of the Respondents of HDFC Bank

Status	*Male*	*Female*	*Total*
Married	145 H(97.97) V(91.20)	3 H(2.03) V(100.00)	**148** **H(100.00)** **V(91.36)**
Single	14 H(100.00) V(8.80)	0	**14** **H(100.00)** **V(8.64)**
Total	**159** **H(98.15)** **V(100.00)**	**3** **H(1.85)** **V(100.00)**	**162** **H(100.00)** **V(100.00)**

Source: Primary Data.

Note:

1. H' indicates to percentages of horizontal totals.
2. 'V' indicates to percentages of vertical totals.

The data in the Table 4.20 furnishes the details of gender and marital status of the respondents of HDFC bank. 148 respondents were married, out of total of the 162 of HDFC bank respondents, and remaining were unmarried. 159 respondents were male and only three respondents were female category and total female respondents were married. Out of the 159 male respondents, 145 respondents indicating nearly 98 per cent were married and remaining 14 respondents were unmarried.

Table 4.21: Bank Wise Gender Wise Marital Status of the Respondents

Status	*SBH*	*TGB*	*HDFC*	*Total*
Married	229 H(38.36) V(95.42)	220 H(36.85) V(96.50)	148 H(24.79) V(91.36)	**597** **H(100.00)** **V(94.76)**
Single	11 H(33.33) V(4.58)	8 H(24.24) V(3.50)	14 H(42.43) V(8.64)	**33** **H(100.00)** **V(5.24)**
Total	**240** **H(38.10)** **V(100.00)**	**228** **H(136.19)** **V(100.00)**	**162** **H(25.71)** **V(100.00)**	**630** **H(100.00)** **V(100.00)**

Source: Primary Data.

Note:

1. H' indicates to percentages of horizontal totals.
2. 'V' indicates to percentages of vertical totals.

The Table 4.21 furnishes the data of bank-wise gender and marital status of the respondents. Out of the total of 630 respondents, 597 respondents signifying 94.76 per cent were married and the rest 33 respondents were unmarried. 229 respondents, out of total of married respondents, belonged to SBH bank, 220 respondents belonged to TGB and 148 respondents belonged to HDFC bank representing 38.36 per cent, 36.85 per cent and 24.79 per cent respectively.

The highest number of respondents, out of the total of unmarried respondents, 14 in number belonged to HDFC bank, 11 respondents belonged to SBH and eight respondents belonged to TGB. With this, it is clear that customers who have more responsible towards their family were chosen to open an account for their financial needs in public sector banks than private sector banks because of their services at low transaction cost.

Types of Banking Service Being Used by Respondents

Table 4.22: Types of Banking Service Using by Respondents

Banking Service	*Types of Banks*			*Total**	*Rank*
	SBH	*TGB*	*HDFC*		
Current Account	51	38	37	126 (12.06)	2
Saving Account	225	204	136	565 (54.07)	1
Investment Account	11	13	2	26 (2.49)	6
Overdraft*	11	5	4	20 (1.91)	8
Personal Loan	5	17	5	27 (2.58)	5
Gold Loan	6	9	10	25 (2.39)	7
Crop Loan	34	39	11	84 (8.04)	4
House loan	6	8	0	14 (1.34)	10
Car Loan	6	0	2	8 (0.76)	11
Mortgage Loan	0	2	0	2 (0.19)	14
Cash Credit	14	5	0	19 (1.82)	9
Tractor Loan	3	1	0	4 (0.38)	13
SHG Linkage Loan	60	58	0	118 (11.29)	3
Others	0	7	0	7 (0.67)	12
Total	**432 (41.34)**	**406 (38.85)**	**207 (19.81)**	**1045 H(100.00) V(100.00)**	
Total No. of Respondents	**240**	**228**	**162**	**630**	
Ratio	**1.8**	**1.78**	**1.28**	**1.66**	

Source: Primary Data.

*A single customer may utilise multiple services, the data reflects multiple responses.

The details of types of banking service used by respondents under study areas depicted in the Table 4.22. Total 630 respondents were utilised 1045 different types of services in their banks. Account in banks is opened and operated by the customers for various reasons. According to their financial needs, respondents opened multiple (two or three) accounts in their respective banks. Saving is the main reason for opening an account in the bank. This is proved in the study. The highest number of respondents i.e. 565 representing 54.07 per cent of the total accounts opened saving account in respective banks. This account opened by all types of respondents i.e. farmers, business people, SHGs and employees. Following this, current account opened and operating by the business people occupied the second position and SHGs linkage loans in the third position and crop loans given to farmers in the next place. Personal loans, long-term deposits (investments), gold loans, overdraft facility and cash credits are in the next positions of fifth, sixth, seventh, eigthth and nineth places respectively.

Usage Period of Banking Services Used by Respondents

The data pertaining to the duration of banking services used by the respondents is furnished in the Table 4.23. This information helps in finding out the relationship between the customer and the bank over a period of time and this leads to devise a strategy to retain the customers for future period. Out of 630 total respondents, the highest numbers of respondents, numbering 246 representing 39 per cent, were utilising the banking services for more than five years for their banking needs. Interesting point to note that, in respect

Table 4.23: Usage Period of Banking Services Using by Respondents

Usage Period	*Bank Type*			*Total*
	SBH	*TGB*	*HDFC*	
Less than One Year	25 H(23.15) V(10.42)	35 H(32.41) V(15.35)	48 H(44.44) V(29.63)	**108** **H(100.00)** **V(17.14)**
One - Three Years	14 H(10.00) V(5.83)	35 H(25.00) H(15.35)	91 H(65.00) V(56.17)	**140** **H(100.00)** **V(22.22)**
Three - Five Years	50 H(36.76) V(20.83)	64 H(47.06) V(28.07)	22 H(16.18) V(13.58)	**136** **H(100.00)** **V(21.59)**
More than Five Years	151 H(61.38) V(62.92)	94 H(38.21) V(41.23)	1 H(0.41) V(0.62)	**246** **H(100.00)** **V(39.05)**
Total	**240** **H(38.10)** **V(100.00)**	**228** **H(36.19)** **V(100.00)**	**162** **H(25.71)** **V(100.00)**	**630** **H(100.00)** **V(100.00)**

Source: Primary Data.

Note:
1. H' indicates to percentages of horizontal totals.
2. 'V' indicates to percentages of vertical totals.

of SBH and TGB, the highest numbers of respondents were utilising their banks and banking services for more than five years. Another important point to note that, in respect of HDFC bank, only one customer has been the customer for more than five years. The reason is that being SBH and TGB, are public sector banks, set up long back and HDFC bank, new generation private bank, was set up recently.

Following this, 140 customers were utilising the banking services for the one to three years, and 136 respondents in between three to five years. Remaining 108 respondents were the customers of the bank for one year or less than one year. Here, in this category, more numbers of customers are in HDFC bank. It indicates that HDFC is attracting new customers more, by offering modern and sophisticated services, than the public sector banks under the study. With this it is assumed that the bank customers have the rich experience with their bank and they were well aware about the services that were offer by their bank in which they opened account.

Frequency of Visiting Banks

The number of times customers transact business with their banks gives a clue about the levels of their frequency in banking, satisfaction and loyalty and has the direct impact on the service quality of the bank in a material way. Owing to this respondents were asked to indicate how often they did

Table 4.24: No. of Times of Visits in a Month* Bank Type Cross Tabulation

Duration	*Bank Type*			*Total*
	SBH	*TGB*	*HDFC*	
One Time or Less	96 H(41.03) V(40.00)	105 H(44.87) V(46.05)	33 H(14.10) V(20.37)	**234** **H(100.00)** **V(37.14)**
2-4 Times	78 H(34.98) V(32.50)	71 H(31.84) V(31.14)	74 H(33.18) V(45.68)	**223** **H(100.00)** **V(35.40)**
5-10 Times	10 H(17.86) V(4.17)	24 H(42.86) V(10.53)	22 H(39.28) V(13.58)	**56** **H(100.00)** **V(8.89)**
More than 10 Times	56 H(47.86) V(23.33)	28 H(23.93) V(12.28)	33 H(28.21) V(20.37)	**117** **H(100.00)** **V(18.57)**
Total	**240** **H(38.10)** **V(100.00)**	**228** **H(36.19)** **V(100.00)**	**162** **H(25.71)** **V(100.00)**	**630** **H(100.00)** **V(100.00)**

Source: Primary Data.

Note:

1. 'H' indicates to percentages of horizontal totals.
2. 'V' indicates to percentages of vertical totals.

business with their banks in a month. The results were presented in the Table 4.24. The details in the table.

These were business people who do frequent transactions with the bank for their business needs. 56 customers do visit their bank five to 10 times in a month. And 234 and 223 customers patronize the bank one time or less and two to four times respectively. In general SHGs visit the bank once in a month to submit monthly SHG report and pay the monthly installment of their loan. Farmers, who visit the bank occasionally at the time of grant the loan which is seasonal based and or to pay the crop loan installments.

Table 4.25: Purpose of Visiting Bank by Respondents*

Purpose of Visiting	*Types of Banks*			*Total*
	SBH	*TGB*	*HDFC*	
Managing Saving A/c	232 H(41.06) V(53.70)	202 H(35.75) V(49.75)	131 H(23.18) V(63.28)	565 H(100.00) V(54.07)
Managing Current A/c	56 H(44.44) V(12.96)	38 H(30.15) V(9.36)	32 H(25.40) V(15.46)	126 H(100.00) V(12.06)
Investment Account (RD/ Fixed)	11 H(42.31) V(2.55)	13 H(50.00) V(3.20)	2 H(7.70) V(0.97)	26 H(100.00) V(2.48)
Operating Loan A/c	122 H(41.08) V(28.24)	144 H(48.48) V(35.48)	31 H(10.43) V(14.98)	297 H(100.00) V(28.42)
Operating Safe Deposit Locker	11 H(35.48) V2.55)	9 H(29.03) V(2.21)	11 H(35.48) V(5.31)	31 H(100.00) V(2.97)
Total	**432** **H(41.34)** **V(100.00)**	**406** **H(38.85)** **V(100.00)**	**207** **H(19.81)** **V(100.00)**	**1045** **H(100.00)** **V(100.00)**

Source: Primary Data.

***A single customer may utilise multiple services, the data reflects multiple responses.**

Note:

1. 'H' indicates to percentages of horizontal totals.
2. 'V' indicates to percentages of vertical totals.

Purpose of Visiting the Bank by Respondents

The details relating to purpose of visiting bank by the respondents were furnished in the Table 4.25. According to the data, total 630 were visited their respective banks for utilisation of 1045 different types of services. Based upon their financial requirement respondents opened accounts and utilised multiple services. The highest number of responses i.e. 54.07 per cent of the total responses was against the saving account. This indicates that customers visit the bank for the purpose of saving their earnings. Saving the money is the primary objective of customers for visiting the bank more times. 297 respondents indicating 28.42 per cent of the total visited the banks for operating loan account. This include different types of loans i.e. SHGs linkage loans of self help groups and crop loans of farmers, personal loans of employees, overdraft of business people, gold loans, vehicle loans, house loans etc. 12 per cent of the total representing 126 number of respondents visited banks to utilise current account. 31 respondents visited banks to utilise safe locker facility with the bank. Remaining 26 respondents visited the bank for the purpose of operating investment account i.e. recurring deposits and fixed deposits.

Out of total 432 respondents of SBH bank, 232 respondents visited this bank to manage their saving account. 122 respondents visited for the purpose of operating loan account. 56 respondents, 11 respondents and 11 respondents visited the bank for managing current account, managing investment account and operating safe deposit locker facility respectively. The similar trend is also seen in case of TGB Bank.

Out of 207 respondents of HDFC bank, 131 respondents visited the bank for the purpose of managing saving account and 32 respondents visited the bank for managing current account. 31 respondents, 11 respondents were visited the bank for the purpose of operating loan account and safe locker deposit. Only two customers visited for the purpose of utilising the investment service.

Having discussed the demographical profile of the respondents of selected banks, an attempt is made to analyse the opinions of customers about awareness of available services in selected banks in the following lines.

Customers' Awareness about Availability of Banking Services

The main objective of any service institution is to delight the customers by providing the modern and sophisticated services and to establish strong relation through proper understanding and fulfilling the requirements of its customers. The banking institution is not exception to this. The bank should tailor the products and services to satisfy the needs of the customers. Some of the core services and innovative services (add-on-services) offered by the most of the banks were divided into three broad categories (a) Accounts (b) Loans and (c) Other Innovative Services, and studied to know the awareness of the selected public and private sector banks' customers. This analysis helps in understanding the customer's awareness about the product or service that offered by the bank and the accessibility of such product or service by the customers in the rural areas.

A. Accounts

Saving Bank Account

Saving bank account is the basic service available in all banks. Through this customers deposit their surplus funds after meeting expenses and withdraw the money as per their requirements. Banks add nominal interest for the amounts deposited in this type of accounts. The opinions of the customers in respect of awareness and access of the saving account in selected banks is presented in the Table 4.26.

Table 4.26: Savings A/c* Bank Type Cross Tabulation

Options	*SBH*	*TGB*	*HDFC*	*Total*
Offered	239 H(38.42) V(99.60)	225 H(36.17) V(98.68)	158 H(25.41) V(97.53)	622 H(100.00) V(98.73)
Not Offered	0	1 H(100.00) V(0.44)	0	1 H(100.00) V(0.16)
Don't Know	1 H(14.29) V(0.42)	2 H(28.57) V(0.88)	4 H(57.14) V(2.50)	7 H(100.00) V(1.11)
Total	**240 H(38.10) V(100.00)**	**228 H(36.19) V(100.00)**	**162 H(25.71) V(100.00)**	**630 H(100.00) V(100.00)**

Source: Primary Data.

Note:

1. 'H' indicates to percentages of horizontal totals.
2. 'V' indicates to percentages of vertical totals.

The data in the Table 4.26 reveals the details about opinion of customers regarding their awareness and access about saving bank account. Out of the total 630 respondents, 622 representing nearly 99 per cent of the total furnished that they were aware of the banks offering saving bank account. Out of 622 respondents, 239, 225 and 158 number of respondents belonged to SBH, TGB and HDFC bank respectively. Only one customer who belonged to TGB bank expressed that the bank had not offered this account and seven (one from SBH, two from TGB and four from HDFC) respondents did not know about the availability of this product in public and private sector banks.

Saving account is a basic account and every customer has to open this account for further transactions. Though eight customers were utilising this banking service, but they did not aware the nature of account because some of the farmers who did not have the formal education and above the age of 60 blindly depend upon the employees of the bank or their nearer.

Current Account

Current account is also another basic service available in all banks. This account, generally, opened by the business people for their business transactions. The opinions of the customers in respect of awareness and access of the saving account in selected banks is presented in the Table 4.27.

Table 4.27: Service Accounts Current A/c* Bank Type Cross Tabulation

Options	*SBH*	*TGB*	*HDFC*	*Total*
Offered	150 H(36.67) V(62.50)	115 H(28.12) V(50.44)	144 H(35.21) V(88.89)	409 H(100.00) V(64.92)
Not Offered	3 H(21.43) V(1.25)	8 H (57.14) V(3.51)	3 H(21.43) V(1.85)	14 H(100.00) V(2.22)
Don't Know	87 H(42.03) V(36.25)	105 H(50.72) V(46.05)	15 H(7.25) V(9.26)	207 H(100.00) V(32.86)
Total	**240** **H(38.10)** **V(100.00)**	**228** **H(36.19)** **V(100.00)**	**162** **H(25.71)** **V(100.00)**	**630** **H(100.00)** **V(100.00)**

Source: Primary Data.

Note:

1. 'H' indicates to percentages of horizontal totals.
2. 'V' indicates to percentages of vertical totals.

The data reveals the details about access of the current account by customers in selected banks in the study area. 65 per cent of the total 630 respondents were expressed that they were well aware about the banks offering this account. The remaining 35 per cent of the total respondents did not have awareness about this account. Though current account is a basic service and offered by all banks, major portion of the respondents did not know about this account. This is very high in case of TGB (nearly 50 per cent) and SBH (nearly 38 per cent) and very low in case of HDFC (10 per cent only). This is because 50 per cent of the respondents belonged to farmers and SHGs group and most of them were illiterates and they visit the bank for particular purpose only.

Demat Account

Demat account refers to dematerialised account. This account is opened by customers to trade (buying and selling) shares on line. This is operated just like a bank account where actual money is replaced by shares. Most of the banks offer this service/facility in collaboration with depository participants (DPs). The opinions in respect of awareness and access of the demat account was offered by selected banks presented below.

Table 4.28: Service Accounts – Demat A/c* Bank Type Cross Tabulation

Demat Account	*Bank Type*			*Total*
	SBH	*TGB*	*HDFC*	
Offered	37 H(33.04) V(15.42)	11 H(9.82) V(4.82)	64 H(57.14) V(39.51)	112 H(100.00) V(17.80)
Not Offered	11 H(20.00) V(4.58)	39 H(70.90) V(17.11)	5 H(9.10) V(3.09)	55 (100.00) V(8.70)
Don't Know	192 H(41.47) V(80.00)	178 H(38.44) V(78.07)	93 H(20.09) V(57.40)	463 (100.00) V(73.50)
Total	**240 H(38.10) V(100.00)**	**228 H(36.19) V(100.00)**	**162 H(25.71) V(100.00)**	**630 H(100.00) V(100.00)**

Source: Primary Data.

Note:

1. 'H' indicates to percentages of horizontal totals.
2. 'V' indicates to percentages of vertical totals.

The Table 4.28 furnishes awareness of the demat account. It is found that only 17.80 per cent of the total 630 respondents expressed that the banks were offering this service. The remaining 82 per cent of the total respondents did not know the availability of this service in the banks. The table also reveals that, 15.42 per cent of the respondents conveyed their opinions that demat account were available and 80 per cent of respondents opined that they did not know the availability of demat account in the both public sector banks i.e. SBH and TGB. 5 per cent in case of SBH and 17 per cent in case of TGB conveyed that these two banks did not offer this type of account. But in case of HDFC bank, private sector bank, 40 per cent of the respondents opined that the demat account was available and 57 per cent opined that they did not have an awareness about the availability of demat account and three per cent of the respondents expressed that the bank did not offer this account.

Safe Locker Facility

This facility, offered by the banks, helps the customers to safeguard their personal valuables. For this banks charge nominal amount from the customers' account. The opinions of banks' customers in respect of awareness about safe locker facility are presented in the following table.

Table 4.29: Service Accounts Safe Locker* Bank Type Cross Tabulation

	Bank Type			*Total*
	SBH	*TGB*	*HDFC*	
Offered	182 H(45.27) V(75.83)	153 H(38.06) V(67.11)	67 H(16.67) V(41.36)	402 H(100.00) V(63.81)
Not Offered	6 H(12.24) V(2.50)	13 H(26.53) V(5.70)	30 H(61.22) V(18.52)	49 H(100.00) V(7.78)
Don't Know	52 H(29.05) V(21.67)	62 H(34.64) V(27.19)	65 H(36.31) V(40.12)	179 H(100.00) V(28.41)
Total	**240** **H(38.10)** **V(100.00)**	**228** **H(36.19)** **V(100.00)**	**162** **H(25.71)** **V(100.00)**	**630** **H(100.00)** **V(100.00)**

Source: Primary Data.

Note:

1. H' indicates to percentages of horizontal totals.
2. 'V' indicates to percentages of vertical totals.

According to the Table 4.29, out of the total 630 respondents the highest number of respondents representing 63.81 per cent expressed their opinion that the safe locker facility was available in all banks in the selected study area. This indicates the customers' awareness about this type of facility/service. 179 respondents i.e. 28.41 per cent conveyed that they did have the knowledge about this facility and only 8 per cent of the total respondents felt that the bank was not offering this facility. 75.83 per cent of SBH customers, 67.11 per cent of TGB customers and 41.36 per cent of HDFC customers expressed that the banks were offering this facility to their customers.

Insurance Facility (Bank Assurance)

Insurance is also a financial service that plays an essential role in the growth of the nation's economy. To provide customer delight banks are offering insurance services through collaboration with insurance companies apart from their normal banking services. These services are provided based on the requirements of the customers by linking with saving deposit accounts. The response in respect of the availability and awareness of customers are presented in the following table.

Table 4.30: Insurance A/c* Bank Type Cross Tabulation

	Bank Type			*Total*
	SBH	***TGB***	***HDFC***	
Offered	143 H(42.06) V(59.58)	83 H(24.41) V(36.40)	114 H(33.53) V(70.37)	340 H(100.00) V(53.97)
Not Offered	21 H(36.21) V(8.75)	34 H(58.62) V(14.91)	3 H(5.17) V(1.85)	58 H(100.00) V(9.21)
Don't Know	76 H(32.76) V(31.67)	111 H(47.84) V(48.68)	45 H(19.40) V(27.78)	232 H(100.00) V(36.82)
Total	**240 H(38.10) V(100.00)**	**228 H(36.19) V(100.00)**	**162 H(25.71) V(100.00)**	**630 H(100.00) V(100.00)**

Source: Primary Data.

Note:
1. 'H' indicates to percentages of horizontal totals.
2. 'V' indicates to percentages of vertical totals.

The data in the above table revealed that the highest number of customers indicating 53.97 (approx. 54) per cent of the total communicated that banks were offering insurance products to their customers. Nearly, 37 per cent of the customers expressed that they did have the knowledge about this product offered by the banks. nine per cent of the respondents clearly expressed that banks did not offer this product in their respective banks. Customers who did not have the sufficient knowledge regarding this insurance product appeared high in number in case of TGB. TGB, as the rural bank which provide financial services particularly rural people who are illiterate in general do not concentrate on the banking affairs.

B. Loans

Personal Loan:

Banks provide personal loans, on conditional basis, to customers to meet their personal financial obligations. The amount of loan, rate of interest and repayment period vary from customer to customer and bank to bank. The opinions of the bank customers in respect of the personal loan were presented in the Table 4.31.

Table 4.31: Personal Loans* Bank Type Cross Tabulation

	Bank Type			*Total*
	SBH	*TGB*	*HDFC*	
Offered	148 H(37.75) V(61.67)	151 H(38.52) V(66.23)	93 H(23.72) V(57.41)	392 H(100.00) V(62.22)
Not Offered	9 H(26.47) V(3.75)	11 H(32.35) V(4.82)	14 H(41.18) V(8.64)	34 H(100.00) V(5.40)
Don't Know	83 H(40.69) V(34.58)	66 H(32.35) V(28.95)	55 H(26.96) V(33.95)	204 H(100.00) V(32.38)
Total	**240 H(38.10) V(100.00)**	**228 H(36.19) V(100.00)**	**162 H(25.71) V(100.00)**	**630 H(100.00) V(100.00)**

Source: Primary Data.

Note:

1. 'H' indicates to percentages of horizontal totals.
2. 'V' indicates to percentages of vertical totals.

From the above data, it is discovered that 62.22 per cent of the total 630 respondents opined that banks were offering personal loan facility to their customers and 34 respondents expressed that the banks were not offering this facility to the customers. 204 respondents representing 32.38 per cent of the total did not have awareness about this facility in banks. In case of SBH, 148 respondents out of 240 expressed that the bank was offering this facility, 83 respondents conveyed that they did not have much knowledge about this facility and only nine respondents, less in number stated that the bank did not offer this type of facility. The similar type opinions were found in respect of TGB and HDFC banks also.

House Loans

House loan is a basic service available in all banks. Banks sanction housc loans on simple conditions to customers for purchase or construction of a new house and renovation of an old existing house. Banks sanction this type of loans against property and reverse mortgage and loans against land holdings. The loans amount is repayable in simple easy monthly installments (EMIs). The opinions of customers in respect of availability of this service in banks are presented in the following Table 4.32.

Table 4.32: House Loans* Bank Type Cross Tabulation

	Bank Type			*Total*
	SBH	*TGB*	*HDFC*	
Offered	187 H(41.46) V(77.92)	171 H(37.91) V(75.00)	93 H(20.62) V(57.41)	451 H(100.00) V(71.59)
Not Offered	6 H(13.64) V(2.50)	11 H(25.00) V(4.82)	27 H(61.36) V(16.67)	44 H(100.00) V(6.98)
Don't Know	47 H(34.81) V(19.58)	46 H(34.07) V(20.18)	42 H(31.11) V(25.92)	135 H(100.00) V(21.43)
Total	**240** **H(38.10)** **V(100.00)**	**228** **H(36.19)** **V(100.00)**	**162** **H(25.71)** **V(100.00)**	**630** **H(100.00)** **V(100.00)**

Source: Primary Data.

Note:

1. 'H' indicates to percentages of horizontal totals.
2. 'V' indicates to percentages of vertical totals.

According to the data in Table 4.32, it is found that the highest number of customers in all the three banks expressed that the house loan service was available in all banks. 135 respondents, out of 630 respondents, opined that they did not aware of this facility and the least number of respondents i.e. 44 in number (SBH-6, TGB-11 and HDFC-27) nearly 7 per cent conveyed that banks did not offer this facility. Out of the total, 78 per cent of SBH respondents, 75 per cent of TGB respondents and 57.41 per cent of HDFC respondents communicated that they were aware of the house loan facility was available in respective banks.

Educational Loans

To pursue higher education in India or abroad, where a person secures admission, banks sanction education loans to Indians. This type of loan is sanctioned for professional courses, post graduate and under graduate courses which approved by the Government of India with excellent employment prospects. This loan includes the expenses such as payment of college fee, purchase of course ware and computer, examination fee and other educational requirements. The loan is repayable after a year of course completion or after six months of securing a job whichever is earlier. The loan is sanctioned at nominal interest rate at collateral. The responses of respondents in the selected areas in respect of availability and awareness of this service in the selected three banks are presented in the following table.

Table 4.33: Educational Loans* Bank Type Cross Tabulation

	Bank Type			*Total*
	SBH	*TGB*	*HDFC*	
Offered	113 H(58.25) V(47.08)	53 H(27.32) V(23.25)	28 H(14.43) V(17.28)	194 H(100.00) V(30.79)
Not Offered	4 H(11.43) V(1.67)	15 H(42.86) V(6.59)	16 H(45.71) V(9.88)	35 H(100.00) V(5.55)
Don't Know	123 H(30.67) V(51.25)	160 H(39.90) V(70.18)	118 H(29.43) V(72.84)	401 H(100.00) V(63.65)
Total	**240 H(38.10) V(100.00)**	**228 H(36.19) V(100.00)**	**162 H(25.71) V(100.00)**	**630 H(100.00) V(100.00)**

Source: Primary Data.

Note: 1. 'H' indicates to percentages of horizontal totals.
2. 'V' indicates to percentages of vertical totals.

According to the Table 4.33, out of 630 respondents the highest number of respondents 401 in number expressed that they did not know this product though banks were offering the product and 30.79 per cent of the respondents conveyed that they had aware of product that banks were offering the education loan. The least number of respondents communicated that banks didn't offer this product.

Vehicle Loans

Banks provide vehicle loans to increase the purchasing power of customers. This loan is provided for two wheelers, four wheeler (car loan) and commercial vehicles (tractor, auto-rikshaw, trucks etc.). The loan amount sanctioned, interest rate, repayment facility depend upon the type of loan and differs from bank to bank and customer to customer. The view of respondents against the various vehicle loans are presented in the following tables.

(a) Two wheeler Loan:

Table 4.34: Two Wheeler Loans* Bank Type Cross Tabulation

	Bank Type			*Total*
	SBH	*TGB*	*HDFC*	
Offered	132 H(37.93) V(55.00)	95 H(27.30) V(41.67)	121 H(34.77) V(74.69)	348 H(100.00) V(55.24)
Not Offered	17 H(48.57) V(7.08)	8 H(22.86) V(3.51)	10 H(28.57) V(6.17)	35 H(100.00) V(5.55)
Don't Know	91 H(36.84) V(37.92)	125 H(50.61) V(54.82)	31 H(12.55) V(19.14)	247 H(100.00) V(39.21)
Total	**240** **H(38.10)** **V(100.00)**	**228** **H(36.19)** **V(100.00)**	**162** **H(25.71)** **V(100.00)**	**630** **H(100.00)** **V(100.00)**

Source: Primary Data.

Note:
1. H' indicates to percentages of horizontal totals.
2. 'V' indicates to percentages of vertical totals.

The Table 4.34 furnishes the details of respondents in respect of awareness of availability of two wheeler loans in the respected bank. Out of the total 55.24 per cent of the respondents, 348 respondents in number (132 of SBH, 95 of TGB and 121 of HDFC), acknowledged that banks were offering two wheeler loans to their customers. 247 respondents indicating 39.21 per cent of the total stated that they did not have the knowledge of availability of this service in their banks and 5.55 per cent of the respondents affirmed that the respective bank did not offer this service to its customers.

(b) Car Loans:

Table 4.35: Car Loans* Bank Type Cross Tabulation

	Bank Type			Total
	SBH	TGB	HDFC	
Offered	141 H(39.06) V(58.75)	96 H(26.59) V(42.11)	124 H(34.35) V(76.54)	361 H(100.00) V(57.30)
Not Offered	11 H(37.93) V(4.58)	11 H(37.93) V(4.82)	7 H(24.14) V(4.32)	29 H(100.00) V(4.60)
Don't Know	88 H(36.67) V(36.67)	121 H(50.42) V(53.07)	31 H(12.92) V(19.14)	240 H(100.00) V(38.10)
Total	**240** **H(38.10)** **V(100.00)**	**228** **H(36.19)** **V(100.00)**	**162** **H(25.71)** **V(100.00)**	**630** **H(100.00)** **V(100.00)**

Source: Primary Data.

Note:
1. 'H' indicates to percentages of horizontal totals.
2. 'V' indicates to percentages of vertical totals.

The Table 4.35 provides the information relating to customers' knowledge about the offering of car loans by respective banks. 361 respondents indicating 57.30 per cent of the total expressed that they had the knowledge about the car loans that were offering by the respective banks. 240 respondents, out of 630 respondents, informed that they did not know this service in their banks and 4.60 per cent of the total respondents, 29 in number, confirmed that respective banks were not offering this facility to their customers.

Commercial Vehicle Loans

The above Table 4.36 furnishes the data relating to opinions of selected respondents in respect of their knowledge against the offering and not offering of commercial vehicle loans by their banks. The highest number of customers 364 representing 57.78 per cent of the total respondents stated that they did not have the knowledge of this product in their respective banks. 37.78 per cent of the total respondents affirmed that banks were offering commercial vehicle loans to their customers. 28 respondents indicating 4.44 per cent of the total confirmed that banks were not offering this service.

Table 4.36: Commercial Vehicle Loans* Bank Type Cross Tabulation

	Bank Type			*Total*
	SBH	*TGB*	*HDFC*	
Offered	88 H(36.97) V(36.66)	72 H(30.25) V(31.58)	78 H(32.77) V(48.15)	238 H(100.00) V(37.78)
Not Offered	13 H(46.43) V(5.42)	10 H(35.71) V(4.39)	5 H(17.86) V(3.09)	28 H(100.00) V(4.44)
Don't Know	139 H(38.19) V(57.92)	146 H(40.11) V(64.03)	79 H(21.71) V(48.76)	364 H(100.00) V(57.78)
Total	**240** **H(38.10)** **V(100.00)**	**228** **H(36.19)** **V(100.00)**	**162** **H(25.71)** **V(100.00)**	**630** **H(100.00)** **V(100.00)**

Source: Primary Data.

Note:
1. 'H' indicates to percentages of horizontal totals.
2. 'V' indicates to percentages of vertical totals.

Gold Loans

In India, gold is seen as the synonym for wealth and the most of Indians love to purchase gold for passion as well as future requirements. If customer owns a sufficient amount of gold and in a need of money then they go for gold loan option.

Gold loan is meant for those people who need fast cash to fulfill their unexpected financial needs. Nowadays, all banks are providing the loan against gold with several benefits and in a very simplified procedure. The response against the awareness of respondents towards availability of this product in respected bank is presented in the following table.

According to the Table 4.37, the highest number of respondents expressed that they had complete knowledge about the product that was offered by respective banks. Few respondents conveyed that they were not aware of gold loan that was offered by the respective bank and very less number, it is zero. In case of TGB bank, indicating only seven in number stated that the banks were not offering gold loan product to its customers.

Table 4.37: Gold Loans* Bank Type Cross Tabulation

	Bank Type			Total
	SBH	TGB	HDFC	
Offered	202 H(35.44) V(84.17)	212 H(37.19) V(92.98)	156 H(27.37) V(96.30)	570 H(100.00) V(90.48)
Not Offered	5 H(71.43) V(2.08)	0	2 H(28.57) V(1.23)	7 H(100.00) V(1.11)
Don't Know	33 H(62.26) V(13.75)	16 H(30.20) V(7.02)	4 H(7.54) V(2.47)	53 H(100.00) V(8.41)
Total	**240** **H(38.10)** **V(100.00)**	**228** **H(36.19)** **V(100.00)**	**162** **H(25.71)** **V(100.00)**	**630** **H(100.00)** **V(100.00)**

Source: Primary Data.

Note:

1. 'H' indicates to percentages of horizontal totals.
2. 'V' indicates to percentages of vertical totals.

Agricultural Loans

As per RBI guidelines banks grant credit to agriculture at a lower rate of interest. Loans are granted for irrigation, purchase of agricultural equipments, inputs, etc. The responses against the product availability in selected banks are presented in the following paragraphs.

Land Mortgage Loan

As per the Table 4.38 the highest number of respondents 393 in number stated that banks under study were offering land mortgage loans. Of which 162 respondents belonged to TGB bank, 149 respondents belonged to SBH bank and 82 respondents were belonged to HDFC bank. 33.81 per cent of the total respondents were stated that they did not have any knowledge about the availability or non-availability of this particular product/service in their banks

Table 4.38: Land Mortgage Loans* Bank Type Cross Tabulation

	Bank Type			*Total*
	SBH	*TGB*	*HDFC*	
Offered	149 H(37.91) V(62.08)	162 H(41.22) V(71.05)	82 H(20.87) V(50.62)	393 H(100.00) V(62.38)
Not Offered	11 H(45.83) V(4.58)	2 H(8.33) V(0.88)	11 H(45.83) V(6.80)	24 H(100.00) V(3.81)
Don't Know	80 H(37.56) V(33.33)	64 H(30.05) V(28.07)	69 H(32.39) V(42.59)	213 H(100.00) V(33.81)
Total	**240** **H(38.10)** **V(100.00)**	**228** **H(36.19)** **V(100.00)**	**162** **H(25.71)** **V(100.00)**	**630** **H(100.00)** **V(100.00)**

Source: Primary Data.

Note:
1. 'H' indicates to percentages of horizontal totals.
2. 'V' indicates to percentages of vertical totals.

where they were opened the account. Out of the total, 24 respondents affirmed that the selected three banks were not offering this service.

Crop Loan

Crop Loans are also called short-term loans for "Seasonal Agricultural Operations." Banks provide the credit to meet the current expenditure for raising the crops on land till the crops are harvested is construed as production or short-term credit for seasonal agricultural operations. The opinions of respondents with regard to the offering or not offering of crop loans by the banks in selected areas are presented in the following table.

As per the data presented in the Table 4.39, out of the total 630 respondents, 62.70 per cent of the respondents expressed that the banks were offering crop loans to the farmers. 209 respondents (76 of SBH, 73 of HDFC and 60 of TGB) representing 33.17 per cent of the total conveyed that they did not have the knowledge that the banks were offering or not offering this product/ service and 26 respondents affirmed that the banks were not offering this service.

Table 4.39: Crop Loans* Bank Type Cross Tabulation

	Bank Type			*Total*
	SBH	*TGB*	*HDFC*	
Offered	152 H(38.48) V(63.33)	166 H(42.02) V(72.81)	77 H(19.49) V(47.53)	395 H(100.00) V(62.70)
Not offered	12 H(46.15) V(5.00)	2 H(7.69) V(0.88)	12 H(46.15) V(7.41)	26 H(100.00) V(4.13)
Don't Know	76 H(36.36) V(31.67)	60 H(28.71) V(26.31)	73 H(34.93) V(45.06)	209 H(100.00) V(33.17)
Total	**240** **H(38.10)** **V(100.00)**	**228** **H(36.19)** **V(100.00)**	**162** **H(25.71)** **V(100.00)**	**630** **H(100.00)** **V(100.00)**

Source: Primary Data.

Note: 1. 'H' indicates to percentages of horizontal totals.
2. 'V' indicates to percentages of vertical totals.

Loan for Agricultural Equipment

Table 4.40: Farming Equipment* Bank Type Cross Tabulation

	Bank Type			*Total*
	SBH	*TGB*	*HDFC*	
Offered	149 H(38.10) V(62.08)	165 H(42.20) V(72.37)	77 H(19.69) V(47.53)	391 H(100.00) V(62.06)
Not Offered	13 H(52.00) V(5.42)	0	12 H(48.00) V(7.41)	25 H(100.00) V(3.97)
Don't Know	78 H(36.45) V(32.50)	63 H(29.44) V(27.63)	73 H(34.11) V(45.06)	214 H(100.00) V(33.97)
Total	**240** **H(38.10)** **V(100.00)**	**228** **H(36.19)** **V(100.00)**	**162** **H(25.71)** **V(100.00)**	**630** **H(100.00)** **V(100.00)**

Source: Primary Data.

Note: 1. 'H' indicates to percentages of horizontal totals.
2. 'V' indicates to percentages of vertical totals.

According to the data in the Table 4.40, 391 respondents, out of total 630 respondents, indicating 62.06 per cent of the total respondents stated that they had the awareness of the product offered by the banks. 214 respondents of which 78 of SBH, 73 of HDFC and 63 of TGB bank were conveyed that they did not have the awareness of product whether banks were offering or not offering this product and 25 respondents representing 3.97 per cent of the total affirmed that the banks were not offering this product.

Loans for Live Stock

Table 4.41: Live Stock* Bank Type Cross Tabulation

	Bank Type			*Total*
	SBH	*TGB*	*HDFC*	
Offered	147 H(39.41) V(61.25)	161 H(43.16) V(70.61)	65 H(100.00) V(40.12)	373 H(100.00) V(59.21)
Not Offered	15 H(46.87) V(6.25)	2 H(6.25) V(0.88)	15 H(46.87) V(9.26)	32 H(100.00) V(5.08)
Don't Know	78 H(34.67) V(32.50)	65 H(28.89) V(28.51)	82 H(50.62)	225 H(100.00) V(35.71)
Total	**240 H(38.10) V(100.00)**	**228 H(36.19) V(100.00)**	**162 H(25.71) V(100.00)**	**630 H(100.00) V(100.00)**

Source: Primary Data.

Note:
1. 'H' indicates to percentages of horizontal totals.
2. 'V' indicates to percentages of vertical totals.

According to the Table 4.41, it is found that the highest number of respondents indicating 59.21 per cent of the total respondents expressed that the banks were offering live stock loans to farmers to purchase live stocks. 35.71 per cent of the total respondents conveyed that they did not know whether banks were offering or not and 32 respondents representing 5.08 per cent of total stated that the banks were not offering this service.

Debit Card or ATM Card (Automic Teller Machine/Any Time Money Card)

The electronic card, which reduces the frequent visits of customers to banks for money withdrawal and makes payment very convenient for purchase of goods and services, issued by the bank to access their account any time is called ATM card. ATM card facilitates immediate transfer of money from customer account to merchant account. The response against the awareness of availability of this facility in selected banks is studied and presented in the Table 4.42.

Table 4.42: Debit Cards* Bank Type Cross Tabulation

	Bank Type			*Total*
	SBH	*TGB*	*HDFC*	
Offered	214 H(56.02) V(89.17)	8 H(2.09) V(3.51)	160 H(41.88) V(98.78)	382 H(100.00) V(60.63)
Not Offered	1 H(0.60) V(0.42)	165 H(99.40) V(72.37)	0	166 H(100.00) V(26.35)
Don't Know	25 H(30.49) V(10.42)	55 H(67.07) V(24.12)	2 H(2.44) V(1.22)	82 H(100.00) V(13.02)
Total	**240 H(38.10) V(100.00)**	**228 H(36.19) V(100.00)**	**162 H(25.71) V(100.00)**	**630 H(100.00) V(100.00)**

Source: Primary Data

Note:
1. 'H' indicates to percentages of horizontal totals.
2. 'V' indicates to percentages of vertical totals.

According to the Table 4.42, the highest number of respondents 60.63 per cent of the total conveyed that they had knowledge about the debit cards and offered by the banks. This product is offered by SBH and HDFC banks and TGB rural bank not offered this product to its customers. TGB bank not established the ATM and does not offer this product. Though TGB, not offering the product, eight respondents replied that the bank was offering this product and 55 respondents expressed that they did not have the knowledge about this product. This indicates that the customers of TGB did not have the knowledge of the bank's products. Hence, the bank should create an awareness of its products to its customers.

Credit Card

It is also an electronic card issued by the bank to selected customers to avail money without having sufficient amount in his account. It is one type of credit facility provided by the bank. The amount used, for purchase of goods and services, by the customer is charged to his account. That means amount will be paid by the bank on behalf of the customer. The availed amount will be repayable to the bank either by installments or total at a time. Bank charges interest for this service. The data relating to the customers' response against the awareness of this product is presented in the following table.

Table 4.43: Credit Cards* Bank Type Cross Tabulation

	Bank Type			***Total***
	SBH	***TGB***	***HDFC***	
Offered	59 H(28.50) V(24.58)	5 H(2.42) V(2.19)	143 H(69.08) V(88.27)	207 H(100.00) V(32.86)
Not Offered	39 H(22.94) V(16.25)	130 H(76.47) V(57.02)	1 H(0.59) V(0.62)	170 H(100.00) V(26.98)
Don't Know	142 H(56.13) V(59.17)	93 H(36.76) V(40.79)	18 H(7.11) V(11.11)	253 H(100.00) V(40.16)
Total	**240 H(38.10) V(100.00)**	**228 H(36.19) V(100.00)**	**162 H(25.71) V(100.00)**	**630 H(100.00) V(100.00)**

Source: Primary Data.

Note:
1. 'H' indicates to percentages of horizontal totals.
2. 'V' indicates to percentages of vertical totals.

The data in the Table 4.43 revealed that 40.16 per cent of the total respondents representing the highest in number, 253 respondents, stated that they did not have awareness of this product. 170 respondents expressed that the bank did not offer this product and 32.86 per cent of the respondents indicating 207 in number (59 of SBH and 143 of HDFC and 5 of TGB customers) communicated that the respective bank was offering this product.

TGB, as regional rural bank, not offered this product. The highest number of this bank customers stated that the bank did not offer this service.

Internet Banking

Nowaday's all banking organisations are offering internet banking facility to their customers. Internet banking has become one of the most important part and sophisticated service of all banks. Because of the busy schedule, customers are not willing to visit banks frequently and spending more time in stand in the queue for banking transaction like, payment and get other facilities. For speed and secure transactions, customers are using internet banking. Banks are also willing to reduce the frequent visits of customers to the bank. To avail this facility, customers have to register with their respective banks' website. At present India has more than two million active internet banking users representing 15 per cent of the internet user population. The responses, in respect of availability and awareness of the internet banking, of the respondents are presented in the following Table 4.44.

Table 4.44: Internet* Bank Type Cross Tabulation

	Bank Type			*Total*
	SBH	*TGB*	*HDFC*	
Offered	130 H(44.37) V(54.17)	24 H(8.19) V(10.53)	139 H(47.44) V(85.80)	293 H(100.00) V(46.51)
Not Offered	6 H(4.80) H(2.50)	119 H(95.20) V(52.19)	0	125 H(100.00) V(19.84)
Don't Know	104 H(49.06) V(43.33)	85 H(40.09) V(37.28)	23 H(10.85) V(14.20)	212 H(100.00) V(33.65)
Total	**240 H(38.10) V(100.00)**	**228 H(36.19) V(100.00)**	**162 H(25.71) V(100.00)**	**630 H(100.00) V(100.00)**
Source: Primary Data.				
Note: 1. 'H' indicates to percentages of horizontal totals. 2. 'V' indicates to percentages of vertical totals.				

The above table revealed that 46.51 per cent of the total respondents 293 (130 respondents of SBH, 24 respondents of TGB and 139 respondents of HDFC) in number conveyed that they are aware of the internet banking service which was provided by the banks under study. 212 respondents expressed that they didn't have the knowledge about this service facility. Out of the total 212 (don't know category) the highest number of respondents 104 belonged to SBH bank, 85 belonged to TGB and 23 respondents belonged to HDFC bank.

Telephone banking

Telephone banking, nowadays, is a service facility provided by all banks and other financial institution. It enables customers to perform financial transactions over the telephone, without visiting a bank branch or automated teller machine. Telephone banking times can be longer than branch opening times, and some financial institutions offer the service on a 24 hour basis. From the bank's point of view, telephone banking reduces the cost of handling transactions by reducing the need for customers to visit a bank branch for non-cash withdrawal and deposit transactions. The response against the availability of tele-banking service in the selected banks is given in the following table.

Table 4.45: Tele Banking* Bank Type Cross Tabulation

	Bank Type			*Total*
	SBH	*TGB*	*HDFC*	
Offered	64 H(34.60) V(26.67)	12 H(6.49) V(5.25)	109 H(58.92) V(67.28)	185 H(100.00) V(29.37)
Not Offered	23 H(15.65) V(9.58)	123 H(83.67) V(53.95)	1 H(0.0.68)) V(0.62)	147 H(100.00) V(23.33)
Don't Know	153 H(51.34) V(63.75)	93 H(31.21) V(40.80)	52 H(17.45) V(32.10)	298 H(100.00) V(47.30)
Total	**240 H(38.10) V(100.00)**	**228 H(36.19) V(100.00)**	**162 H(25.71) V(100.00)**	**630 H(100.00) V(100.00)**

Source: Primary Data.

Note:
1. 'H' indicates to percentages of horizontal totals.
2. 'V' indicates to percentages of vertical totals.

The Table 4.45 shows the details of responses against awareness of telephone banking by respondents of selected banks. According to the data, the highest number of respondents conveyed that they did not have the awareness of telephone banking service whether banks were providing or not. Out of the total, 147 respondents representing 23.33 per cent of the total, expressed that the banks were not offering this facility and the remaining 185 respondents, indicating 29.37 per cent of the total, stated that they knew that banks were providing telephone banking service.

In case of SBH bank, out of the total 240 respondents, the highest number of respondents did have the knowledge about the availability of this service. 23 respondents confirmed that the bank was not offering this facility and 26.67 per cent of the total SBH respondents had the knowledge about that the bank was offering this service to its customers.

In case of TGB the highest number of customers expressed that the bank was not providing this facility. 40.80 per cent of the respondents 93 in number did not know this service. Only 12 respondents had the knowledge of this service in this bank.

In case of HDFC, the highest number of respondents 67.28 per cent of the total 162 respondents had the knowledge that the bank was offering this service. 52 respondents did not have the knowledge of this service and only one respondent expressed that the bank was not providing this service.

Mobile Banking

At present, with the help of modern technology, customer need not visit bank branches for their monetary requirements. By using their mobile phones, customers can be able to do most of their banking transactions to save valuable time and money. Now, all banks are providing this service.

Mobile banking is a system that allows customers of a bank or financial institution to conduct a number of financial transactions through a mobile device such as a mobile phone or personal digital assistant. Mobile banking differs from mobile payments, which involve the use of a mobile device to pay for goods or services either at the point of sale or remotely, analogously to the use of a debit or credit card to effect an electronic fund transfer at point

Table 4.46: Mobile Banking* Bank Type Cross Tabulation

	Bank Type			*Total*
	SBH	*TGB*	*HDFC*	
Offered	103 H(40.23) V(42.92)	22 H(8.60) V(9.65)	131 H(51.17) V(80.09)	256 H(100.00) V(40.63)
Not Offered	11 H(8.40) V(4.58)	117 H(89.31) V(51.31)	3 H(2.30) V(1.85)	131 H(100.00) V(20.80)
Don't Know	126 H(51.85) V(52.50)	89 H(36.63) V(39.03)	28 H(11.52) V(17.28)	243 H(100.00) V(38.57)
Total	**240** **H(38.10)** **V(100.00)**	**228** **H(36.19)** **V(100.00)**	**162** **H(25.71)** **V(100.00)**	**630** **H(100.00)** **V(100.00)**

Source: Primary Data.

Note:
1. 'H' indicates to percentages of horizontal totals.
2. 'V' indicates to percentages of vertical totals.

of sale (EFTPOS) payment. The earliest mobile banking services were offered over SMS, a service known as SMS banking. With the introduction of smart phones with Wireless Application Protocol (WAP) support enabling the use of the mobile web in 1999, the first European banks started to offer mobile banking on this platform to their customers.

The details of the respondents' views about availability of the mobile banking service were presented in the Table 4.46. The data inferred that the highest number of respondents, 256 in number, stated that they were well aware of the availability of this mobile banking service in the banks. This represents about 41 per cent of the total respondents. 243 respondents indicating 38.57 per cent of the total did not have knowledge about this service. The remaining 131 respondents confirmed that the banks were not offering this service.

Electronic Funds Transfer (EFT)

With the computerised networking of bank branches, customer can transfer their saving/ funds from one place to other places or one bank to other banks easily. This EFT facility is very useful to customers to pay their utility bills like electricity bill, phone bill, taxes to government, credit card bill payment, railway/air/bus ticket reservation etc., online purchases and loans. The response of respondents of selected bank customers against the awareness of availability and non-availability of EFT facility in their respective banks is furnished with the help of following table.

Table 4.47: EFT* Bank Type Cross Tabulation

	Bank Type			*Total*
	SBH	*TGB*	*HDFC*	
Offered	147 H(40.50) V(61.25)	98 H(27.00) V(42.98)	118 H(32.51) V(72.84)	363 H(100.00) V(57.62)
Not Offered	1 H(2.78) V(0.42)	35 H(97.22) V(15.35)	0	36 H(100.00) V(5.71)
Don't Know	92 H(39.83) V(38.33)	95 H(41.12) V(41.67)	44 H(19.05) V(27.16)	231 H(100.00) V(36.67)
Total	**240** **H(38.10)** **V(100.00)**	**228** **H(36.19)** **V(100.00)**	**162** **H(25.71)** **V(100.00)**	**630** **H(100.00)** **V(100.00)**

Source: Primary Data.

Note:
1. 'H' indicates to percentages of horizontal totals.
2. 'V' indicates to percentages of vertical totals.

As per the information furnished in the above table, out of the total 630 respondents the highest number of respondents representing 57.62 per cent avowed that they were aware about the availability of this facility in their respective banks. Nearly 37 per cent of the total respondents stated that they did not have the awareness of this facility in their banks. Very less number i.e. 5.71 per cent, 36 in number, affirmed that the banks were not offering this facility. Interesting point is that, in case of HDFC bank no single respondent confirmed that the bank was not offering this facility. But, in case of TGB, 35 respondents out of 36 declared that the bank was not offering this facility.

Table – 4.48: Products and Services Offered by the All Banks

		Offered	*Not Offered*	*Don't Know*	*Total*
Savings Account	Count	622	1	7	630
	per cent	98.7	.2	1.1	100.0
Current Account	Count	409	14	207	630
	per cent	64.9	2.2	32.9	100.0
Demat. Account	Count	112	55	463	630
	per cent	17.8	8.7	73.5	100.0
Safe Locker Facility	Count	402	49	179	630
	per cent	63.8	7.8	28.4	100.0
Insurance	Count	340	58	232	630
	per cent	54.0	9.2	36.8	100.0
Personal Loan	Count	392	34	204	630
	per cent	62.2	5.4	32.4	100.0
House Loan	Count	451	44	135	630
	per cent	71.6	7.0	21.4	100.0
Two-Wheeler Loan	Count	348	35	247	630
	per cent	55.2	5.6	39.2	100.0
Car Loans	Count	361	29	240	630
	per cent	57.3	4.6	38.1	100.0
Commercial Vehicle Loan	Count	238	28	364	630
	per cent	37.8	4.4	57.8	100.0
Land Mortgage Loan	Count	393	24	213	630
	per cent	62.4	3.8	33.8	100.0
Crop Loans	Count	395	26	209	630
	per cent	62.7	4.1	33.2	100.0
Live Stock Loan	Count	373	32	225	630
	per cent	59.2	5.1	35.7	100.0
Farming Equipment Loan	Count	391	25	214	630
	per cent	62.1	4.0	34.0	100.0
Educational Loan	Count	194	35	401	630
	per cent	30.8	5.6	63.7	100.0
Gold Loans	Count	570	7	53	630
	per cent	90.5	1.1	8.4	100.0
Credit Card	Count	207	170	253	630
	per cent	32.9	27.0	40.2	100.0
Debit Card	Count	382	166	82	630
	per cent	60.6	26.3	13.0	100.0
Smart Card	Count	31	206	393	630
	per cent	4.9	32.7	62.4	100.0

(Contd...)

Agri. Card	Count	14	210	406	630
	per cent	2.2	33.3	64.4	100.0
Kisan Credit Card	Count	18	208	404	630
	per cent	2.9	33.0	64.1	100.0
Internet Banking	Count	293	125	212	630
	per cent	46.5	19.8	33.7	100.0
Tele Banking	Count	185	147	298	630
	per cent	29.4	23.3	47.3	100.0
Mobile Banking	Count	256	131	243	630
	per cent	40.6	20.8	38.6	100.0
EFT	Count	363	36	231	630
	per cent	57.6	5.7	36.7	100.0
Total Average	**per cent**	**49.00**	**12.00**	**39.00**	**100.00**

Source: Primary Data.

The data in the above table furnishes the details of opinions of respondents regarding their awareness about services, facilities and amenities provided by their respective bank where they had bank account. Out of 630 respondents bellow 50 per cent i.e. only 49 per cent have awareness about the services offered by the bank. The rest 51 per cent of the total respondents do not have knowledge about the service and products offered by the bank.

Necessary steps to be taken by the bank authorities by arranging awareness programmes frequently and proper display of services and products that are offering by the bank to create awareness on their services and products.

Summary

The chapter demographic profile of the respondents, under study, revealed that gender was almost evenly split in the proportions of 78.25 per cent males and 21.75 per cent females 22.22 per cent of the respondents were below the age group of 30 years 39.21 per cent of respondents were in between 31 – 40 years, 23.49 per cent of respondents were in between the age group of 41 – 50 years, 10.16 per cent in between the age group of 51 – 60 and 4.44 per cent respondents belonged to above 60 years. 94.76 per cent of respondents were married and 5.24 per cent respondents were unmarried.

The highest number of respondents i.e. 28.73 per cent of the total respondents possessed the degree qualification, 19.68 per cent have 10th class qualification, 16.35 per cent respondents had completed intermediate education 15.71 per cent of respondents had possessed only formal education i.e. less than 10th class and 8.10 per cent possessed master degree qualification. The remaining 8.73 per cent of the total respondents did not have any formal education. These were illiterates and mostly belonged to farmers and SHGs categories.

The data relating to occupation shows that 28.57 per cent of the total respondents belonged to business category, 27.62 per cent belonged to employees category, 25.08 per cent belonged to farmers category and the remaining 18.73 per cent of the total 118 in number belonged to self-help groups (SHGs) category who spread to SBH and DGB bank only. The SHGs loan linkage scheme was offered by these two public sector banks. SHGs were nil in HDFC bank as it is a private sector and deos not offer SHG linkage scheme.

This chapter also explained the customers' awareness about the services that are offered by the selected banks in the study area.

Chapter - 5

Customers' Satisfaction of Service Quality

Introduction

Having discussed the demographical profile of the respondents and customer's awareness about availability services in banks in the selected Karimnagar district in the above chapter, an attempt is made to study the opinions of bank customers on service quality aspects. This chapter deals with opinions of 630 rural customers of selected banks under the study area, against the awareness of respondents about the services or products that are available in banks, influencing factors, service timings of the banks, service encounters, service quality by using SERVQUAL, and opinions about overall service quality.

Influencing Factors to Open Bank Account by Respondents

Table 5.1: Influencing Factors for Opening Bank Account

Sl. No.	*Influencing Factors*	*Total*	
		Mean	*Rank*
1.	Place of the Bank Branch	7.34	2
2.	Banking Business Hours	7.22	3
3.	Employees Attitude/Behaviour	6.69	4
4.	Bank Advertisement in T.V.s/News Papers etc.	4.95	6
5.	Mobile Messages alerts	4.94	7
6.	References of friends/relatives	4.48	9
7.	Prompt Services of Bank	7.82	1
8.	Value Added Services	4.71	8
9.	Less Transactions Cost	5.72	5
10.	Govt. Benefit/Others	4.14	10

Source: Primary Data.

Table 5.2: Bank wise Influencing Factors for Opening Bank Account

Sl. No.	*Influencing Factors*	*SBH*		*TGB*		*HDFC*		*TOTAL*	
		Mean	*Ranks*	*Mean*	*Rank*	*Mean*	*Rank*	*Mean*	*Ranks*
1.	Location of the Bank Branch	7.72	2	6.90	3	7.40	3	7.34	2
2.	Banking Business Hours	7.41	3	7.05	2	7.18	4	7.22	3
3.	Employees Attitude/Behavior	6.09	4	6.78	4	7.46	2	6.69	4
4.	Bank Advertisement in T.V.s/News Papers etc.	4.88	7	5.02	7	4.96	8	4.95	6
5.	Mobile Messages alerts	4.71	8	4.59	8	5.76	6	4.94	7
6.	References of friends/relatives	4.26	9	4.50	9	4.79	5	4.48	9
7.	Prompt Services of Bank	7.98	1	7.87	1	7.52	1	7.82	1
8.	Value Added Services	4.23	10	4.16	10	6.20	5	4.71	8
9.	Less Transactions Cost.	5.34	5	6.23	5	5.57	7	5.72	5
10.	Govt. Benefit/Others	5.21	6	5.96	6	0.00	10	4.14	10

Source: Primary Data.

The influencing factors or motivational factors are varying from customer to customer and bank to bank. Choosing the bank to open an account is mainly depend upon the need of the customer, though, some factors like value added services, offering government benefits convenient location of the bank and convenient business hours, quality services rendered by the bank, employee behaviour etc. will influence the customer greatly in selected the bank to open an account. Some of the most important influencing factors to open an account, in general, are selected and studied the priorities given by the customers in choosing the bank for their financial needs. The mean values and ranks based on priority of influencing factors for choosing a bank are presented with the help of the Table 5.1.

The data in the Table 5.1 furnishes the details of ranks based on priority of influencing factors for choosing a bank. The prompt services of the banks and location of the bank branch have been ranked first and second respectively. The third, fourth and fifth ranks have been given to business timing of the bank and behavioural attitude of the bank employees and less transaction cost respectively. Respondents, under the study, have given less priority to the remaining factors such as advertisements of the particular bank, mobile messages, and value added services. It is noted that those factors, references of friends and relatives and other factors are the least prioritized by the respondents. With this, it is inferred that the rendering service at prompt time is most significant factor to attract more number of customers to open their bank account to meet their financial requirements.

The Table 5.2 presents the details about bank-wise factors that are influencing for opening an account in SBH, TGB and HDFC bank. In case of SBH, prompt services are provided by the bank, location of the bank branch and business hours are the highly influencing factors to choose the bank for opening an account. These factors were ranked first, second and third by the customers. In case of TGB prompt services, business hours of the bank and location of the bank were ranked as first, second and third respectively by its customers. Prompt services provided by the bank and employee attitude/ behaviour were ranked first and second respectively by HDFC bank customers. Location of the bank and business hours of the bank were ranked 3rd and 4th by the customers of HDFC bank.

Spearman Rank Correlation	
In Between	***Co-efficient***
SBH and TGB	0.95
SBH and HDFC	0.58
TGB and HDFC	0.48

Table 5.4: Customers-wise Influencing Factors for Opening Bank Account

Sl. No.	Influencing Factors	Farmers		SHGs		Business		Employees		Total	
		Mean	Ranks	Mean	Ranks	Mean	Ranks	Mean	Ranks	Mean	Ranks
1.	Place of the Bank Branch	6.38	4	8	2	8.03	2	8.45	1	7.72	2
2.	Banking Business Hours	7.55	2	7.23	3	7.27	3	7.58	3	7.41	3
3.	Employees Attitude/Behaviour	6.17	5	5.98	5	6.38	4	5.82	4	6.09	4
4.	Bank Advertisement in T.V.s/News Papers etc.	4.95	7	4.6	6	4.73	7	5.25	7	4.88	7
5.	Mobile Messages alerts	4.25	9	4.1	9	5.15	6	5.35	6	4.71	8
6.	References of friends/relatives	4.78	8	4.18	8	4	9	4.08	9	4.26	9
7.	Prompt Services of Bank	7.57	1	8.3	1	8.22	1	7.83	2	7.98	1
8.	Value Added Services	4.05	10	4.08	10	4.53	8	4.25	8	4.23	10
9.	Less Transactions Cost	5.6	6	4.42	7	5.53	5	5.8	5	5.34	5
10.	Govt. Benefit/Others	6.77	3	7.17	4	3.47	10	3.45	10	5.21	6

Source: Primary Data.

and friends (9th rank) and very near opinions expressed against some other factors.

The data also reviewed with the help of SPSS and inferred that factors such as Employee Attitude and Behaviour, Advertisements, Prompt Services, and Government Benefits were highly influencing variables and differ from bank to bank in choosing the bank to open an account.

The Table 5.4 presents the details about customer-wise factors that are influencing for opening an account in selected banks. In case of farmers, prompt services are provided by the bank and business hours of the bank branch and government benefits were the highly influencing factors to choose the bank for opening an account. These factors were ranked first, second and third by the customers respectively. In case of SHGs prompt services, location of the bank branch and business hours of the bank were highly influencing and ranked as first, second and third respectively. Prompt services provided by the bank, location of the bank and business hours of the bank were greatly influencing business category customers and ranked as first, second and third respectively. Location of the bank, prompt services provided by the bank and business hours of the bank were ranked first, second and third ranks respectively by the employee type of customers.

Spearman Rank Correlation	
In Between	***Co-efficient***
Farmers and SHGs	0.93
Farmers and Business	0.63
Farmers and Employees	0.61
SHGs and Business	0.7
SHGs and Employees	0.7
Business and Employees	0.98

The ranks of the various influencing factors given by the selected customers to the banks were tested with the help of spearman rank correlation and proved that there was a positive correlation i.e. the similarity in opinions among the ranks given by various types of customers. The high positive correlation was established in respect of views between business and employee customers and farmer and SHG customers. Because of similar opinions expressed against many influencing factors (eight factors i.e. Banking Business Hours, Employees Attitude/Behaviour, Bank Advertisement in T.V.s/News Papers etc., Mobile Messages alerts, References of friends/relatives, Value Added Services, Less Transactions Cost, and Govt. Benefit/Others. In case of business and employee customers and four factors i.e. Employees Attitude/ Behaviour, Mobile Messages alerts, References of friends/relatives, Value Added Services in case of farmer and SHG customers) by these customers.

Importance of Facilities and Amenities Provided by the Bank

The bank is the place where different kinds of customers visit and avail different banking services for different purposes. Customers also expect different facilities and amenities, like Location of the Bank, Parking Facility, Information about working hours, Information about service timings, Availability of personal assistance/guidance, Display of identification boards at counters, May I Help You Counter, Proper Lighting, Information about available services and products, Electronic token number display and audio announcement system, Waiting Room/Place, ATM facility at the branch, Attractive Flooring, Drinking Water, A/C Facility, Dust Bins, Toilets Facility, Complaint and Suggestion Box etc., in addition to general banking services. With this customers can make transactions for their needs, with the bank, without any discomfort. Therefore, it is considered that customers' convenience is to be an important criterion for evaluating the service quality and customers satisfaction towards service provided by the banks. Opinions from customers were gathered to study the gap between the expectations of facilities and amenities expected to be provided and actual facilities and amenities that were provided by the selected banks. The responses regarding these facilities and amenities were presented and analysed in the form of mean values and ranks in the following lines.

Importance of Facilities and Amenities Provided by the Selected Banks

The data in the Table 5.6 presents the details of customers' opinions of selected banks (SBH, TGB and HDFC) regarding the Expectations of facilities and amenities to be provided by the bank for convenient of customers. Bank customers gave the first rank to 'information about working hours' second rank to 'information about service timings', and third rank given to 'Proper lighting'. The fourth rank and fifth rank were given to 'Information about available services' and products', and 'Availability of personal assistance/ guidance'. 'Complaint and suggestion box', 'Location of the bank where it located' and 'drinking water' were ranked sixth, seventh and eighth ranks respectively. Ninth, tenth, eleventh, twelfth and thirteenth ranks were given to 'display of identification boards at counters for easy identification', 'parking facility' 'waiting room/place in the bank' 'ATM facility at the bank branch' and 'Attractive Flooring' respectively. 'May I Help You counter', 'electronic token number display and audio announcement system', 'Dust Bins, 'Toilets Facility' and 'A/C facility', were ranked as fourteenth, fifteenth, sixteenth, seventeenth and eighteenth ranks respectively.

Table 5.6: Importance of Facilities and Amenities provided by Selected Banks in KARIMNAGAR

Sl.No.	*Variables*	*Mean*	*Std. Deviation*	*Ranks*
1.	Location of the Bank	4.79	.500	7
2.	Parking Facility	4.73	.616	10
3.	Information about working hours	4.93	.302	1
4.	Information about service timings	4.91	.339	2
5.	Availability of personal assistance/guidance	4.89	.474	5
6.	Display of identification boards at counters	4.77	.617	9
7.	May I Help You Counter	4.65	.841	14
8.	Proper Lighting	4.90	.356	3
9.	Information about available services and products	4.89	.444	4
10.	Electronic token number display and audio announcement system	4.61	.926	15
11.	Waiting Room/Place	4.71	.631	11
12.	ATM facility at the branch	4.69	.716	12
13.	Attractive Flooring	4.65	.760	13
14.	Drinking Water	4.77	.555	8
15.	A/C Facility	4.28	1.315	18
16.	Dust Bins	4.60	.839	16
17.	Toilets Facility	4.49	1.007	17
18.	Complaint and Suggestion Box	4.80	.597	6

Source: Primary Data.

Customers of selected banks in Karimnagar district were given high priority to items like 'Information about working hours', 'Information about service timings', 'proper lighting', 'Availability of personal assistance/ guidance', 'Complaint and suggestion box', and 'Location of the bank where it located' which were ranked one to seventh ranks respectively, were very common required facilities in every banking organisations.

Actual Quality of Facilities and Amenities Provided by Selected Banks

The data in the Table 5.7 presents the details of customers' opinions of bank customers regarding the actual facilities and amenities provided by the selected banks for the convenient of their customers. Customers of selected banks gave the first rank to 'Proper lighting', second rank to 'Location of the bank where it located' and third rank given to 'Attractive Flooring'. The fourth rank and fifth rank were given to 'information about working hours' and 'Availability of personal assistance/guidance' respectively. 'Information about available services and products', 'waiting room/place in the bank' and

Table 5.7: Actual Quality of Facilities and Amenities Provided by Selected Banks

Sl.No.	*Variables*	*Mean*	*Std. Deviation*	*Ranks*
1.	Location of the Bank	4.60	.781	2
2.	Parking Facility	2.89	1.059	11
3.	Information about working hours	3.84	.809	4
4.	Information about service timings	3.28	1.108	8
5.	Availability of personal assistance/guidance	3.77	1.055	5
6.	Display of identification boards at counters	3.16	1.245	9
7.	May I Help You Counter	1.82	1.328	16
8.	Proper Lighting	4.60	.644	1
9.	Information about available services and products	3.40	1.050	6
10.	Electronic token number display and audio announcement system	1.62	1.312	17
11.	Waiting Room/Place	3.30	1.159	7
12.	ATM facility at the branch	2.86	1.835	12
13.	Attractive Flooring	4.33	.762	3
14.	Drinking Water	3.09	1.529	10
15.	A/C Facility	1.96	1.609	15
16.	Dust Bins	2.40	1.448	13
17.	Toilets Facility	1.21	.718	18
18.	Complaint and Suggestion Box	2.36	1.499	14

Source: Primary Data.

'information about service timings' were ranked as sixth, seventh and eighth ranks respectively. Ninth, tenth, eleventh, twelfth and thirteenth ranks were given to 'Display of identification boards at counters for easy identification', 'Drinking water', 'parking facility', 'ATM facility at the bank branch' and 'Dust Bins' respectively. 'Complaint and suggestion box', 'A/C facility', 'May I Help You counter', 'electronic token number display and audio announcement system' and Toilets Facility' were ranked as fourteenth, fifteenth, sixteenth, seventeenth and eighteenth ranks respectively.

Gap between Importance and Actual

An attempt was made to analyse customers' opinions with regard to importance of facilities and amenities that are required to a bank and actual facilities and amenities provided by the selected banks in Karimnagar District. The above table shows that the mean score of important and actual and gap between the two. The level of importance of customers with regard to facilities and amenities were rated between 'four' and 'five' indicate that the respondents

by the bank for service is the key factor to the customers. Customers do not like to wait for long time. Taking long time, to give service, leads dissatisfaction among customers. Opinions of customers on service timings of the bank were collected and presented in the following lines.

Cash Receipt

Collection of the deposits is the primary function of the bank. The bank collects money from different customers for different purposes. In general, all customers deposit money in their account either saving/current account or loans account for their future needs. Saving account holders visit the bank, occasionally, and deposit their savings in their accounts. Frequently, business people visit the bank to deposit their daily business collections. It is tested that how much time is taken by the banker to complete the cash transactions in their banks. Opinions of the customers were collected, in this regard, and analysed in the following lines.

Table 5.9: Cash Receipt - Selected Banks

		Total		
	Mid Values	***Frequency***	***per cent***	
0 - 15 Min.	7.5	331	52.54	
15 - 30 Min.	22.5	212	33.65	Standard Time 10-20 Min.
30 - 45 Min.	37.5	82	13.02	
Don't Know	-	5	0.79	
Total		**630**	**100.00**	
Mean Time (Min.)		**16.52**		**15.00**

Source: Primary Data.

The above table presents the details of opinions of the customers about the time taken for the cash receipt (cash payment in terms of customer) by the banker. The highest number of customers represents 331 customers indicating 52.54 per cent of the total, informed that the transaction would be completed within the 15 minutes and as per 212 customers opined that the transaction would be completed between 15-30 minutes. An average of 16.52 minutes, against standard average time 15.00 minutes, is taken by selected banks (SBH, TGB and HDFC bank) in the study area to receipt the cash from customers.

Cash Payment

The table 5.10 presents the details of opinions of the customers about the time taken for the cash payment (cash receipt in terms of customer) by the banker. Out of 630 customers, 256 customers indicating 40.63 per cent of the total stated that the cash payment service will be completed within the

Table 5.10: Cash Payment - Selected Banks

		Total		
	Mid Values	*Frequency*	*per cent*	
0 - 15 Min.	7.5	256	40.63	Standard Time 10-20 Min.
15 - 30 Min.	22.5	203	32.22	
30 - 45 Min.	37.5	139	22.06	
Don't Know		32	5.08	
Total		**630**	**100.00**	
Mean Time (Min.)		**19.56**		**15.00**

Source: Primary Data.

15 minutes. 203 customers i.e. 32.22 per cent informed that the service will be completed in between 15-30 minutes and 139 customers expressed that the transaction will be completed in between 30-45 minutes. 32 customers do not know this service timing. An average of 19.56 minutes, against standard average time 15.00 minutes, is taking by selected banks (SBH, TGB and HDFC bank) in the study area to pay the cash to customers.

Issue of Draft

Table 5.11 - Issue of Draft - Selected Banks

		Total		
	Mid Values	*Frequency*	*per cent*	
0 - 15 Min.	7.5	45	7.14	Standard Time 15-25 Min.
15 – 30 Min.	22.5	104	16.51	
30 - 45 Min.	37.5	142	22.54	
Don't Know		339	53.81	
Total		**630**	**100.00**	
Mean Time (Min.)		**27.50**		**20.00**

Source: Primary Data.

The above table presents the details of opinions of respondents about issuance of the demand draft. The normal standard time for issuance of DD is 15 – 25 minutes. The highest number of the customers in all selected bank branches in Karimnagar district i.e. 53.81 per cent of the total does not have awareness about this service timing. Rural customers do not require the Demand Draft. Only some of the business people and employees demand the demand draft for their payment purposes. 23.60 per cent of the total indicating 149 in number stated that the service timing for this service is within 30 minutes. 142 customers representing 22.54 per cent of the total informed that the time taken by the banks for this service is in between 30 – 45 minutes. An average of 27.50 minutes, against standard average time 20.00 minutes, is taken by selected banks (SBH, TGB and HDFC bank) in the study area to issue the demand draft to customers.

Collection of Outstation Cheques

The data relating to the opinions of the selected banks' customers on collection of outstation cheques were presented in the following table. The highest number of customers does not have awareness of this service timing. Rural customers do not go with the cheque transactions. Only some of business and employee category customers may use this service from the banker for their collections or payments.

Table 5.12: Collection of Outstation Cheques - Selected Banks

		Total		
	Days	*Frequency*	*per cent*	
1 - 3 Days	2	52	8.25	Standard Time 10-14 Days
4 - 8 Days	6	113	17.94	
8 - 12 Days	10	136	21.59	
Don't Know		329	52.22	
Total		**630**	**100.00**	
Mean Time (Days)		**7.12**		**12 Days**

Source: Primary Data.

They only expressed their opinion about the collection of out station cheques. 136 customers in number representing 21.60 per cent of the total customers informed that the outstation cheques were collected and credited by the banker after 14 days. On an average banks collecting the outstation cheques and depositing them in customers' account in 7.12 days, against standard average time 12 days, by selected banks (SBH, TGB and HDFC bank) in the study area.

Updating Pass Book

Table 5.13: Updating Pass Book - Selected Banks

		Total		
	Mid Values	*Frequency*	*per cent*	
0 - 15 Min.	7.5	242	38.41	Standard Time 5-15 Min.
15 - 30 Min.	22.5	95	15.08	
30 - 45 Min.	37.5	122	19.37	
Don' t Know		171	27.14	
Total		**630**	**100.00**	
Mean Time (Min.)		**18.58**		**10**

The data in the Table 5.13 presents the details of service timing for 'updating the pass book' in selected banks under study. Banker updates the information in the pass book further information to the customers to check the availability amount in their accounts. The highest number of customers indicating 38.41 per cent of the total stated that the banker update the pass book information within the 15 minutes. 171 customers representing 27.14 per cent of the total informed that they did not have the awareness about this service. 122 customers stated that the time taken by the banker to finish this service in between 30-45 minutes. 95 customers i.e. 15.08 per cent of the total customers stated that this service was done by the banker in between 15-30 minutes. To update the pass book, selected banks are taking much time than the standard average time.

Issue of Cheque Book

Table 5.14: Issue of Cheque Book - Selected Banks

		Total		
Particulars	*Mid Values*	*Frequency*	*per cent*	
0 - 7 Days	3.50	69	11.00	Standard Time 7-15 Min.
8 - 15 Days	11.50	123	19.50	
16 - 21 Days	18.50	136	21.60	
Don't Know		302	47.90	
Total		**630**	**100.00**	
Mean Time (Days)		**12.72**		**11**

Source: Primary Data.

The details of opinions of customers about the issue of check book were presented in the above table. Majority of the customers i.e. 47.90 per cent of the total 630 customers do not have the knowledge of the cheque book service. This service also utilised by some of the business and employee type of customers only. 136 customers indicating 21.60 per cent of the total informed that the banks are taking above 14 days to issue the cheque book. The remaining customers stated that banks issue the cheque book within the standard time i.e. 15 days. Selected banks in the study area are taking average time to issue the cheque book to customers.

Service Encounters

Most services are characterised by an encounter between a service provider and a customer. This interaction, which defines the quality of the service in the mind of the customer, has been called a service encounter or "moment of truth". The often brief encounter is a moment in time when the customer is evaluating the service and a forming an opinion of its quality. A service encounter is defined as the period of time that a customer interacts with a service provider (Shostack, 1985). The definition of a service encounter is broad and includes a customer's interaction with customer-contact employees, machines, automated systems, physical facilities, and any other service provider visible elements. A customer experiences many encounters with a variety of service providers, and each moment of truth is an opportunity to influence the customer's perception of the service quality.

From the customers' point of view, vivid impressions about service encounter or moment of truth in respect of the service provider when the customer interacts with the service firm. It is in these encounters that customers receive a snapshot of the organisation's service quality, and each encounter contributes to the customers overall satisfaction and willingness to continue the business with the organisation. From the organisation's point of view, service encounters are where promises are kept of broken and where the proverbial rubber meets the road. Each encounter, thus, presents an opportunity to improve its potential as a quality service provider and to increase customer loyalty.

Thus, the environment in which the customer directly interacts with the bank employees during the period of time is one of the measuring tool of the service quality of a bank.

An attempt is made to measure the service quality of selected three banks (SBH-public sector, HDFC-private sector and TGB-rural bank) in selected areas (six mandals) through selected service encounter statements usually taking place between the customers and the bank employees during the banking transactions are mentioned in the questionnaire. The opinions of the bank's customers in respect of the service encounter are analysed with their mean, ranks, factor analysis test and also conducted **KMO and Bartlett's Test,** and **ANOVA PostHoc** tests are presented in the following lines.

Analysis of Service Encounters in Selected Banks

Table 5.15: Ranks Based on Service Encounters in Selected Bank (Relationship between Bank Employees and Customers)

Sl.No.	*Particulars*	*Mean*	*Std. Deviation*	*Rank*
1.	Front Office Employee (Receptionist) notices, welcomes and greets the customers.	1.93	1.442	14
2.	Receptionist asks customer May I Help You sir.	1.94	1.456	13
3.	Receptionist asks customer to be seated	2.01	1.512	12
4.	Required suggestion, help and cooperation are provided by the bank employees.	4.47	.798	5
5.	Bank staff speaks pleasantly with smiling face.	4.48	.793	3
6.	Bank staffs are friendly with customers.	4.49	.771	2
7.	Bank staffs are informative.	4.50	.750	1
8.	It is easy to approach or meet Bank Manager or other superiors in the Bank.	4.45	.879	6

(Contd...)

9.	Bank staff responds properly to the phone calls.	3.85	.959	10
10.	Bank staff shows reasonable interest in me as a customer.	4.37	.795	8
11.	Bank staff thanks me for transacting with them	2.98	1.369	11
12.	Bank staff handles any problems/interruptions efficiently.	4.33	.852	9
13.	I enjoy myself dealing with the employees of this bank.	4.37	.784	7
14.	I wish to continue my relationship with this bank for long.	4.47	.703	4

Source: Primary Data.

The Table 5.15 furnishes the details about ranks based on service encounters in selected banks of Karimnagar district. It is found that the statement **"bank staff are informative"** ranked first by the customers/ respondents of selected banks. They ranked **"bank staff are friendly with customers", "bank staff speak pleasantly with smiling face"**, and **"I wish to continue my relationship with this bank for long"**, and "**required suggestion, help and co-operation are provided by the bank staff"** as second, third, fourth and fifth ranks respectively. Sixth, seventh, eighth and ninth ranks given to "**It is easy to approach or meet bank manager or other superiors in the bank", "I enjoy myself dealing with the employees of this bank", "bank staff show reasonable interest in me as a customer"**, and "**bank staff handle any problem or interruptions efficiently"** respectively.

Statements **"bank staff respond properly to the phone calls", "bank staff thanks me for transacting with them", "receptionist asks customer to be seated"** were ranked as tenth, eleventh and twelfth respectively. Thirteenth rank was posted to **receptionist asks customer May I Help you sir"** and statement **"front office staff notices, welcomes and greets the customers"** was ranked fourteenth.

The variables i.e. statements relating to the service encounter of the selected banks under study were measured with the help of statistical tool 'Factor Analysis'. The statements were arranged as per their loading according to factor analysis. The results of the factor analysis are presented in the following table.

The application of the factor analysis reduced fourteen variables of service encounter into three predominant factors based on their factor loading. Factor loadings to the variables are considered on the basis of the 'rotated component matrix'. The first factor includes of three variables like 'front office employee asks the customer May I Help You sir', 'receptionist notices, welcomes and greets the customer' and 'receptionist asks the customer to be seated' have

Table 5.16: Factor Analysis of Service Encounters in Selected Banks (Relationship between Bank Employees and Customers)

Sl. No.	*Statements*	*Factor Loading*	*Factors*	*Eigen Values*	*Individual Variance*	*Cumulative Variance*
1.	Receptionist asks customer May I Help You sir.	0.974	**Highly Significant**	7.097	76.127	99.999
2.	Front Office Employee (Receptionist) notices, welcomes and greets the customers.	0.968		2.654		
3.	Receptionist asks customer to be seated.	0.965		0.907		
4.	Bank staffs are informative.	0.869	**Significant**	0.394	18.337	
5.	I enjoy myself dealing with the employees of this bank.	0.866		0.052		
6.	Bank staff s are friendly with customers.	0.854		0.413		
7.	Bank staff speak pleasantly with smiling face.	0.849		0.649		
8.	Bank staff shows reasonable interest in me as a customer.	0.814		0.221		
9.	I wish to continue my relationship with this bank for long.	0.792		0.24		
10.	Required suggestion, help and cooperation are provided by the bank employees.	0.789		0.743		
11.	Bank staff handles any problems/interruptions efficiently.	0.753		0.071		
12.	It is easy to approach or meet Bank Manager or other superiors in the Bank.	0.678	**Low Significant**	0.320	5.535	
13.	Bank staff responds properly to the phone calls.	0.489		0.297		
14.	Bank staff thanks me for transacting with them.	0.485		0.159		

the loading of above 0.9 or near to 0.9. These are treated as **high significant** factors.

The second factor treated as **significant** as these are having factor loading between 0.7 – 0.8. This include eight factors such as 'bank staff are informative', 'I enjoy myself dealing with the employees of this bank', 'bank staff are friendly with customers', 'bank staff speak pleasantly with smiling face', 'bank staff shows reasonable interest in me as a customer', 'I wish to continue my relationship with this bank for long', 'required suggestion, help and cooperation are provided by the bank employees', and 'bank employees handles any problems/interruptions efficiently'.

The three variables 'it is easy to approach or meet bank manager or other superiors in the bank' and 'bank employees responds properly to the phone calls' and 'bank employees thanks me for transacting with them' having the factor loading of less than 0.7, are fall under the category of **low significant.**

Hypothesis

H_0:- There is no significant difference among service encounter variable of selected bank.

H_A:- There is a significant difference among service encounter variable of selected bank.

Table 5.17: KMO and Bartlett's Test

Kaiser-Meyer-Olkin Measure of Sampling Adequacy.		.891
Bartlett's Test of Sphericity	Approx. Chi-Square	9202.284
	Df	91
	Sig.	0.000

The above table shows the Kaiser-Meyer-Olkin measure of sampling adequacy and Bartlett's test of sphericity. The KMO statistic varies between 0 and 1. Value 0 indicates that the sum of partial correlations is large relative to the sum of correlations, indicating diffusion in the pattern of correlation (hence, factor analysis is likely to be inappropriate). Value closes to 1 indicates that pattern of correlations are relatively compact and so factor analysis should yield distinct and reliable factors. Kaiser recommends accepting values greater than 0.5 as acceptable (values below this should lead to either collect more data or rethink which variables to include). Furthermore, according to Hutcheson and Sofroniou, values between 0.5 and 0.7 are mediocre, values between 0.7 and 0.8 are good, values between 0.8 and 0.9 are great and values above 0.9 superb.

For the present data the value of KMO Measure of sampling adequacy is 0.891, which falls into the range of being great: so it is said that, it should be confident that factor analysis is appropriate for this data, and the Bartlett's test also highly significant (p = 0.000), and therefore factor analysis is appropriate.

Bartlett's measure tests the null hypothesis that the original correlation matrix is an identity matrix. For factor analysis, there is a need for some relationships between variables and if the R-matrix were an identity matrix then all correlation coefficients would be zero. Therefore, this test to be significant (i.e. have a significance value less than 0.05). A significant test tells that the R - matrix is not an identity matrix; therefore, there are some relationships between the variables to include in the analysis. For this data, Bartlett's test is highly significant (p = 0.000), and therefore factor analysis is appropriate.

With this analysis it is said the null hypothesis is rejected and proved that there is some difference among service encounter variable of selected bank.

Measuring Service Quality

The Service Quality of SBH, TGB and HDFC banks is measured through SERVQUAL scale. The Service Quality elements are Tangibles, Reliability, Responsiveness, Assurance and Empathy. Since these elements are standardised in nature, it is indispensible to extract the factors of SERVQUAL elements for SBH, TGB and HDFC banks in the present rural environment. The SERVQUAL elements comprise various individual variables as the true representation of SERVQUAL elements. Factor analysis by principal component method is found suitable to extract the underline predominant factors in each elements of SERVQUAL. These would be useful to compare the service quality of SBH, TGB and HDFC banks based on their customer perception. The difference emergence of the factors would be useful to compare them text of proportion anatomically.

"SERVQUAL" is a method designed by Parasuraman *et al* (1988) to identify the gaps between the expectations of the customers from the best service supplier/provider and service perceived by the customers from their present service supplier/provider. The structured questionnaire as used by the Parasuraman et al (1988) has been personalised and used for this study with 20 statements under five service quality dimensions. The responses of customers had been confined in five point Likert Scale and gap was calculated by taking the difference between service quality expectation and service perceived (E - P). The results were analysed with the help of statistical tools like percentages, paired sample test and to derive the logical conclusions.

Evaluation of Service Quality in All Selected Banks in Karimnagar

Table 5.18: Assessment of Service Quality in All Selected Banks in Karimnagar

Sl. No.	Expected Quality (E)	Mean	Perceived Quality (P)	Mean	Gap (E-P)	per cent of Gap
			A. TANGIBLES			
1	The Bank must possess the sophisticated and good looking infrastructure.	4.93	My Bank has the sophisticated and good looking infrastructure.	4.09	0.85	16.92
2	Physical facilities at banks should be visual and attractive.	4.91	Physical facilities at my banks are visual and attractive.	4.10	0.80	16.03
3	Bank employees has to be in neat dress and appear dignified.	4.87	My Bank employees is in neat dress and appearing dignified.	4.35	0.52	10.35
4	Materials (statements or passbook) with bank should be visual and excellent.	4.86	Materials (statements or passbook) with my bank are visual and excellent.	4.19	0.67	13.40
	Total	19.56	**Total**	16.73	2.83	
Average		**4.89**		**4.18**	0.71	14.17
			B. RELIABILTY			
5	If the bank promises something, it will do.	4.87	If my bank promises something, it will certainly do.	4.22	0.65	13.08
6	If customers have problems, the bank has to show sincere interest in solving them.	4.89	If customers have problems, my bank will show sincere interest in solving it.	4.33	0.56	11.24
7	The bank ought to perform the services at right time.	4.90	My bank performs the services at right time. As per time mentioned.	4.34	0.57	11.33
8	The bank should provide service at the time it promises to do so.	4.89	My Bank provides service at the time it promises to do so.	4.28	0.61	12.25
9	The Bank should keep accurate/error-free records.	4.88	My Bank keeps accurate/error-free records.	4.50	0.38	7.68
	Total	24.44	**Total**	21.66	2.78	
Average		**4.89**		**4.33**	0.56	11.12

(Contd...)

C. RESPONSIVENESS						
10	Employees of the bank ought to inform customers exactly when service will be performed.	4.83	Employees of my bank inform customers exactly when service will be performed.	3.98	0.86	17.17
11	The Bank employees ought to give excellent service to its customers	4.88	My Bank employees give excellent service to its customers	4.43	0.45	8.92
12	The Bank employees must be willing to help the customers.	4.87	My Bank employees are always willing to help customers.	4.42	0.45	8.95
13	The Bank employees should be always ready to respond to customers' requests.	4.89	Bank employees always ready to respond to customers' requests.	4.41	0.48	9.52
	Total	19.47	**Total**	17.24	2.23	44.57
Average		**4.87**		**4.31**	0.56	11.14
D. ASSURANCE						
14	Bank employees should always try to infuse confidence in the customers.	4.85	My Bank employees always tries to instill confidence in customers.	4.42	0.43	8.67
15	Customers (you) have to feel safe in transactions with the Bank's employees.	4.89	Customers (me) always feel safe in transactions with my bank's employees.	4.49	0.40	8.00
16	The Bank employees always ought to be courteous and polite with customers.	4.91	My Bank employees always courteous and polite with customers.	4.53	0.37	7.49
17	Bank must possess employees have complete knowledge to answer queries of customers.	4.89	My Bank employees has complete knowledge to answer queries of customers.	4.37	0.53	10.54
	Total	19.54	**Total**	17.80	1.73	
Average		**4.88**		**4.45**	0.43	8.67

(Contd...)

E. EMPATHY						
18	The Bank has to give individual attention to customers.	4.85	My Bank gives individual attention to customers.	4.10	0.75	14.98
19	The Bank operating hours must be convenient to all customers.	4.86	My Bank operating hours is convenient to all the customers.	4.48	0.38	7.68
20	Bank employees ought to understand the specific needs of their customers.	4.87	Bank employees understands the specific needs of customers.	4.19	0.68	13.59
	Total	14.59	**Total**	12.77	1.81	
Average		**4.86**		**4.26**	0.60	12.08

Source: Primary Data.

by the bank. This was presented and analysed, in the following table, in the form of mean and ranks. Rank is awarded to the each factor on the basis of weighted average mean and standard deviation.

Importance of Facilities and Amenities Provided by SBH Bank

Table 5.20: Importance of Facilities and Amenities Provided by SBH Bank

Sl. No.	*Factors*	*Mean*	*Std. Deviation*	*Rank*
1.	Location of the Bank	4.78	0.51	9
2.	Parking Facility	4.73	0.59	13
3.	Information about working hours	4.90	0.40	4
4.	Information about service timings	4.91	0.37	2
5.	Availability of personal assistance/guidance	4.93	0.41	1
6.	Display of identification boards at counters	4.86	0.50	7
7.	May I Help You Counter	4.74	0.67	12
8.	Proper Lighting	4.89	0.43	6
9.	Information about available services and products	4.90	0.39	3
10.	Electronic token number display and audio System	4.65	0.80	15
11.	Waiting Room/Place	4.75	0.55	10
12.	ATM facility at the branch	4.75	0.57	11
13.	Attractive Flooring	4.66	0.71	14
14.	Drinking Water	4.78	0.49	8
15.	A/C Facility	4.50	1.13	18
16.	Dust Bins	4.64	0.84	16
17.	Toilets Facility	4.57	0.92	17
18.	Complaint and Suggestion Box	4.89	0.38	5

Source: Primary Data.

The Table 5.20 presents the details of customers' opinions of SBH bank regarding the expectations of facilities and amenities to be provided by the bank for convenience of customers. Customers of SBH bank gave the first rank to personal assistance/guidance and second rank to information about service timings and third rank given to information about available services and products. The fourth rank and fifth rank were given to information about working hours and complaint and suggestion box respectively. Proper lighting, display of identification boards at counters for easy identification and drinking water facilities were ranked sixth, seventh and eighth ranks respectively. Ninth, tenth, eleventh, twelfth and thirteenth ranks were given to drinking water facility at banks, location of the bank where it is located, waiting place in the bank, ATM facility at the bank branch, May I Help You counter and display of information about working hours of the bank respectively. Attractive Flooring, Electronic token number display and audio announcement system, Dust Bins, Toilets Facility were ranked as fourteenth, fifteenth, sixteenth and seventeenth ranks respectively. SBH bank customers were given eighteenth rank to A/C facility. Customers of SBH bank recognised and given high importance to the basic items like. 'Availability of personal assistance/guidance', 'Information about service timings', Information about available services and products, Information about working hours and Complaint and Suggestion Box, which were ranked one to fifth respectively, were very essential facilities every organisation must provide. Interestingly these customers had given least priority to the A/C facility in the bank.

Actual Quality of Facilities and Amenities Provided by SBH Bank

The customers' views with regard to the actual quality of facilities and amenities perceived by customers of SBH bank were collected by using five point Likert Scale ranging from Excellent to Very Poor mentioning different statements relating to facilities and amenities provided by the bank. This was presented and analysed, in the following table, in the form of mean and ranks. Rank is awarded to the each factor on the basis of weighted average mean and standard deviation.

From the Table 5.21, it is noted that "Location of the Bank" ranked as first, "Proper Lighting" facility was ranked as second, "Attractive Flooring" as third rank, "Drinking Water Facility" as fourth rank, "Information about Working Hours" as fifth rank, "Waiting Room/Place in the bank" as sixth rank. "ATM facility at the branch", "Availability of personal assistance/ guidance", "Display of identification boards at counters", "Information about available services and products", "Information about service timings", "Parking Facility" were ranked as seventh, eighth, ninth, tenth, eleventh and twelfth ranks respectively.

Table 5.21: Actual Facilities and Amenities Provided by SBH Bank

Sl. No.	*Factors*	*Mean*	*Std. Deviation*	*Ranks*
1.	Location of the Bank	4.80	.535	1
2.	Parking Facility	2.82	1.046	12
3.	Information about working hours	3.67	.780	5
4.	Information about service timings	2.98	1.203	11
5.	Availability of personal assistance/guidance	3.31	1.097	8
6.	Display of identification boards at counters	3.13	1.088	9

(Contd...)

7.	May I Help You Counter	1.31	.731	16
8.	Proper Lighting	4.55	.719	2
9.	Information about available services and products	3.03	.981	10
10.	Electronic token number display and audio announcement system	2.54	1.718	13
11.	Waiting Room/Place	3.62	1.044	6
12.	ATM facility at the branch	3.46	1.628	7
13.	Attractive Flooring	4.53	.671	3
14.	Drinking Water	4.02	1.187	4
15.	A/C Facility	1.09	.349	18
16.	Dust Bins	2.38	1.259	14
17.	Toilets Facility	1.15	.556	17
18.	Complaint and Suggestion Box	2.06	1.414	15
	Average Score	**3.03**		

Source: Primary Data.

Thirteenth, fourteenth, fifteenth, sixteenth, seventeenth and eighteenth ranks to "Electronic token number display and audio announcement system", "Dust Bins", "Complaint and Suggestion Box", "May I Help You Counter", "Toilets Facility", and "A/C Facility" respectively.

Gap between Importance and Actual Facilities and Amenities Provided by the SBH Bank

An attempt was made to analyse customers' opinions with regard to Importance of facilities and amenities that required to a bank and actual facilities and amenities provided by the bank. The following table shows that the mean score of expectations and actual facilities and amenities and gap between the two. The level of expectations of customers with regard to facilities and amenities were rated between '4' and '5' indicates that the respondents rated these factors between 'Important and Very Important, The level of actual facilities and amenities provided by the bank were rated between '1 and 5' implies that the respondents rated these factors between 'Very Poor to Excellent'. Since the gap score was negative in respect of 'location of the bank', reveals that the customers were very much satisfied with location of the bank where it was established and also indicates that the bank was located in convenience to the customers.

The highest gap score in respect of factors 'May I Help You (3.43)', 'Toilet Facilities (3.42)' and 'A/C Facility (3.41)' reveal dissatisfaction of customers towards these facilities and amenities.

2. Independent Variables:
   a. Location of the Bank (X1)
   b. Parking Facility (X2)
   c. Information about working hours (X3)
   d. Information about service timings (X4)
   e. Availability of personal assistance/guidance (X5)
   f. Display of identification boards at counters (X6)
   g. May I Help You Counter (X7)
   h. Proper Lighting (X8)
   i. Information about available services and products (X9)
   j. Electronic token number display and audio announcement system (X10)
   k. Waiting Room/Place (X11)
   l. ATM facility at the branch (X12)
   m. Attractive Flooring (X13)
   n. Drinking Water (X14)
   o. A/C Facility (X15)
   p. Dust Bins (X16)
   q. Toilets Facility (X17)
   r. Complaint and Suggestion Box (X18)
3. Linear R Value : 0.606
4. R Square Value : 0.367
5. F Value : 7.120
6. P Value : 0.000**

The data in the Table 5.24 furnishes the details of Variables in Linear Regression Equation of Overall service quality on Actual Quality of Facilities and Amenities provided by SBH Bank. Linear correlation coefficient R = 0.606 measures the degree of relationship between the actual values (X) and predicted values of overall service quality (Y) because the overall service quality (Y) values are obtained as linear combination of 18 variables of actual facilities and amenities provided by the selected SBH bank. They were Location of the Bank (X1), Parking Facility (X2), Information about working hours (X3). Information about service timings (X4), Availability of personal assistance/guidance (X5), Display of identification boards at counters (X6), May I Help You Counter (X7), Proper Lighting (X8), Information about available services and products (X9), Electronic token number display and audio announcement system (X10), Waiting Room/Place (X11), ATM facility

Table – 5.23: Linear Regression Equation of Overall service quality of SBH Model Summary

Model	R	R Square	Adjusted R Square	Std. Error of the Estimate	Change Statistics				
					R Square Change	F Change	df1	df2	Sig. F Change
1	.606[a]	.367	.315	.689	.367	7.120	18	221	.000

a. Predictors: (Constant), Actual 1, Actual 2, Actual 3, Actual 4, Actual 5, Actual 6, Actual 7, Actual 8, Actual 9, Actual 10, Actual 11, Actual 12, Actual 13, Actual 14, Actual 15, Actual 16, Actual 17, Actual 18

Y = b0 0.332+b1 0.259X1+b2 0.014X2+b3 0.122X3-b 40.118X4+b5 0.272X5-b6 0.057X6+b7 0.99X7+b80.171X8+b90.062X9-b10 0.026X10+b11 0.145X11+b12 0.128X12-b13 0.024X13-b14 0.122X14 + b15 0.100X15+b16 0.103X16-b17 0.024X17-b18 0.092X18.

Table 5.24: Variables in Linear Regression Equation of Overall service quality on Actual Quality of Facilities and Amenities provided by SBH Bank

Sl. No.	*Variables*	*Unstandardized Coefficients*		*Standardized Coefficients*	*t-Value*	*Sig.*	*Correlations*		
		B	*Std. Error*	*Beta*			*Zero-order*	*Partial*	*Part*
b.	**Customers' Overall SQ (Constant)**	**.332**	**.629**		**.528**	**.598**			
X1	Location of the Bank	.259	.089	.166	2.914	.004	.182	.192	.156
X2	Parking Facility	.014	.056	.018	.251	.802	.171	.017	.013
X3	Information about working hours	.122	.078	.114	1.558	.121	.215	.104	.083
X4	Information about service timings	-.118	.061	-.170	-1.919	.056	.154	-.128	-.103
X5	Availability of personal assistance/guidance	.272	.060	.358	4.533	.000	.447	.292	.243
X6	Display of identification boards at counters	-.057	.056	-.075	-1.028	.305	.226	-.069	-.055
X7	May I Help You Counter	.099	.075	.087	1.330	.185	.203	.089	.071
X8	Proper Lighting	.171	.069	.148	2.486	.014	.177	.165	.133
X9	Information about available services and products	.062	.059	.073	1.046	.297	.334	.070	.056
X10	Electronic token number display and audio announcement system	-.026	.039	-.053	-.662	.509	.200	-.044	-.035
X11	Waiting Room/Place	.145	.051	.181	2.857	.005	.202	.189	.153
X12	ATM facility at the branch	.128	.038	.251	3.351	.001	.274	.220	.179
X13	Attractive Flooring	-.024	.080	-.019	-.294	.769	.047	-.020	-.016
X14	Drinking Water	-.122	.043	-.173	-2.827	.005	-.050	-.187	-.151
X15	A/C Facility	.100	.147	.042	.676	.500	.068	.045	.036
X16	Dust Bins	.103	.045	.156	2.280	.024	.196	.152	.122
X17	Toilets Facility	-.024	.097	-.016	-.248	.804	.155	-.017	-.013
X18	Complaint and Suggestion Box	-.092	.040	-.157	-2.311	.022	.059	-.154	-.124

a. Dependent Variable: Overall SQ

at the branch (X12), Attractive Flooring (X13), Drinking Water (X14), A/C Facility (X15), Dust Bins (X16), Toilets Facility (X17), Complaint and Suggestion Box (X18). The coefficient value 0.606 indicates that the relationship between overall service quality and the actual quality of facilities and amenities is positive and strong.

1. **b_1 = 0.259** represents the partial effect of 'Location of the Bank' on overall service quality holding parking facilities constant. The estimated positive sign implies that such effect is positive while the absolute value implies that overall service quality has direct impact of 25.9 per cent.
2. **b2 = 0.014** indicates the partial effect of 'Parking Facility' on overall service quality holding other independent variables constant. The estimated positive sign implies that such effect is positive while the absolute value implies that overall service quality has direct impact of 1.40 per cent.
3. **b3 = 0.122** represents the partial effect of 'Information about Working Hours' on overall service quality holding other independent variables constant. The estimated positive sign implies that such effect is positive while the absolute value implies that overall service quality has the direct impact of 12.20 per cent.
4. **b4 = -0.118** represents the partial effect of 'Information about Service Timings' on overall service quality holding other independent variables constant. The estimated negative sign implies that such effect is negative while the absolute value implies that overall service quality has inverse impact of 11.80 per cent.
5. **b5 = 0.272** represents the partial effect of 'Availability of Personal Assistance/Guidance' on overall service quality holding other independent variables constant. The estimated positive sign implies that such effect is positive while the absolute value implies that overall service quality has the direct impact of 27.20 per cent.
6. **b6 = -0.057** represents the partial effect of display of 'Identification Boards at Counters' on overall service quality holding other independent variables constant. The estimated negative sign implies that such effect is negative while the absolute value implies that overall service quality has the inverse impact of 5.70 per cent.
7. **b7 = 0.099** represents the partial effect of 'May I Help You' on overall service quality holding other independent variables constant. The estimated positive sign implies that such effect is positive while the absolute value implies that overall service quality has the direct impact of 9.90 per cent.

8. **b8 = 0.171** represents the partial effect of 'Proper Lighting' on overall service quality holding other independent variables constant. The estimated positive sign implies that such effect is positive while the absolute value implies that overall service quality has the direct impact of 17.10 per cent.
9. **b9 = 0.062** represents the partial effect of 'Information about Available Services and Products' on overall service quality holding other independent variables constant. The estimated positive sign implies that such effect is positive while the absolute value implies that overall service quality has the direct impact of 6.20 per cent.
10. **b10 = -0.026** represents the partial effect of 'Electronic Token Number Display and Audio Announcement System' on overall service quality holding other independent variables constant. The estimated negative sign implies that such effect is negative while the absolute value implies that overall service quality would decrease by 2.60 per cent.
11. **b11 = 0.145** represents the partial effect of 'Waiting Room/Place' on overall service quality holding other independent variables constant. The estimated positive sign implies that such effect is positive while the absolute value implies that overall service quality would increase by 1.45 per cent.
12. **b12 = 0.128** represents the partial effect of 'ATM Facility at Bank' on overall service quality holding other independent variables constant. The estimated positive sign implies that such effect is positive while the absolute value implies that overall service quality has the direct relation of 12.80 per cent.
13. **b13 = -0.024** represents the partial effect of 'Attractive Flooring' on overall service quality holding other independent variables constant. The estimated negative sign implies that such effect is negative while the absolute value implies that overall service quality has the inverse relation of 0.24 per cent.
14. **b14 = -0.122** represents the partial effect of 'Drinking Water Facility' on overall service quality holding other independent variables constant. The estimated negative sign implies that such effect is negative while the absolute value implies that overall service quality would decrease by 12.20 per cent.
15. **b15 = 0.100** represents the partial effect of 'A/C Facility' on overall service quality holding other independent variables constant. The estimated positive sign implies that such effect is positive while the absolute value implies that overall service quality has the direct impact of 10.00 per cent.

16. **b16 = 0.103** represents the partial effect of 'Dustbins' on overall service quality holding other independent variables constant. The estimated positive sign implies that such effect is positive while the absolute value implies that overall service quality would increase by 10.30 per cent.
17. **b17 = -0.024** represents the partial effect of 'Toilets Facility' on overall service quality holding other independent variables constant. The estimated negative sign implies that such effect is negative while the absolute value implies that overall service quality has the inverse relation of 2.40 per cent.
18. **b18 = -0.092** represents the partial effect of 'Complaint and Suggestion Box' on overall service quality holding other independent variables constant. The estimated negative sign implies that such effect is negative while the absolute value implies that overall service quality would decrease by 9.20 per cent.

Since the significant value is less than 0.05 in b1 'location of the bank' (0.004), b5 'availability of personal assistance' (0.00), b8 'proper lighting' (0.014), b13 'attractive flooring', b14 'drinking water', b17 'toilets facility' (-0.013), and b11 'waiting room/place' (0.005), b12 'ATM facility' (0.001), b14 'drinking water' (0.005), b16 'Dust bins' (0.024) and b18 'Complaint and Suggestion Box' (0.22). Hence, the Linear regression analysis reveals that the above said facilities and amenities may lead to influence the overall service quality.

Hypothesis

H_0:-There is no significant relation between service quality and actual facilities and amenities provided by SBH Bank.

H_A:- There is significant relation between service quality and actual facilities and amenities provided by SBH Bank.

ANOVA[a]

	Model	*Sum of Squares*	*df*	*Mean Square*	*F*	*Sig.*
1	Regression	60.833	18	3.380	7.120	1.61
	Residual	104.901	221	0.475		
	Total	**165.733**	**239**			

a. Dependent Variable: Overall Satisfaction

b Predictors: (Constant), Actual 1, Actual 2, Actual 3, Actual 4, Actual 5, Actual 6, Actual 7, Actual 8, Actual 9, Actual 10, Actual 11, Actual 12, Actual 13, Actual 14, Actual 15, Actual 16, Actual 17, Actual 18

The above ANOVA table shows that the calculated value of *F* is 7.120 which is greater than the significance value at 0.05 level of significance is

1.61 with degree of freedom being $v_1 = 18$ and $v_2 = 221$. This analysis rejects the null hypothesis of no significant relation between customers' satisfactions towards service quality and actual facilities and amenities provided by SBH bank. Therefore it may conclude that the difference in customers' satisfaction due to actual facilities and amenities provided by SBH bank is significant and is just not a matter of chance.

Hence, the bank officials need to focus on improving the facilities and amenities which have high and positive impact on customers' satisfaction.

Service Timings of SBH Bank

Cash Receipt

Table 5.25: Service Timing for Cash Receipt in SBH

		SBH		
Time	**Mid Values**	**Frequency**	**per cent**	
0 - 15 Min.	7.5	55	22.92	Standard Time 10-20 Min.
15 - 30 Min.	22.5	113	47.08	
30 - 45 Min.	37.5	72	30.00	
Don't Know	-	0	0.00	
Total		**240**	**100.00**	
Mean Time (Min.)	**23.56**		**15.00**	

Source: Primary Data.

The data in the above table furnishes that the highest number of customers of SBH expressed the time taken by the banker for cash receipt was 15 – 30 minutes. 72 customers indicating 30 per cent of the total expressed that the transaction would be completed within 30 – 45 min. and 55 customers expressed that the transaction would be completed within 15 minutes. An average of 23.56 minutes is taking by SBH to receipt the cash from customers against standard average time 15 minutes.

Cash Payment

Table 5.26: Service Timing for Cash Payment in SBH

Time	***Mid Values***	***Frequency***	***per cent***	
0 - 15 Min.	7.5	43	17.92	Standard Time 10-20 Min.
15 - 30 Min.	22.5	90	37.50	
30 - 45 Min.	37.5	99	41.25	
Don't Know		8	3.33	
Total		**240**	**100.00**	
Mean Time (Min.)		**26.12**		**15.00**

Source: Primary Data.

From the above table it is found that the highest number of customers, in SBH, informed that the service timing of the bank for cash payment was 30-45 minutes. Following these 90 customers of the same bank accepted that the timing for this service was 15-30 minutes. 73.90 of the total SBH customers said that the service timing for this transaction was below 15 minutes. eight customers do not have the awareness about this service timing. An average of 26.12 minutes is taking by SBH to pay the cash to customers against standard average time 15 minutes.

Issue of Draft

Table 5.27: Service Timing for Issue of Draft in SBH

Time	*Mid Values*	*Frequency*	*per cent*	
0 - 15 Min.	7.5	4	1.67	Standard Time 15-25 Min.
15 – 30 Min.	22.5	35	14.58	
30 - 45 Min.	37.5	94	39.17	
Don't Know		107	44.58	
Total		**240**	**100.00**	
Mean Time (Min.)		**32.65**		**20.00**

Source: Primary Data.

The details in the table shows that 39.20 per cent of the total SBH customers and customers representing 94 in number respectively stated that the service timing for the issue of DD was in between 30 – 45 minutes. 39 customers of SBH indicating 16.30 per cent and 16.70 per cent informed that the DD was issued by the banks within 30 minutes. To issue the DD to customers, the bank is taking an average of 32.65 minutes against standard average time 20 minutes.

Collection of Outstation Cheques

The data relating to the opinions of SBH customers on collection of outstation cheques is presented in the Table 5.28. The highest number of customers does not have awareness of this service timing. 71 customers in number representing 29.58 per cent of the total customers informed that the outstation cheques were collected and credited by the banker in between 8-12 days and 20.42 per cent of the total representing 49 in number stated that the service time for this service is 4-8 days. On an average banks collecting the outstation cheques and depositing them in customers' account in 8.88 approx. 9 days, against standard average time 12 days, by SBH bank.

Table 5.28: Service Timing for Collection of Outstation Cheques in SBH

Days	**Mid Values**	***Frequency***	***per cent***	
1 - 3 Days	2	8	3.33	Standard Time 10-14 Days
4 - 8 Days	6	49	20.42	
8 - 12 Days	10	71	29.58	
Don't Know		112	46.67	
Total		**240**	**100.00**	
Mean Time (Days)		**8.88**		**12 Days**

Updating Pass Book

Table 5.29: Service Timing for Updating Pass Book in SBH

Time	**Mid Values**	**Frequency**	**per cent**	
0 - 15 Min.	7.5	101	42.08	Standard Time 5-15 Min
15 - 30 Min.	22.5	45	18.75	
30 - 45 Min.	37.5	73	30.42	
Don' t Know		21	8.75	
Total		**240**	**100.00**	
Mean Time (Min.)		**20.58**		**10**

Source: Primary Data.

The data in the above table presents the details of service timing for 'updating the pass book' in SBH bank. The highest number of customers indicating 42.08 per cent of the total stated that the banker update the pass book information within the 15 minutes. 45 customers i.e. 18.75 per cent of the total customers stated that this service was done by the banker in between 15 – 30 minutes. 73 customers stated that the time taken by the banker to finish this service in between 30 – 45 minutes. 21 customers representing 8.75 per cent of the total informed that they did not have the awareness about this service. To update the pass book SBH bank is taking much time than the standard average time.

Issue of Cheque Book

Table 5.30: Service Timing for Issue of Cheque Book in SBH

	Mid Values	Frequency	per cent	
0 - 7 Days	3.50	25	10.40	Standard Time 7-15 Days.
8 - 15 Days	11.50	39	16.30	
16 - 21 Days	18.50	71	29.60	
Don't Know		105	43.80	
Total		**240**	**100.00**	
Mean Time (Days)		**13.70**		**11**

Source: Primary Data.

The details of opinions of customers about the issue of check book were presented in the above table. Majority of the customers i.e. 43.80 per cent of the total 240 customers do not have the knowledge of the check book service. This service also utilised by some of the business and employee type of customers only. 71 customers indicating 29.60 per cent of the total informed that the banks are taking 16-21 days to issue the check book. The remaining customers stated that banks issue the check book within the standard time i.e. 15 days. SBH bank is taking above average time to issue the cheque book to customers.

SBH bank, a public sector bank which is established long back and offering all types of services including government schemes, the number of visitors to this bank for various purposes is heavy on busy days like Mondays and first week of the month. To meet the needs of customers, the bank have not had the sufficient number of employees. This is the reason why banks are taking much time in providing this service.

Service Encounters in SBH

The data presented in the below table furnishes the details about ranks based on service encounters in selected public sector bank SBH. It is found that the "I wish to continue my relationship with this bank for long" ranked first by the customers/respondents of SBH bank. They ranked "bank staff are informative" as second, third and forth ranks were given to "required suggestion, help and co-operation are provided by the bank staff" and "It is easy to approach or meet bank manager or other superiors in the bank" respectively. Statements "bank staff handles any problem or interruptions efficiently" and "bank staffs are friendly with customers" were ranked as five and six. Seven and eight ranks were given to "I enjoy myself dealing with the employees of this bank" and "bank staff speaks pleasantly with customers" respectively.

Ranks Based on Service Encounters in - SBH

Table 5.31: Ranks Based on Service Encounters in - SBH

Sl. No.	*Statements*	*SBH*		
		Mean	***Std. Deviation***	***Rank***
1.	Front Office Employee (Receptionist) notices, welcomes and greets the customers.	1.11	0.384	13
2.	Receptionist asks customer May I Help You sir.	1.1	0.37	14
3.	Receptionist asks customer to be seated.	1.13	0.462	12
4.	Required suggestion, help and cooperation are provided by the bank employees.	4.06	0.901	3
5.	Bank staff speak pleasantly with smiling face.	4.02	0.933	8
6.	Bank staff are friendly with customers.	4.03	0.898	6
7.	Bank staff are informative.	4.12	0.855	2
8.	It is easy to approach or meet Bank Manager or other superiors in the Bank.	4.06	1.035	4
9.	Bank staff responds properly to the phone calls.	3.46	0.909	10
10.	Bank staff shows reasonable interest in me as a customer.	3.95	0.883	9
11.	Bank staff thanks me for transacting with them.	2.49	1.186	11
12.	Bank staff handles any problems/interruptions efficiently.	4.04	0.891	5
13.	I enjoy myself dealing with the employees of this bank.	4.02	0.858	7
14.	I wish to continue my relationship with this bank for long.	4.14	0.814	1

Customers ranked ninth, tenth and eleventh ranks to **"bank employees show reasonable interest in me as a customer"**, **"bank employees respond properly to the phone calls"** and **"bank staff thanks me for transacting with them"** respectively. Statements **"receptionist asks customer to be seated"**, **"front office employee notices, welcomes and greets the customers"** were ranked as twelfth, thirteenth respectively. Fourteenth rank was posted to **"receptionist asks customer May I Help you sir."**

Factor Analysis of Service Encounters in SBH Bank

Table 5.32: Factor Analysis of Service Encounters in SBH Bank
(Relationship between Bank Employees and Customers)

Sl. No.	*Statements*	*Factor Loading*	*Factors*	*Eigen Values*		*Individual Variance*	*Cumulative Variance*
1.	Receptionist asks customer May I Help You sir.	0.971	**High Significant**	2.754	11.628	83.06	98.89
2.	Front Office Employee (Receptionist) notices, welcomes and greets the customers.	0.963		7.130			
3.	Bank Staffs are informative.	0.923		0.354			
4.	Receptionist asks customer to be seated	0.909		0.962			
5.	I enjoy myself dealing with the employees of this bank.	0.901		0.052			
6.	Bank Staffs are friendly with customers.	0.895		0.376			
7.	Bank Staff shows reasonable interest in me as a customer.	0.880	**Significant**	0.196	1.979	12.20	
8.	Bank staffs speak pleasantly with smiling face.	0.872		0.614			
9.	Required suggestion, help and cooperation are provided by the bank employees.	0.866		0.760			
10.	I wish to continue my relationship with this bank for long.	0.816		0.30			
11.	Bank staff handles any problems/interruptions efficiently.	0.793		0.109			
12.	It is easy to approach or meet Bank Manager or other superiors in the Bank.	0.706	**Low Significant**	0.278	0.508	3.63	
13.	Bank Staff responds properly to the phone calls.	0.631		0.230			
14.	Bank staff thanks me for transacting with them	**Not significant**					

The application of the factor analysis reduced fourteen variables of service encounter into four predominant factors based on their factor loading. Factor loadings to the variables are considered on the basis of the 'rotated component matrix'. The first factor includes of six variables like 'front office employee asks the customer May I Help You sir', 'receptionist notices, welcomes and greets the customer', 'bank staffs are informative', 'receptionist asks the customer to be seated', 'I enjoy myself dealing with the staffs of this bank' and 'bank staffs are friendly with customers' have the loading of above 0.9 or near to 0.9. These are treated as **high significant** factors.

The second factor treated as **significant** as these are having factor loading between 0.7 – 0.8. This include five factor such as 'bank Employees shows reasonable interest in me as a customer', 'bank staffs speak pleasantly with smiling face', 'required suggestion, help and cooperation are provided by the bank employees', 'I wish to continue my relationship with this bank for long', and 'bank employees handles any problems/interruptions efficiently'.

The two variables, 'it is easy to approach or meet bank manager or other superiors in the bank' and 'bank employees responds properly to the phone calls', having the factor loading of less than 0.7, are fall under the category of **low significant.**

The remaining one variable i.e. 'bank staffs thanks me for transacting with them' is not significant in factor analysis because component matrix not given the any loading to this variable. That means this variable is not correlating with other variables in the factor analysis.

Table 5.33: KMO and Bartlett's Test

Kaiser-Meyer-Olkin Measure of Sampling Adequacy.		.868
Bartlett's Test of Sphericity	Approx. Chi-Square	3448.455
	Df	91
	Sig.	0.000

Hypothesis

H_0:- Service Encounter variables do not vary in importance significantly in respect of SBH bank.

H_A:- Service Encounter variables do vary in importance significantly in respect of SBH bank.

For the present data the value is 0.869, which falls into the range of being great: so it is said that, it should be confident that factor analysis is appropriate for this data.

With this analysis it said that the null hypothesis is rejected and proved that Service Encounter variables do vary in importance significantly in respect of SBH bank.

Measuring Service Quality - SBH.

Table – 5.34: Assessment of Service Quality in SBH

Sl. No.	*Expected Quality (E)*	*Mean*	*Perceived Quality (P)*	*Mean*	*Gap (E-P)*	*per cent of Gap*
			A. TANGIBLES			
1.	The Bank must possess the sophisticated and good looking infrastructure.	4.92	My Bank has the sophisticated and good looking infrastructure.	4.03	0.89	17.80
2.	Physical facilities at banks should be visual and attractive.	4.90	Physical facilities at my banks are visual and attractive.	4.03	0.87	17.40
3.	Bank employees have to be in neat dress and appear dignified.	4.90	My Bank employees are in neat dress and appearing dignified.	4.29	0.62	12.40
4.	Materials (statements or passbook) with bank should be visual and excellent.	4.88	Materials (statements or passbook) with my bank are visual and excellent.	4.03	0.84	16.80
	Total	19.60	**Total**	16.38	3.22	
	Average (19.60/4)	**4.90**	**Average (16.38/4)**	**4.09**	0.81	**16.20**
			B. RELIABILTY			
5.	If the bank promises something, it will do.	4.87	If my bank promises something, it will certainly do.	3.91	0.96	19.20
6.	If customers have problems, the bank has to show sincere interest in solving them.	4.88	If customers have problems, my bank will show sincere interest in solving it.	4.02	0.86	17.20
7.	The bank ought to perform the services at right time.	4.90	My bank performs the services at right time. As per time mentioned.	4.00	0.91	18.20
8.	The bank should provide service at the time it promises to do so.	4.88	My Bank provides service at the time it promises to do so.	3.95	0.93	18.60
9.	The Bank should keep accurate/error-free records.	4.88	My Bank keeps accurate/error-free records.	4.25	0.63	12.60
	Total	24.42	**Total**	20.13	4.29	
	Average (24.42/5)	**4.88**	**Average (20.13/5)**	**4.02**	0.86	17.20

C. RESPONSIVENESS						
10.	Employees of the bank ought to inform customers exactly when service will be performed.	4.87	Employees of my bank inform customers exactly when service will be performed.	3.61	1.26	25.20
11.	The Bank employees ought to give excellent service to its customers	4.88	My Bank employees give excellent service to its customers	4.03	0.85	17.00
12.	The Bank employees must be willing to help the customers.	4.88	My Bank employees are always willing to help customers.	4.02	0.85	17.00
13.	The Bank employees should be always ready to respond to customers' requests.	4.90	Bank employees always ready to respond to customers' requests.	4.04	0.86	17.20
	Total	19.52	**Total**	15.70	3.82	
Average (19.52/4)		**4.88**	**Average (15.70/4)**	**3.92**	0.96	19.20
D. ASSURANCE						
14.	The Bank employees should always try to infuse confidence in the customers.	4.88	My Bank employees always try to instill confidence in customers.	4.02	0.86	17.20
15.	Customers (you) have to feel safe in transactions with the Bank's employees.	4.91	Customers (me) always feel safe in transactions with my bank's employees.	4.15	0.75	15.00
16.	The Bank employees always ought to be courteous and polite with customers.	4.88	My Bank employees always courteous and polite with customers.	4.13	0.75	15.00
17.	The Bank must possess employees have complete knowledge to answer queries of customers.	4.91	My Bank employees have complete knowledge to answer queries of customers.	4.09	0.82	16.40
	Total	19.58	**Total**	16.40	3.18	
Average (19.58/4)		**4.90**	**Average (16.40/4)**	**4.10**	0.80	16.00
E. EMPATHY						
18.	The Bank has to give individual attention to customers.	4.89	My Bank gives individual attention to customers.	3.72	1.17	23.40
19.	The Bank operating hours must be convenient to all customers.	4.90	My Bank operating hours is convenient to all the customers.	4.35	0.55	11.00
20.	Bank employees ought to understand the specific needs of their customers.	4.88	Bank employees understand the specific needs of customers.	3.91	0.97	19.40
	Total	14.67	**Total**	11.99	2.68	
Average (14.67/3)		**4.89**	**Average (11.99/3)**	**4.00**	0.89	17.80

Source: Primary Data.

Table 5.36: Paired Sample Test (Repeated Measures T-TEST)

TANGIBLES									
Paired Variables		*Paired Differences*					t	df	Sig. (2-tailed) @ 0.05
		Mean	*Std. Deviation*	*Std. Error Mean*	*95 per cent Confidence Interval of the Difference*				
					Lower	*Upper*			
Pair 1	EQ1 - PQ1	.892	.816	.053	.788	.995	16.926	239	.000
Pair 2	EQ2 - PQ2	.871	.810	.052	.768	.974	16.645	239	.000
Pair 3	EQ3 - PQ3	.617	.681	.044	.530	.703	14.035	239	.000
Pair 4	EQ4 - PQ4	.842	.924	.060	.724	.959	14.114	239	.000
RELIABILITY									
Pair 1	EQ5 - PQ5	.958	.984	.064	.833	1.084	15.082	239	.000
Pair 2	EQ6 - PQ6	.863	.929	.060	.744	.981	14.376	239	.000
Pair 3	EQ7 - PQ7	.908	.964	.062	.786	1.031	14.601	239	.000
Pair 4	EQ8 - PQ8	.883	.987	.064	.758	1.009	13.868	239	.000
Pair 5	EQ9 - PQ9	.629	.782	.050	.530	.729	12.471	239	.000
RESPONSIVENESS									
Pair 1	EQ10 - PQ10	1.258	1.059	.068	1.124	1.393	18.410	239	.000
Pair 2	EQ11 - PQ11	.846	.895	.058	.732	.960	14.647	239	.000
Pair 3	EQ12 - PQ12	.854	.946	.061	.734	.974	13.988	239	.000
Pair 4	EQ13 - PQ13	.863	.893	.058	.749	.976	14.968	239	.000
ASSURANCE									
Pair 1	EQ14 - PQ14	.863	.952	.061	.741	.984	14.040	239	.000
Pair 2	EQ15 - PQ15	.754	.893	.058	.641	.868	13.087	239	.000
Pair 3	EQ16 - PQ16	.750	.912	.059	.634	.866	12.733	239	.000
Pair 4	EQ17 - PQ17	.817	.933	.060	.698	.935	13.564	239	.000
EMPATHY									
Pair 1	EQ18 - PQ18	1.171	1.105	.071	1.030	1.311	16.410	239	.000
Pair 2	EQ19 - PQ19	.546	.689	.044	.458	.633	12.271	239	.000
Pair 3	EQ20 - PQ20	.967	1.030	.067	.836	1.098	14.534	239	.000

Hypothesis

H_0 = There is no significant difference between opinions of customers of SBH in respect of expected and perceived quality.

H_A = There is significant difference between opinions of customers of SBH in respect of expected and perceived quality.

Paired Sample Test (PST) was used to test the hypothesis on opinions, of customers, in respect of expected quality and perceived quality of SBH bank in selected mandal areas. At a = 0.05 level of significance, there exists enough evidence to conclude that there is a difference between expected and perceived service quality dimensions that are 'Tangibles', ' Reliability', 'Responsiveness', 'Assurance' and 'Empathy'. It clearly establishes the significant difference between expected and perceived service quality dimensions of SBH bank.

It is clear that there is difference in customers' opinions of SBH in respect of the service quality, so it is very important that the bank officials should be more responsive and respond immediately to the queries and provide the needed information to the customers. Satisfaction of customers will increase if bank officials give individual attention and adjust the bank operating timing that is convenient to all type of customers and make a focus on the needs of customers.

Overall Service Quality

Having discussed the demographical details of the customers and opinions of customers on various aspects of bank service variables like influencing factors for opening bank account, services, facilities and amenities provided by the bank to the customers, service encounters, facilities and amenities provided by the bank to customers and dimensions of service quality of selected banks in rural areas. Karimnagar district in the above lines, an attempt has been made to analyse the overall opinions of customers on banks' performance where they are maintaining account in the following lines.

Overall Service Quality of SBH Bank

Table 5.37: Overall Service Quality of SBH Bank

Particulars	*Weights*	*Frequency*	*Per cent*	*Mean*	*SD*
Very Poor	1	3	1.25		
Poor	2	12	5.00		
Average	3	33	13.75	3.97	0.83
Good	4	134	55.83		
Very Good	5	58	24.17		
Total		**240**	**100.00**		

Source: Primary Data.

The above tables reveals that the opinions of the customers on overall service quality of SBH bank in Karimnagar district. The opinions are rated

Paired Samples Test – Profile of Respondents and Overall Service Quality

		Paired Differences					***t***	***df***	***Sig. (2-tailed)***
		Mean	***Std. Deviation***	***Std. Error Mean***	***95 per cent Confidence Interval of the Difference***				
					Lower	***Upper***			
Pair 1	Area of Bank and Overall SQ	-.467	1.970	.127	-.717	-.216	-3.669	239	0.000
Pair 2	Gender and Overall SQ	-2.688	.927	.060	-2.805	-2.570	-44.893	239	0.000
Pair 3	Age and Overall SQ	-.500	1.486	.096	-.689	-.311	-5.211	239	0.000
Pair 4	Qualification and Overall SQ	.021	2.040	.132	-.239	.280	.158	239	0.000
Pair 5	Occupation and Overall SQ	-1.467	1.387	.090	-1.643	-1.290	-16.383	239	0.000
Pair 6	Annual Income and Overall SQ	-1.800	1.207	.078	-1.954	-1.646	-23.096	239	0.000
Pair 7	Marital Status and Overall SQ	-2.921	.847	.055	-3.029	-2.813	-53.418	239	0.000

with the help of five point Liker Scale' ranging 1 – 5 points indicating 'Very Poor – Very Good'. Repondents of SBH bank averagely rated the Overall Service Quality between 3 – 4 implies 'Average to Good' for the services provided by the bank. The highest number of respondents representing 55.83 per cent of the total had expressed that the service quality of the bank as 'good' and following 24.17 per cent indicating 58 in number rated as 'very good'. Customer opined overall service quality as 'average' by 33 representing 13.75 per cent of the total. The service quality rated as 'poor and very poor' by 12 and 3 respondents respectively showing very less per cent i.e. 5 per cent and 1.25 per cent of the total.

According to Table 5.35, the gap score was high in respect of 'Responsiveness and Empathy' factors. This reflected the overall service quality of the bank. These factors need more attention by the bank officials to improve the service quality in State Bank of Hyderabad.

It is tested to prove the relation between service quality (dependent variable) and demographical details of respondents (independent variables) of selected banks through paired sample t- test.

H_0 – There is no significant relation between service quality and bank type, area of the bank, age, gender, qualification, occupation, annual income and marital status of the respondents of SBH Bank.

H_1– There is significant relation between service quality and bank type, area of the bank, age, gender, qualification, occupation, annual income and marital status of the respondents of SBH bank.

The significance value at 0.05 is zero, hence it is rejected the null hypothesis and concluded that the difference in opinions of customers about service quality due to bank type, area of the bank, age, gender, educational qualification, occupation, annual income and marital status of respondents is significant and is just not a matter of chance.

Service Quality Meeting Needs of the Customers

Table 5.38: Service Quality Meeting Needs of the Customers

Scale	*Weights*	*Frequency*	*Per cent*	*Mean*	*SD*
Strongly Disagree	1	2	0.83		
Disagree	2	20	8.33		
Neutral	3	6	2.50	4.05	0.837
Agree	4	148	61.67		
Strongly Agree	5	64	26.67		
Total		**240**	**100.00**		

Every person opens an account in the bank to meet his personal or business financial needs. The above table furnishes the details of the opinions of the respondents that whether the services provided by the bank were meeting their needs. The opinions are rated with the help of five point Liker Scale' ranging 1 – 5 points indicating 'Strongly Disagree – Strongly Agree'. Respondents of SBH bank rated the Service Quality meeting their financial needs in between 4 – 5 implies 'agree to Strongly Agree' for the services provided by the bank. The highest number of respondents representing 61.67 per cent of the total had agreed that the service quality of the bank as 'Agree' and following 26.67 per cent indicating 64 in number rated as 'strongly agree' and meeting their needs. Customer opined overall service quality as 'disagree' by 20 in number representing 8.33 per cent. The service quality rated as 'neutral and strongly disagree' by six and two respondents repectively.

Overall Satisfaction against the Service Quality

Table 5.39: Overall Satisfaction Against the Service Quality

Scale	*Frequency*	*Per cent*	*Mean*	*SD*
Very Unsatisfied	3	1.25	4.04	0.886
Slightly Unsatisfied	20	8.33		
Neutral	11	4.58		
Satisfied	136	56.67		
Very Satisfied	70	29.17		
Total	**240**	**100.00**		

Source: Primary Data.

After studying the responses of respondents of SBH against various aspects of service quality, an attempt is made to know their satisfaction level and furnished in the above table. The opinions are rated with the help of five point Liker Scale' ranging 1 – 5 points indiciating 'Very Unsatisfied – Very Satisfied'. The average of satisfaction level of repondents of SBH lied between 4 – 5 implies 'satisfied to very satisfied' for the services provided by the bank. The highest number of respondents representing 56.67 per cent of the total had expressed their satisfaction against service quality of the bank and following 29.17 per cent indicating 70 in number were very much satisfied. Customer who slightly unsatisfied were 20 in number representing 8.33 per cent and 3 customers in number were unsatisfied. 11 Customers were neutral and not expressed their opinion against satisfaction with service quality.

Paired Samples Test									
		Paired Differences					t	df	Sig. (2-tailed)
		Mean	Std. Deviation	Std. Error Mean	95 per cent Confidence Interval of the Difference				
					Lower	Upper			
Pair 1	Area of Bank and Overall Satisfaction	-.542	2.014	.130	-.798	-.286	-4.166	239	0.000
Pair 2	Gender and Overall Satisfaction	-2.763	.988	.064	-2.888	-2.637	-43.301	239	0.000
Pair 3	Age and Overall Satisfaction	-.575	1.421	.092	-.756	-.394	-6.268	239	0.000
Pair 4	Qualification and Overall Satisfaction	-.054	2.042	.132	-.314	.205	-.411	239	0.000
Pair 5	Occupation and Overall Satisfaction	-1.542	1.452	.094	-1.726	-1.357	-16.454	239	0.000
Pair 6	Annual Income and Overall Satisfaction	-1.875	1.271	.082	-2.037	-1.713	-22.849	239	0.000
Pair 7	Marital Status and Overall Satisfaction	-2.996	.894	.058	-3.110	-2.882	-51.917	239	0.000

It is also tested to prove the relation between customers' overall satisfaction towards service quality (dependent variable) and demographical details of respondents (independent variables) of selected banks through paired sample t- test.

H_0 – Customers' satisfaction does not vary in respect of bank type, area of the bank, age, gender, qualification, occupation, annual income and marital status of the respondents of SBH bank.

H_1 – Customers' satisfaction varies in respect of bank type, area of the bank, age, gender, qualification, occupation, annual income and marital status of the respondents of bank.

The significance value at 0.05 is zero, hence it is rejected the null hypothesis and concluded that the difference in customers' satisfaction towards service quality due to bank type, area of the bank, age, gender, educational qualification, occupation, annual income and marital status of respondents is significant and is just not a matter of chance.

5.11.4 Loyalty towards Bank

Table 5.40 Loyalty Towards Bank

Scale	*Frequency*	*Per cent*	*Mean*	*SD*
Very Low Probability	5	2.1	4.35	0.897
Low Probability	13	5.4		
Probability	98	40.8		
Very High Probability	124	51.7		
Total	**240**	**100.0**		

Source: Primary Data.

Customers were tested to know whether they remain loyal towards the bank and continue with bank in future also. It is fact that the satisfied customers definitely loyal towards the banks and also continue their financial transactions with the bank in the future. Respondents opinions were collected and presented in the above table. The opinions were rated with the help of 'five point Liker Scale' ranging 1 – 5 points indicating 'Very Low Probability–Very High Probability'. Repondents of SBH bank expressed their opinion averagely in between 4 – 5 implies 'Probability to Very High Probability' to continue with the bank in the future. The highest number of respondents representing agreed and expressed positive opinion that definitely loyal to the bank and continue in the future with the bank. Again, with this, it is proved that the highest number of customers were very satisfied with services of the bank. Very less per cent of the total respondents i.e. 2.10 per cent indicate five in number had expressed that they did not continue with the banks and switch off to other bank. Customers who did not satisfied with the services of bank try to switch off the bank.

5.11.5 Recommendations to Relatives and Friends

Table 5.41: Recommendations to Relatives and Friends

Scale	*Frequency*	*Per cent*	*Mean*	*SD*
Very Low Probability	7	2.9	4.20	0.952
Low Probability	13	5.4		
Neutral	8	3.3		
Probability	109	45.4		
Very High Probability	103	42.9		
Total	**240**	**100.0**		

Again it is tried to know whether satisfied customer recommend the bank to their friends, relatives to open an account in the bank and utilise the services. Opinions of the same were collected and presented in the above table. The opinions were rated with the help of five point Liker Scale' ranging 1–5 points indicating 'Very Low Probability–Very High Probability'. Repondents of SBH bank expressed their opinion averagely in between 4 – 5 implies 'Probability to Very High Probability' to suggest others to open account in the bank. The highest number of respondents representing agreed that they definitely suggest their friends and relatives to use the services of the bank. This indicates that the highest number of customers were very satisfied with services of the bank. Very less per cent of the total respondents i.e. 2.90 per cent indicate seven in number had expressed that they did not sugggest any person to open an account in the bank and 13 customers were expressed doubtfulness in suggesting their relatives and friends. Eight customers were in neutral position that they either suggest or do not suggest to their friends and relatives. With this analysis it is inferred that the highest number of customers were satisfied with the services provided by SBH bank.

5.12 Facilities and Amenities Provided by TGB Bank

The data in the below table presents the details of customers' opinions of TGB Bank with regard to the importance of facilities and amenities to be provided by the bank for convenience of customers.

5.12.1 Importance of Quality of Facilities and Amenities Provided by TGB Bank

Table 5.42: Importance of Facilities and Amenities Provided by TGB Bank

Sl.No.	*Variables*	*Mean*	*Std. Deviation*	*Ranks*
1.	Location of the Bank	4.78	0.483	6
2.	Parking Facility	4.66	0.694	8
3.	Information about working hours	4.95	0.224	1
4.	Information about service timings	4.88	0.374	3
5.	Availability of personal assistance/guidance	4.80	0.637	5
6.	Display of identification boards at counters	4.62	0.744	10
7.	May I Help You Counter	4.45	1.075	14
8.	Proper Lighting	4.89	0.335	2
9.	Information about available services and products	4.87	0.497	4
10.	Electronic token number display and audio announcement system	4.43	1.146	15
11.	Waiting Room/Place	4.52	0.793	12
12.	ATM facility at the branch	4.50	0.941	13
13.	Attractive Flooring	4.53	0.877	11
14.	Drinking Water	4.69	0.640	7
15.	A/C Facility	3.68	1.570	18
16.	Dust Bins	4.39	0.981	16
17.	Toilets Facility	4.22	1.168	17
18.	Complaint and Suggestion Box	4.64	0.780	9

Customers of TGB Bank gave the first rank to 'information about working hours', second rank to 'Proper lighting', and third rank given to 'information about service timings'. The fourth rank and fifth rank were given to 'information about available services' and products and 'Availability of personal assistance/guidance'. 'Location of the bank where it located', 'drinking water', 'parking facility', were ranked sixth, seventh and eighth ranks respectively. Ninth, tenth, eleventh, twelfth and thirteenth ranks were given to facility at banks, 'complaint and suggestion box', 'display of identification boards at counters for easy identification' and 'Attractive Flooring', 'waiting place in the bank', and 'ATM facility at the bank branch' respectively. 'May I Help You counter', 'electronic token number display and audio announcement system', 'Dust Bins', and 'Toilets Facility' were ranked as fourteenth, fifteenth, sixteenth and seventeenth ranks respectively. TGB customers also were given the least and last eighteenth rank to A/C facility.

Customers of TGB recognised basic items like 'Information about working hours', 'proper lighting', 'Information about service timings', 'Information about available services and products', and 'Availability of personal assistance/ guidance', which were ranked one to fifth respectively, were very essential facilities, every organisation must provide. Interestingly these customers also had given least priority to the A/C facility in the bank.

5.12.2 Actual Quality of Facilities and Amenities Provided by TGB Bank

Table 5.43: Actual Quality Facilities and Amenities Provided by TGB Bank

Sl.No.	*Variables*	*Mean*	*Std. Deviation*	*Ranks*
1	Location of the Bank	4.68	.634	1
2	Parking Facility	3.05	.935	9
3	Information about working hours	3.90	.882	4
4	Information about service timings	3.26	1.083	8
5	Availability of personal assistance/guidance	4.02	.883	3
6	Display of identification boards at counters	2.47	1.143	9
7	May I Help You Counter	1.12	.525	14
8	Proper Lighting	4.51	.619	2
9	Information about available services and products	3.55	1.083	6
10	Electronic token number display and audio announcement system	1.01	.148	18
11	Waiting Room/Place	3.41	1.027	7
12	ATM facility at the branch	1.03	.303	17
13	Attractive Flooring	3.86	.752	5
14	Drinking Water	2.11	1.289	11
15	A/C Facility	1.03	.197	16
16	Dust Bins	1.43	.774	13
17	Toilets Facility	1.04	.227	15
18	Complaint and Suggestion Box	1.94	1.206	12
	Average Score	**2.64**		

Opinions of TGB customers against quality of facilities and amenities provided by the bank are presented in the Table 5.43. It is inferred that "Location of the bank" ranked as first, "Proper Lighting" facility was ranked as second. They ranked "Availability of personal assistance/guidance" as third rank, "Information about working hours" as fourth rank, "Attractive Flooring" as fifth rank, "Information about available services and products" as sixth rank. "Waiting Room/Place", "Information about service timings", "Parking

provided by the bank were rated between '1 and 5' implies that the respondents rated these factors between 'Very Poor to Excellent'. Since the gap score was very less in respect of 'location of the bank', reveals that the customers were very much satisfied with location of the bank where it was established and also indicates that the bank was located in convenience to the customers. The highest gap score in respect of factors 'ATM Facility' (3.47), 'Electronic token number display and audio announcement system' (3.42), 'May I Help You Counter' (3.33) and 'Toilet Facilities' (3.18) reveal dissatisfaction of customers against these factors.

The Table also indicate that the customers were very much satisfied in respect of factors those had gap score was very less i.e. less than '1'. Customers were more expecting those facilities having gap score more than '1' and bank officials need to pay attention on the above factors which have the gap score more than one to understand the requirements of the customers and satisfy their needs.

5.13.4 Linear Regression Equation of Overall service quality on Actual Quality of Facilities and Amenities provided by TGB

Table 5.45: Linear Regression Equation of Overall service quality in TGB Model Summary

Model	*R*	*R Square*	*Adjusted R Square*	*Std. Error of the Estimate*	*Change Statistics*				
					R Square Change	*F Change*	*df1*	*df2*	*Sig. F Change*
1	.479[a]	.230	.163	.518	.230	3.460	18	209	.000
b Predictors: (Constant), Actual 1, Actual 2, Actual 3, Actual 4, Actual 5, Actual 6, Actual 7, Actual 8, Actual 9, Actual 10, Actual 11, Actual 12, Actual 13, Actual 14, Actual 15, Actual 16, Actual 17, Actual 18									

Y = b0 3.301-b1 0.072X1+b2 0.125X2+b3 0.029X3-b4 0.085X4+b5 0.276X5+b6 0.18X6-b7 0.098X7-b8 0.040X8-b9 0.012X9+b10 0.72X10-b11 0.099X11+b12 0.282X12-b13 0.05X13+b14 0.10X14 + b15 0.215X15-b16 0.17X16+b17 0.215X17-b18 0.25X18.

The Table 5.46 furnishes the details of Variables in Linear Regression Equation of Overall service quality on Actual Quality of Facilities and Amenities provided by TGB Bank. Linear correlation coefficient R = 0.479 measures the degree of relationship between the actual values and predicted values of overall service quality (Y) because the overall service quality (Y) values are obtained as linear combination of 18 variables of actual facilities and amenities provided by the selected TGB Bank. They were Location of the Bank (X1), Parking Facility (X2), Information about working hours (X3), Information about service timings (X4), Availability of personal assistance/ guidance (X5), Display of identification boards at counters (X6), May I Help You Counter (X7), Proper Lighting (X8), Information about available services and products (X9), Electronic token number display and audio announcement system (X10), Waiting Room/Place (X11), ATM facility at the branch (X12), Attractive Flooring (X13), Drinking Water (X14), A/C Facility (X15), Dust Bins (X16), Toilets Facility (X17), Complaint and Suggestion Box (X18). The coefficient value 0.479 indicates that the relationship between overall service quality and the actual quality of facilities and amenities is positive.

Table–5.46 Variables in Linear Regression Equation of Overall service quality on Actual Quality of Facilities and Amenities provided by TGB

Sl. No.	Variables	Unstandardized Coefficients		Standardized Coefficients	t-Value	Sig.	Correlations		
		B	Std. Error	Beta			Zero-order	Partial	Part
	Service Quality (Constant)	3.301	.579		5.703	.000			
1.	Location of the Bank	-.072	.062	-.080	-1.162	.247	-.110	-.080	-.071
2.	Parking Facility	.125	.050	.206	2.517	.013	.179	.172	.153
3.	Information about working hours	.029	.057	.046	.518	.605	.020	.036	.031
4.	Information about service timings	-.085	.046	-.162	-1.838	.068	.085	-.126	-.112
5.	Availability of personal assistance/guidance	.276	.046	.430	6.048	.000	.370	.386	.367
6.	Display of identification boards at counters	.018	.046	.037	.394	.694	.033	.027	.024
7.	May I Help You Counter	-.098	.073	-.091	-1.332	.184	-.004	-.092	-.081
8.	Proper Lighting	-.040	.066	-.043	-.602	.548	-.078	-.042	-.037
9.	Information about available services and products	-.012	.040	-.022	-.292	.771	.051	-.020	-.018
10.	Electronic token number display and audio announcement system	.072	.250	.019	.288	.774	.042	.020	.017
11.	Waiting Room/Place	-.099	.045	-.180	-2.180	.030	-.015	-.149	-.132
12.	ATM facility at the branch	.282	.129	.151	2.181	.030	.056	.149	.132
13.	Attractive Flooring	-.005	.052	-.007	-.097	.923	-.048	-.007	-.006
14.	Drinking Water	.010	.038	.023	.273	.785	.015	.019	.017
15.	A/C Facility	.210	.185	.073	1.130	.260	.086	.078	.069
16.	Dust Bins	-.017	.060	-.024	-.291	.771	-.026	-.020	-.018
17.	Toilets Facility	.215	.159	.086	1.351	.178	.095	.093	.082
18.	Complaint and Suggestion Box	-.025	.033	-.053	-.754	.452	-.114	-.052	-.046

a. Dependent Variable: Overall SQ

1. **b1 = -0.072** represents the partial effect of 'Location of the Bank' on overall service quality holding other independent variables constant. The estimated negative sign implies that such effect is negative while the absolute value implies that overall service quality has inverse impact of 7.20 per cent.

2. **b2 = 0.125** indicates the partial effect of 'Parking Facility' on overall service quality holding other independent variables constant. The estimated positive sign implies that such effect is positive while the absolute value implies that overall service quality has direct impact of 12.50 per cent.

3. **b3 = 0.029** represents the partial effect of 'Information about Working Hours' on overall service quality holding other independent variables constant.

The estimated positive sign implies that such effect is positive while the absolute value implies that overall service quality has the direct impact of 2.90 per cent.

4. b4 = -0.085 represents the partial effect of 'Information about Service Timings' on overall service quality holding other independent variables constant. The estimated negative sign implies that such effect is negative while the absolute value implies that overall service quality has inverse relation of 8.50 per cent.

5. b5 = 0.276 represents the partial effect of 'Availability of Personal Assistance/Guidance' on overall service quality holding other independent variables constant. The estimated positive sign implies that such effect is positive while the absolute value implies that overall service quality would has the direct impact of 27.60 per cent.

6. b6 = 0.018 represents the partial effect of display of 'Identification Boards at Counters' on overall service quality holding other independent variables constant. The estimated positive sign implies that such effect is positive while the absolute value implies that overall service quality has the direct relation of 1.80 per cent.

7. b7 = -0.098 represents the partial effect of 'May I Help You' on overall service quality holding other independent variables constant. The estimated negative sign implies that such effect is negative while the absolute value implies that overall service quality has the inverse relation of 9.80 per cent.

8. b8 = -0.040 represents the partial effect of 'Proper Lighting' on overall service quality holding other independent variables constant. The estimated negative sign implies that such effect is negative while the absolute value implies that overall service quality has the inverse relation of 4.00 per cent.

9. b9 = -0.012 represents the partial effect of 'Information about Available Services and Products' on overall service quality holding other independent variables constant. The estimated negative sign implies that such effect is negative while the absolute value implies that overall service quality would have the inverse impact of 1.20 per cent.

10. b10 = 0.072 represents the partial effect of 'Electronic Token Number Display and Audio Announcement System' on overall service quality holding other independent variables constant. The estimated positive sign implies that such effect is positive while the absolute value implies that overall service quality has direct relation of 7.20 per cent.

11. b11 = -0.099 represents the partial effect of 'Waiting Room/Place' on overall service quality holding other independent variables constant. The estimated negative sign implies that such effect is negative while the absolute value implies that overall service quality would decrease by 9.90 per cent.

12. b12 = 0.282 represents the partial effect of 'ATM Facility at Bank' on overall service quality holding other independent variables constant. The estimated positive sign implies that such effect is positive while the absolute value implies that overall service quality has the direct relation of 28.20 per cent.

13. b13 = -0.005 represents the partial effect of 'Attractive Flooring' on overall service quality holding other independent variables constant. The estimated negative sign implies that such effect is negative while the absolute value implies that overall service quality has the inverse relation of 0.50 per cent.

14. b14 = 0.010 represents the partial effect of 'Drinking Water Facility' on overall service quality holding other independent variables constant. The estimated positive sign implies that such effect is positive while the absolute value implies that overall service quality would increase by 1.00 per cent.

15. b15 = 0.210 represents the partial effect of 'A/C Facility' on overall service quality holding other independent variables constant. The estimated positive sign implies that such effect is positive while the absolute value implies that overall service quality has the direct impact of 21.00 per cent.

16. b16 = -0.017 represents the partial effect of 'Dustbins' on overall service quality holding other independent variables constant. The estimated negative sign implies that such effect is negative while the absolute value implies that overall service quality 1.70 per cent.

17. b17 = 0.215 represents the partial effect of 'Toilets Facility' on overall service quality holding other independent variables constant. The estimated positive sign implies that such effect is positive while the absolute value implies that overall service quality has the direct relation of 21.50 per cent.

18. b18 = -0.025 represents the partial effect of 'Complaint and Suggestion Box' on overall service quality holding other independent variables constant. The estimated negative sign implies that such effect is negative while the absolute value implies that overall service quality would decrease by 2.50 per cent.

Since the significant value is less than 0.05 in b2 'Parking Facility' (0.013), b5 'Availability of Personal Assistance/Guidance' (0.00), b11 'Waiting room/ Place' (-0.03) and b12 'ATM Facility' (0.03). Hence, the Linear regression analysis reveals that a slight increase in the above said facilities and amenities may lead to influence the overall service quality.

Hypothesis

H_0:- There is no significant relation between service quality and actual facilities and amenities provided by TGB Bank.

H_1:- There is significant relation between service quality and actual facilities and amenities provided by TGB Bank.

ANOVA[a]

	Model	*Sum of Squares*	*df*	*Mean Square*	*F*	*Sig.*
1	Regression	16.730	18	.929	3.460	1.61
	Residual	56.147	209	.269		
	Total	72.877	227			
a. Dependent Variable: Overall Satisfaction						
b Predictors: (Constant), Actual 1, Actual 2, Actual 3, Actual 4, Actual 5, Actual 6, Actual 7, Actual 8, Actual 9, Actual 10, Actual 11, Actual 12, Actual 13, Actual 14, Actual 15, Actual 16, Actual 17, Actual 18						

The above ANOVA table shows that the calculated value of *F* is 3.460 which is greater than the significance value at 0.05 level of significance is 1.61 with degree of freedom being $v_1 = 18$ and $v_2 = 209$. This analysis rejects the null hypothesis of no significant relation between customers' satisfactions towards service quality and actual facilities and amenities provided by TGB Bank. Therefore, it may conclude that the difference in customers' satisfaction due to actual facilities and amenities provided by TGB Bank is significant and is just not a matter of chance.

Hence, the bank officials need to focus on improving the facilities and amenities which have high and positive impact on customers' satisfaction.

5.13 Service Timings of TGB

5.13.1 Cash Receipt

Table 5.47: Service Timings for Cash Receipt in TGB

	Mid Values	*Frequency*	*Per cent*	
0 - 15 Min.	7.5	133	58.33	**Standard Time 10-20 Min.**
15 - 30 Min.	22.5	84	36.84	
30 - 45 Min.	37.5	10	4.39	
Don't Know	-	1	0.44	
Total		**228**	**100.00**	
	Mean Time (Min.)	**14.37**		**15**

Source: Primary Data.

From the Table 5-47 it is inferred that, out of 228 TGB customers, the highest numbers of customers, 133 customers informed that the cash receipt of the transaction would be completed within the 15 minutes. Following these

84 customers informed that time taking for cash receipt transaction in between 15-30 minutes by TGB bank officials. Only one customer did not know the when the service timing of the cash receipt. The bank is providing this service (14.37 minutes) within the specified average time (15 minutes).

5.13.2 Cash Payment

Table 5.48: Service Timings for Cash Payment in TGB

	Mid Values	*Frequency*	*Per cent*	
0 - 15 Min.	7.5	97	42.54	**Standard Time 10-20 Min.**
15 - 30 Min.	22.5	91	39.91	
30 - 45 Min.	37.5	40	17.54	
Don't Know		0	0.00	
Total		**228**	**100.00**	
Mean Time (Min.)		**18.75**		**15**

Source: Primary Data.

As per the table-5.48, the cash payment service in TGB would be completed within the 15 minutes according to 97 customers of the bank. The service timing for the cash payment is in between 15-30 minutes according to 91 customers. 17.50 per cent of total 228 customers expressed that the service timing for the service is in between 30-45 minutes. An average of 18.75 minutes is taking by TGB to pay the cash to customers against standard average time 15 minutes.

5.13.3 Issue of Draft

Table 5.49: Service Timings for Issue of Draft in TGB

Minutes	*Mid Values*	*Frequency*	*Per cent*	
0 - 15 Min.	7.5	12	5.26	**Standard Time 15-25 Min.**
15 – 30 Min.	22.5	26	11.40	
30 - 45 Min.	37.5	47	20.61	
Don't Know		143	62.72	
Total		**228**	**100.00**	
Mean Time (Min.)		**28.67**		**20**

Source: Primary Data.

The details in respect of opinions of customers against service timing of issue of demand draft, 20.61 per cent of the total TGB customers representing 47 in number stated that the service timing for the issue of DD was in between

30 – 45 minutes. 38 customers 16.66 per cent informed that the DD was issued by the banks within 30 minutes. TGB bank is taking average time of 28.67 minutes as against standard average time 20 minutes.

5.13.4 Collection of Outstation Cheques

Table 5.50: Service Timings for Collection of Outstation Cheques in TGB

Days	*Mid Values*	*Frequency*	*Per cent*	
1 - 3 Days	2	15	6.58	**Standard Time 10-14 Days**
4 - 8 Days	6	29	12.72	
8 - 12 Days	10	47	20.61	
Don't Know		137	60.09	
Total		**228**	**100.00**	
Mean Time (Days)		**7.41**	**7.41**	**12**

Source: Primary Data.

The data relating to the opinions of TGB customers on collection of outstation cheques is presented in the above table. The highest number of customers does not have awareness of this service timing. 47 customers in number representing 20.61 per cent of the total customers informed that the outstation cheques were collected and credited by the banker in between 8–12 days and 12.72 per cent of the total representing 29 in number stated that the service time for this service is 4-8 days. On an average bank is collecting the outstation cheques and depositing them in customers' account in 7.41 days, against standard average time 12 days.

5.13.5 Updating Pass Book

Table 5.51: Service Timings for Updating Pass Book in TGB

	Mid Values	*Frequency*	*Per cent*	
0 - 15 Min.	7.5	125	54.82	**Standard Time 5-15 Min**
15 - 30 Min.	22.5	38	16.67	
30 - 45 Min.	37.5	45	19.74	
Don't Know		20	8.77	
Total		**228**	**100.00**	
Mean Time (Min.)		**16.73**		**10**

Source: Primary Data.

The data in the Table 5.51 presents the details of service timing for 'updating the pass book' in TGB. The highest number of customers indicating 54.82 per cent of the total stated that the banker update the pass book information within the 15 minutes. 38 customers i.e. 16.67 per cent of the total customers stated that this service was done by the banker in between 15–30 minutes. 45 customers stated that the time taken by the banker to finish this service in between 30 – 45 minutes. 20 customers representing 8.77 per cent of the total informed that they did not have the awareness about this service. To update the pass book TGB is taking much time than the standard average time.

5.13.6 Issue of Cheque Book

Table 5.52: Service Timing for Issue of Cheque Book in TGB

<table>
<tr><th></th><th>Mid Values</th><th>Frequency</th><th>Per cent</th><td rowspan="6">Standard Time 7 - 15 Days.</td></tr>
<tr><td>0 - 7 Days</td><td>3.50</td><td>22</td><td>9.60</td></tr>
<tr><td>8 - 15 Days</td><td>11.50</td><td>23</td><td>10.10</td></tr>
<tr><td>16 - 21 Days</td><td>18.50</td><td>50</td><td>21.90</td></tr>
<tr><td>Don't Know</td><td></td><td>133</td><td>58.30</td></tr>
<tr><td>Total</td><td></td><td>228</td><td>100.00</td></tr>
<tr><td colspan="2">Mean Time (Days)</td><td>13.33</td><td></td><td>11</td></tr>
</table>

Source: Primary Data.

The details of opinions of customers about the issue of cheque book were presented in the above table. Majority of the customers i.e. 58.30 per cent of the total 228 customers do not have the knowledge of the cheque book service. 50 customers indicating 21.90 per cent of the total informed that the banks are taking 16-21 days to issue the cheque book. The remaining customers stated that banks issue the cheque book within the standard time i.e. 15 days. TGB bank is taking above average time to issue the cheque book to customers.

TGB bank, a public sector bank which is established long back and offering all types of services including government schemes, the number of visitors to this bank for various purposes is heavy on busy days like Mondays and first week of the month. To meet the needs of customers, the bank have not had the sufficient number of employees. This is the reason why banks are taking much time in providing this service.

5.14. Service Encounters

5.14.1 Ranks Based on Service Encounters in TGB

The table furnishes the details about ranks based on service encounters in selected TGB rural banks. It is found that the "bank employees speak pleasantly with smiling face" ranked first by the customers/respondents of TGB Bank. They ranked "bank staffs are friendly with customers" and "I wish to continue my relationship with this bank for long", "bank staffs are informative" and "required suggestion, help and co-operation are provided by the bank staffs". as second and third and fourth and fifth ranks respectively.

Table 5.53: Ranks based on Service Encounters in TGB Bank (Relationship between Bank Employees and Customers)

Sl. No.	*Statements*	*TGB*		
		Mean	*Std. Deviation*	*Rank*
1	Front Office Employee (Receptionist) notices, welcomes and greets the customers.	1.33	0.618	14
2	Receptionist asks customer May I Help You sir.	1.36	0.690	13
3	Receptionist asks customer to be seated.	1.40	0.804	12
4	Required suggestion, help and cooperation are provided by the bank employees.	4.72	0.683	5
5	Bank staff speaks pleasantly with smiling face.	4.79	0.514	1
6	Bank staffs are friendly with customers.	4.77	0.506	2
7	Bank staffs are informative.	4.73	0.510	4
8	It is easy to approach or meet Bank Manager or other superiors in the Bank.	4.71	0.624	6
9	Bank staff responds properly to the phone calls.	3.89	0.903	10
10	Bank staff shows reasonable interest in me as a customer.	4.62	0.635	8
11	Bank staff thanks me for transacting with them.	2.88	1.393	11
12	Bank staff handles any problems/interruptions efficiently.	4.56	0.691	9
13	I enjoy myself dealing with the employees of this bank.	4.64	0.565	7
14	I wish to continue my relationship with this bank for long.	4.75	0.436	3

Source: Primary Data.

Sixth, seventh, eighth and ninth ranks given to "It is easy to approach or meet bank manager or other superiors in the bank", "I enjoy myself dealing with the employees of this bank", "bank employees show reasonable interest in me as a customer", and "bank staffs handle any problem or interruptions efficiently" respectively. Statements "bank staffs respond properly to the phone calls", "bank staffs thanks me for transacting with them" and "receptionist asks customer to be seated" ranked as tenth, eleventh and twelfth ranks respectively. Thirteenth rank was posted to "receptionist asks customer May I Help you sir" and statement "front office employee notices, welcomes and greets the customers" was ranked fourteenth. The variables i.e. statements relating to the service encounter of TGB Bank under study were measured with the help of statistical tool 'Factor Analysis'. The statements were arranged as per their loading according to factor analysis. The results of the factor analysis are presented in the following table.

5.14.2 Factor Analysis of Service Encounters in TGB Bank

The application of the factor analysis reduced fourteen variables of service encounter into three predominant factors based on their factor loading. Factor loadings to the variables are considered on the basis of the 'rotated component matrix'. The first factor includes of five variables like 'front office employee asks the customer May I Help You sir', 'receptionist asks the customer to be seated', 'bank staffs speak pleasantly with smiling face', 'bank staffs are friendly with customers' and 'receptionist notices, welcomes and greets the customer' have the loading of above 0.9 or near to 0.9. These are treated as **high significant** factors.

The second factor treated as **significant** as these are having factor loading between 0.7–0.8. This include four factor such as 'bank staffs responds properly to the phone calls', 'I wish to continue my relationship with this bank for long', 'I enjoy myself dealing with the staffs of this bank' and 'bank staffs are informative'.

Table 5.54: Factor Analysis of Service Encounters in TGB Bank (Relationship between Bank Employees and Customers)

Sl. No.	*Statements*	*Factor Loading*	*Factors*	*Eigen Values*		*Individual Variance*	*Cumulative Variance*
1.	Receptionist asks customer May I Help You sir.	0.965	**High Significant**	2.633	10.394	74.242	100.00
2.	Receptionist asks customer to be seated	0.917		1.428			
3.	Bank staffs speak pleasantly with smiling face.	0.916		0.847			
4.	Bank Staffs are friendly with customers.	0.915		0.620			
5.	Front Office Employee (Receptionist) notices, welcomes and greets the customers.	0.909		4.866			
6.	Bank Staff responds properly to the phone calls.	0.877	**Significant**	0.456	1.204	8.598	
7.	I wish to continue my relationship with this bank for long.	0.826		0.066			
8.	I enjoy myself dealing with the employees of this bank.	0.772		0.121			
9.	Bank Staffs are informative.	0.742		0.561			
10.	Bank Staff thanks me for transacting with them.	0.685	**Low Significant**	0.267	2.403	17.16	
11.	Required suggestion, help and cooperation are provided by the bank employees.	0.669		1.113			
12.	It is easy to approach or meet Bank Manager or other superiors in the Bank.	0.609		0.501			
13.	Bank staff handles any problems/interruptions efficiently.	0.588		0.234			
14.	Bank Staff shows reasonable interest in me as a customer.	0.565		0.288			

Source: Primary Data.

Table 5.56: Assessment of Service Quality in TGB

Sl. No.	*Expected Quality (E)*	*Mean*	*Perceived Quality (P)*	*Mean*	*Gap (E-P)*	*%of Gap*
			A. TANGIBLES			
1.	The Bank must possess the sophisticated and good looking infrastructure.	4.93	My Bank has the sophisticated and good looking infrastructure.	3.89	1.04	20.80
2.	Physical facilities at banks should be visual and attractive.	4.88	Physical facilities at my banks are visual and attractive.	3.98	0.89	17.80
3.	Bank employees have to be in neat dress and appear dignified.	4.76	My Bank employees are in neat dress and appearing dignified.	4.20	0.56	11.20
4.	Materials (statements or passbook) with bank should be visual and excellent.	4.76	Materials (statements or passbook) with my bank are visual and excellent.	4.03	0.74	14.80
	Total	**19.33**	**Total**	**16.09**	**3.24**	
	Average (19.33/4)	**4.83**	**Average (16.09/4)**	**4.02**	**0.81**	**16.20**
			B. RELIABILTY			
5.	If the bank promises something, it will do.	4.81	If my bank promises something, it will certainly do.	4.43	0.38	7.60
6.	If customers have problems, the bank has to show sincere interest in solving them.	4.83	If customers have problems, my bank will show sincere interest in solving it.	4.51	0.32	6.40
7.	The bank ought to perform the services at right time.	4.85	My bank performs the services at right time. As per time mentioned.	4.49	0.36	7.20
8.	The bank should provide service at the time it promises to do so.	4.85	My Bank provides service at the time it promises to do so.	4.42	0.43	8.60
9.	The Bank should keep accurate/error-free records.	4.83	My Bank keeps accurate/error-free records.	4.64	0.19	3.80
	Total	**24.17**	**Total**	**22.49**	**1.68**	
	Average (24.17/5)	**4.83**	**Average (22.49/5)**	**4.50**	**0.34**	**6.80**

(Contd...)

C. RESPONSIVENESS						
10	Employees of the bank ought to inform customers exactly when service will be performed.	4.71	Employees of my bank inform customers exactly when service will be performed.	4.03	0.68	13.60
11	The Bank employees ought to give excellent service to its customers	4.83	My Bank employees give excellent service to its customers	4.64	0.19	3.80
12	The Bank employees must be willing to help the customers.	4.79	My Bank employees are always willing to help customers.	4.61	0.18	3.60
13	The Bank employees should be always ready to respond to customers' requests.	4.83	Bank employees always ready to respond to customers' requests.	4.57	0.26	5.20
	Total	**19.16**	**Total**	**17.85**	**1.31**	
Average (19.16/4)		**4.79**	**Average (17.85/4)**	**4.46**	**0.33**	**6.60**
D. ASSURANCE						
14	The Bank employees should always try to infuse confidence in the customers.	4.75	My Bank employees always try to instill confidence in customers.	4.65	0.11	2.20
15	Customers (you) have to feel safe in transactions with the Bank's employees.	4.82	Customers (me) always feel safe in transactions with my bank's employees.	4.69	0.13	2.60
16	The Bank employees always ought to be courteous and polite with customers.	4.89	My Bank employees always courteous and polite with customers.	4.78	0.11	2.20
17	The Bank must possess employees have complete knowledge to answer queries of customers.	4.82	My Bank employees have complete knowledge to answer queries of customers.	4.46	0.36	7.20
	Total	**19.29**	**Total**	**18.58**	**0.71**	
Average (19.29/4)		**4.82**	**Average (18.58/4)**	**4.65**	**0.18**	**3.60**

(Contd...)

E. EMPATHY						
18	The Bank has to give individual attention to customers.	4.75	My Bank gives individual attention to customers.	4.29	0.46	9.20
19	The Bank operating hours must be convenient to all customers.	4.77	My Bank operating hours is convenient to all the customers.	4.58	0.18	3.60
20	Bank employees ought to understand the specific needs of their customers.	4.79	Bank employees understand the specific needs of customers.	4.36	0.43	8.60
	Total	**14.31**	**Total**	**13.24**	**1.07**	
Average (14.31)		**4.77**	**Average (13.24/3)**	**4.41**	**0.36**	**7.20**

Table 5.57: Average Score of Service Quality Factors of TGB

Sl. No.	Categories	Expected SQ (E)	Actual SQ (P)	SQ Gap (E-P)	per cent of Gap
1	Tangibles	4.83	4.02	0.81	16.20
2	Reliability	4.83	4.5	0.33	6.60
3	Responsiveness	4.79	4.46	0.33	6.60
4	Assurance	4.82	4.65	0.17	3.40
5	Empathy	4.77	4.41	0.36	7.20
	Total	**24.04**	**22.04**	**2.00**	**40.00**
	Average	**4.808**	**4.408**	**0.4**	**8.00**

The above tables and graph reveal that the level of expectation of the service quality of the customers and perceived quality by the customers for dimentions namely tangibles, reliability, responsiveness, assurance and empathy are rated between four and five points implies that the respondents rated these dimensions in between 'agree and strongly agree', and the level of percieved quality for the above five dimensions rated by respendents between four and five points implies that the respondents rated these dimensions in between 'agree and strongly agree' for the services provided by TGB bank. The gap score is very less in 'Assurance' reveals that customers are highly satisfied with the assurance aspects associated with the service. Tangibles have the greater average gap score 0.81 than others dimensions, implying dissatifaction of customers.

Table 5.58: Paired Sample Test (Repeated Measures T-test)

		Paired Differences					t	df	Sig. (2-tailed)
		Mean	Std. Deviation	Std. Error Mean	95 per cent Confidence Interval of the Difference: Lower	Upper			
TANGIBLES									
Pair 1	EQ1 - PQ1	1.044	.784	.052	.942	1.146	20.102	227	.000
Pair 2	EQ2 - PQ2	.895	.778	.052	.793	.996	17.361	227	.000
Pair 3	EQ3 - PQ3	.561	.751	.050	.463	.659	11.283	227	.000
Pair 4	EQ4 - PQ4	.737	.866	.057	.624	.850	12.849	227	.000
RELIABILITY									
Pair 1	EQ5 - PQ5	.382	.914	.061	.262	.501	6.301	227	.000
Pair 2	EQ6 - PQ6	.325	.796	.053	.221	.428	6.154	227	.000
Pair 3	EQ7 - PQ7	.360	.935	.062	.238	.482	5.807	227	.000
Pair 4	EQ8 - PQ8	.430	.905	.060	.312	.548	7.172	227	.000
Pair 5	EQ9 - PQ9	.189	.765	.051	.089	.288	3.722	227	.000
RESPONSIVENESS									
Pair 1	EQ10 - PQ10	.684	1.031	.068	.550	.819	10.021	227	.000
Pair 2	EQ11 - PQ11	.189	.619	.041	.108	.269	4.603	227	.000
Pair 3	EQ12 - PQ12	.180	.689	.046	.090	.270	3.943	227	.000
Pair 4	EQ13 - PQ13	.259	.756	.050	.160	.357	5.169	227	.000
ASSURANCE									
Pair 1	EQ14 - PQ14	.105	.635	.042	.022	.188	2.504	227	.013
Pair 2	EQ15 - PQ15	.132	.609	.040	.052	.211	3.265	227	.001
Pair 3	EQ16 - PQ16	.110	.631	.042	.027	.192	2.626	227	.009
Pair 4	EQ17 - PQ17	.360	.877	.058	.245	.474	6.194	227	.000
EMPATHY									
Pair 1	EQ18 - PQ18	.461	.892	.059	.344	.577	7.795	227	.000
Pair 2	EQ19 - PQ19	.184	.786	.052	.082	.287	3.539	227	.000
Pair 3	EQ20 - PQ20	.430	.829	.055	.322	.538	7.832	227	.000

Hypothesis

H_0 = There is no significant difference between opinions of customers of TGB Bank in respect of expected and perceived quality.

H_A = There is significant difference between opinions of customers of TGB Bank in respect of expected and perceived quality.

At the a = 0.05 level of significance, there exists enough evidence to conclude that there is a difference between expected and perceived service quality dimensions that are 'Tangibles', 'Reliability', 'Responsiveness', 'Assurance' and 'Empathy'. It clearly establishes that the significant difference between expected and perceived service quality dimensions of TGB bank.

It is clear that there is difference in customers' opinions of customers TGB Bank in respect of the service quality. It is essential that the bank officials should more focus on the issues relating to the tangibility and maintain sophisticated and good looking infrastructure to attract the customers and bank employees should more focus on their appearance and should maintain neat dress. All the material with the bank should be visible and available, to reduce the service quality gap which lead to increase the satisfaction level of customers.

5.16 Interpretation of Overall Service Quality

5.16.1 Overall Service Quality of TGB Bank

Table 5.59: Overall Service Quality of TGB Bank

Particulars	*Frequency*	*Per cent*	*Mean*	*SD*
Very Poor	0	0	4.40	0.567
Poor	0	0		
Average	9	3.90		
Good	118	51.80		
Very Good	101	44.30		
Total	**228**	**100.00**		

Source: Primary Data.

The above tables reveals that the opinions of the customers on overall service quality of TGB bank in Karimnagar district. The opinions are rated with the help of '5 point Liker Scale' ranging 1–5 points indicating 'Very Poor–Very Good'. Repondents of TGB bank averagely rated the Overall Service Quality between 4–5 implies 'Good to Very Good' for the services provided by the bank. The highest number of respondents representing

51.80 per cent of the total had expressed that the service quality of the bank as 'good' and following 44.30 per cent indicating 101 in number rated as 'very good'. Customer opined overall service quality as 'average' by nine representing 3.90 per cent. No customer rated the service quality as 'poor and very poor'.

It is tested to prove the relation between service quality (dependent variable) and demographical details of respondents (independent variables) of TGB banks through paired sample t-test.

H_0– There is no significant relation between service quality and bank type, area of the bank, age, gender, qualification, occupation, annual income and marital status of the respondents of TGB bank.

H_1– There is significant relation between service quality and bank type, area of the bank, age, gender, qualification, occupation, annual income and marital status of the respondents of TGB bank.

Paired Samples Test

		Paired Differences					*t*	*df*	*Sig. (2-tailed)*
		Mean	*Std. Deviation*	*Std. Error Mean*	*95 per cent Confidence Interval of the Difference*				
					Lower	*Upper*			
Pair 1	Area of Bank - Overall Service Quality	-1.035	1.860	.123	-1.278	-.792	-8.401	227	.000
Pair 2	gender - Overall Service Quality	-3.110	.740	.049	-3.206	-3.013	-63.464	227	.000
Pair 3	Age - Overall Service Quality	-.961	1.203	.080	-1.118	-.804	-12.054	227	.000
Pair 4	Qualification - Overall Service Quality	0.000	1.926	.128	-.251	.251	0.000	227	1.000
Pair 5	Occupation - Overall Service Quality	-1.904	1.266	.084	-2.069	-1.738	-22.702	227	.000
Pair 6	Annual Income - Overall Service Quality	-2.285	1.112	.074	-2.430	-2.140	-31.041	227	.000
Pair 7	Marital Status - Overall Service Quality	-3.368	.590	.039	-3.445	-3.291	-86.188	227	.000

The significance value at 0.05 is zero, hence it is rejected the null hypothesis and concluded that the difference in opinions of customers about service quality due to bank type, area of the bank, age, gender, educational qualification, occupation, annual income and marital status of respondents is significant and is just not a matter of chance.

5.16.2 Service Quality Meeting Needs of Customers

Table 5.60: Service Quality Meeting Needs of the Customers

Scale	*Frequency*	*Per cent*	*Mean*	*SD*
Strongly Disagree	0	0	4.45	0.557
Disagree	2	0.90		
Neutral	1	0.40		
Agree	118	51.80		
Strongly Agree	107	46.90		
Total	**228**	**100.00**		

Source: Primary Data.

Every person opens an account in the bank to meet his personal or business financial needs. The above table furnishes the details of the opinions of the respondents that whether the services provided by the bank were meeting their needs. The opinions are rated with the help of '5 point Liker Scale' ranging 1–5 points indicating 'Strongly Disagree–Strongly Agree'. Respondents of TGB bank rated the Service Quality Meeting their financial needs in between 4–5 implies 'agree to strongly agree' for the services provided by the bank. The highest number of respondents representing 51.80 per cent of the total had agreed that the service quality of the bank as 'agree' and following 46.90 per cent indicating 107 in number rated as 'strongly agree' and meeting their needs. Only two customer opined overall service quality meeting their needs as 'disagree'. No customer expressed his opinion as 'strongly disagree'.

5.16.3 Overall Satisfaction against the Service Quality

Table 5.61: Overall Satisfaction Against the Service Quality

Scale	*Frequency*	*Percent*	*Mean*	*SD*
Unsatisfied	0	0	4.53	0.534
Slightly Unsatisfied	1	0.40		
Neutral	1	0.40		
Satisfied	102	44.70		
Very Satisfied	124	54.40		
Total	**228**	**100.0**		

Source: Primary Data.

After studying the responses of respondents of TGB against various aspects of service quality, an attempt is made to know their satisfaction level and furnished in the above table. The opinions are rated with the help of '5 point

Liker Scale' ranging 1–5 points indicating 'Very Unsatisfied – Very Satisfied'. The average of satisfaction level of repondents of TGB lied between 4 – 5 implies 'satisfied to very satisfied' for the services provided by the bank. The highest number of respondents representing 54.40 per cent of the total were very satisfied and following 44.70 per cent indicating 102 in number were satisfied. Only one customer who slightly unsatisfied and who was neutral and was not expressed his opinion in respect of satisfaction level.

It is also tested to prove the relation between customers' overall satisfaction towards service quality (dependent variable) and demographical details of respondents (independent variables) of selected banks through paired sample t-test.

H_0 – Customers' satisfaction does not vary in respect of bank type, area of the bank, age, gender, qualification, occupation, annual income and marital status of the respondents selected bank.

H_1 – Customers' satisfaction varies in respect of bank type, area of the bank, age, gender, qualification, occupation, annual income and marital status of the respondents selected bank.

Paired Samples Test

		Paired Differences					*t*	*df*	*Sig. (2-tailed)*
		Mean	*Std. Deviation*	*Std. Error Mean*	*95 per cent Confidence Interval of the Difference*				
					Lower	*Upper*			
Pair 1	Area of Bank - Overall Satisfaction	-1.162	1.814	.120	-1.399	-.926	-9.675	227	.000
Pair 2	gender - Overall Satisfaction	-3.237	.725	.048	-3.331	-3.142	-67.444	227	.000
Pair 3	Age - Overall Satisfaction	-1.088	1.188	.079	-1.243	-.933	-13.828	227	.000
Pair 4	Qualification - Overall Satisfaction	-.127	1.973	.131	-.385	.130	-.974	227	.331
Pair 5	Occupation - Overall Satisfaction	-2.031	1.232	.082	-2.192	-1.870	-24.880	227	.000
Pair 6	Annual Income - Overall Satisfaction	-2.412	1.035	.069	-2.547	-2.277	-35.187	227	.000
Pair 7	Marital Status - Overall Satisfaction	-3.496	.567	.038	-3.570	-3.422	-93.080	227	.000

The significance value at 0.05 is zero, hence it is rejected the null hypothesis and concluded that the difference in customers' satisfaction towards service quality due to bank type, area of the bank, age, gender, educational qualification, occupation, annual income and marital status of respondents is significant and is just not a matter of chance.

5.16.4 Loyalty towards Bank

Table 5.62: Loyalty Towards Bank

Scale	*Frequency*	*Per cent*	*Mean*	*SD*
Very Less Probability	0	0	4.65	0.504
Low Probability	1	0.40		
Neutral	0	0.00		
Probability	76	33.30		
Very High Probability	151	66.30		
Total	**228**	**100.00**		

Source: Primary Data.

Customers were tested to know whether they remain loyal towards the bank and continue with bank in future also. It is fact that the satisfied customers definitely loyal towards the banks and also continue their financial transactions with the bank in the future. Respondents opinions were collected and presented in the above table. The opinions were rated with the help of '5 point Liker Scale' ranging 1–5 points indicating 'Very Low Probability–Very High Probability'. Repondents of TGB bank expressed their opinion averagely in between 4–5 implies 'Probability to Very High Probability' to continue with the bank in the future. The highest number of respondents representing 151 respondents in number strongly agreed and expressed positive opinion that definitely loyal to the bank and continue in the future with the bank. Again, with this, it is proved that the highest number of customers were very satisfied with services of the bank. Only one customer expressed his doubt to continue with the bank.

5.16.5 Recommendations to Relatives and Friends

Table 5.63: Recommendations to Relatives and Friends

Scale	*Frequency*	*Per cent*	*Mean*	*SD*
Very Less Probability	0	0	4.61	0.579
Low Probability	3	1.30		
Neutral	2	0.90		
Probability	75	32.90		
Very High Probability	148	64.90		
Total	**228**	**100.00**		

Source: Primary Data.

An attempt is made to know whether satisfied customer recommend his friends, relatives to open an account in the bank and utilize the services.

Opinions of the same were collected and presented in the above table. The opinions were rated with the help of '5 point Liker Scale' ranging 1–5 points indicating 'Very Less Probability–Very High Probability'. Repondents of TGB bank expressed their opinion averagely in between 4–5 implies 'Probability to Very High Probability' to suggest others to open account in the bank. The highest number of respondents representing 148 in number strongly agreed that they definitely suggest their friends and relatives to use the services of the bank. This indicates that the highest number of customers were very satisfied with services of the bank. Very less per cent of the total respondents i.e. 1.30 per cent indicate three customers in number were expressed doubtfulness in suggesting their relatives and friends and two customers were in neutral position. With this analysis it is inferred that the most number of customers were satisfied with the services provided by TGB bank.

5.17 HDFC Bank

5.17.1 Importance of Facilities and Amenities Provided by HDFC Bank

The data presented in the Table–5.4 presents the details of customers' opinions of HDFC bank regarding the importance of facilities and amenities to be provided by the bank for convenience of customers. Customers of HDFC bank gave the first rank to 'information about service timings', second rank to 'information about working hours' and third rank given to 'Availability of personal assistance/guidance'. The fourth rank and fifth rank were given to 'Proper lighting', and 'waiting room/place in the bank' respectively.

'Information about available services' and products', 'ATM facility at the bank branch' and 'drinking water' were ranked sixth, seventh and eighth ranks respectively. Ninth, tenth, eleventh, twelfth and thirteenth ranks were given to 'complaint and suggestion box', 'display of identification boards at counters for easy identification', 'Dust Bins, 'Location of the bank where it located' and 'parking facility' respectively. 'Attractive Flooring', 'May I Help You counter', 'electronic token number display and audio announcement system', 'A/C facility', and 'Toilets Facility' were ranked as fourteenth, fifteenth, sixteenth, seventeenth and eighteenth ranks respectively.

Table–5.64 Importance of Facilities and Amenities Provided by HDFC Bank

Sl.No.	*Variables*	*Mean*	*Std. Deviation*	*Ranks*
1	Location of the Bank	4.83	.502	12
2	Parking Facility	4.83	.514	13
3	Information about working hours	4.94	.230	2
4	Information about service timings	4.96	.204	1
5	Availability of personal assistance/guidance	4.93	.298	3

(Contd...)

6	Display of identification boards at counters	4.85	.537	10
7	May I Help You Counter	4.81	.616	15
8	Proper Lighting	4.93	.263	4
9	Information about available services and products	4.90	.449	6
10	Electronic token number display and audio announcement system	4.81	.683	16
11	Waiting Room/Place	4.91	.349	5
12	ATM facility at the branch	4.88	.414	7
13	Attractive Flooring	4.81	.606	14
14	Drinking Water	4.87	.500	8
15	A/C Facility	4.80	.732	17
16	Dust Bins	4.85	.480	11
17	Toilets Facility	4.73	.786	18
18	Complaint and Suggestion Box	4.87	.512	9

Customers of HDFC bank were given the high priority to items like 'Information about service timings', 'Information about working hours', 'Availability of personal assistance/guidance', 'proper lighting', 'waiting room/ place in the bank', and Information about available services and products, and which were ranked one to sixth ranks respectively, were very essential and common required facilities in every banking organisations.

5.17.2 Actual Quality of Facilities and Amenities Provided by HDFC Bank

The data presented in the following table presents the details of customers' opinions of HDFC bank regarding the actual facilities and amenities provided by the bank for the convenient of their customers. Customers of HDFC bank gave the first rank to 'Proper lighting', second rank to 'Attractive Flooring', and third rank given to 'ATM facility at the bank branch'. The fourth rank and fifth rank were given to, 'A/C facility', and 'Location of the bank where it located' respectively. 'Display of identification boards at counters for easy identification', 'Availability of personal assistance/guidance', 'information about working hours' were ranked as sixth, seventh and eighth ranks respectively.

Table 5.65: Actual Quality of Facilities and Amenities Provided by HDFC Bank

Sl. No.	*Variables*	*Mean*	*Std. Deviation*	*Ranks*
1	Location of the Bank	4.19	1.070	5
2	Parking Facility	2.77	1.212	15
3	Information about working hours	4.00	.696	8

(Contd...)

4	Information about service timings	3.76	.794	10
5	Availability of personal assistance/guidance	4.09	.981	7
6	Display of identification boards at counters	4.18	.855	6
7	May I Help You Counter	3.56	1.266	12
8	Proper Lighting	4.81	.501	1
9	Information about available services and products	3.75	.928	11
10	Electronic token number display and audio announcement system	1.10	.501	18
11	Waiting Room/Place	2.67	1.255	16
12	ATM facility at the branch	4.56	.959	3
13	Attractive Flooring	4.69	.538	2
14	Drinking Water	3.07	1.434	14
15	A/C Facility	4.55	.878	4
16	Dust Bins	3.78	1.317	9
17	Toilets Facility	1.57	1.141	17
18	Complaint and Suggestion Box	3.39	1.521	13

Ninth, tenth, eleventh, twelfth and thirteenth ranks were given to 'Dust Bins', 'information about service timings', 'Information about available services and products', 'May I Help You counter' and 'complaint and suggestion box' respectively. 'Drinking water', 'parking facility', 'waiting room/place in the bank', 'Toilets Facility' and 'electronic token number display and audio announcement system' were ranked as fourteenth, fifteenth, sixteenth, seventeenth and eighteenth ranks respectively.

An attempt was made to analyse customers' opinions with regard to importance of facilities and amenities that required to a bank and actual facilities and amenities provided by the bank. The above table shows that the mean score of important and actual and gap between the two. The level of importance of customers with regard to facilities and amenities were rated between '4' and '5' indicate that the respondents rated these factors between 'Importance and Very Important'. The level of actual facilities and amenities provided by the bank were rated between '1 and 5' implies that the respondents rated these factors between 'Very Poor to Very Good'. Since the gap score was very less in respect of 'Proper Lighting', 'Attractive Flooring', 'A/C Facility', 'ATM facility at the branch', 'location of the bank', 'Display of identification boards at counters'.

5.18.4 Linear Regression Equation of Overall Service Quality on Actual Quality of Facilities and Amenities Provided by HDFC Bank

1. Dependent Variable: Overall service quality (Y)
2. Independent Variables:
   a. Location of the Bank (X1)
   b. Parking Facility (X2)
   c. Information about working hours (X3)
   d. Information about service timings (X4)
   e. Availability of personal assistance/guidance (X5)
   f. Display of identification boards at counters (X6)
   g. May I Help You Counter (X7)
   h. Proper Lighting (X8)
   i. Information about available services and products (X9)
   j. Electronic token number display and audio announcement system (X10)
   k. Waiting Room/Place (X11)
   l. ATM facility at the branch (X12)
   m. Attractive Flooring (X13)
   n. Drinking Water (X14)
   o. A/C Facility (X15)
   p. Dust Bins (X16)
   q. Toilets Facility (X17)
   r. Complaint and Suggestion Box (X18)
3. Linear R Value : 0.517
4. R Square Value : 0.267
5. F Value : 2.893
6. P Value : 1.61

Table 5.67: Linear Regression Equation of Overall Service Quality on Actual Quality Model Summary

Model	*R*	*R Square*	*Adjusted R Square*	*Std. Error of the Estimate*	*Change Statistics*				
					R Square Change	*F Change*	*df1*	*df2*	*Sig. F Change*
1	.517[a]	.267	.175	.520	.267	2.893	18	143	1.61

a. Dependent Variable: Overall Satisfaction b. Predictors: (Constant), Actual 1, Actual 2, Actual 3, Actual 4, Actual 5, Actual 6, Actual 7, Actual 8, Actual 9, Actual 10, Actual 11, Actual 12, Actual 13, Actual 14, Actual 15, Actual 16, Actual 17, Actual 18

Y = b0 2.105 + b1 0.05X1 + b2 0.115X2 - b3 0.047X3 + b4 0.062X4 + b5 0.039X5 + b6 0.012X6 + b7 0.059X7 + b8 0.122X8 + b9 0.047X9 + b10 0.012X10 - b11 0.036X11 + b12 0.039X12 + b13 0.020X13 - b14 0.056X14 + b15 0.096X15 + b16 0.104X16 - b17 0.044X17 - b18 0.78X18.

The above table furnishes the details of Variables in Linear Regression Equation of Overall Service Quality on Actual Quality of Facilities and Amenities provided by HDFC Bank. Linear correlation coefficient R = 0.517 measures the degree of relationship between the actual values and predicted values of overall service quality (Y) because the overall service quality (Y) values are obtained as linear combination of 18 variables of actual facilities and amenities provided by the selected HDFC bank. They were Location of the Bank (X1), Parking Facility (X2), Information about working hours (X3), Information about service timings (X4), Availability of personal assistance/ guidance (X5), Display of identification boards at counters (X6), May I Help You Counter (X7), Proper Lighting (X8), Information about available services and products (X9), Electronic token number display and audio announcement system (X10), Waiting Room/Place (X11), ATM facility at the branch (X12), Attractive Flooring (X13), Drinking Water (X14), A/C Facility (X15), Dust

Table 5.68: Variables in Linear Regression Equation of Overall Service Quality on Actual Quality of Facilities and Amenities provided by HDFC Bank

Sl. No.	*Variables*	*Unstandardized Coefficients*		*Standardized Coefficients*	*t-Value*	*Sig.*	*Correlations*		
		B	*Std. Error*	*Beta*			*Zero-order*	*Partial*	*Part*
	Service Quality (Constant)	2.105	.577		3.645	.000			
1	Location of the Bank	.005	.044	.009	.113	.910	.042	.009	.008
2	Parking Facility	.115	.040	.244	2.889	.004	.310	.235	.207
3	Information about working hours	-.047	.081	-.057	-.574	.567	.109	-.048	-.041
4	Information about service timings	.062	.079	.085	.779	.437	.088	.065	.056
5	Availability of personal assistance/guidance	.039	.054	.067	.719	.473	.216	.060	.051
6	Display of identification boards at counters	.012	.058	.018	.205	.838	.172	.017	.015
7	May I Help You Counter	.059	.043	.130	1.357	.177	.158	.113	.097
8	Proper Lighting	.122	.097	.107	1.263	.209	.148	.105	.090
9	Information about available services and products	.047	.053	.077	.893	.373	.201	.075	.064
10	Electronic token number display and audio announcement system	.201	.092	.176	2.197	.030	.166	.181	.157
11	Waiting Room/Place	-.036	.041	-.079	-.866	.388	.077	-.072	-.062
12	ATM facility at the branch	.039	.053	.065	.733	.465	.005	.061	.052
13	Attractive Flooring	.020	.108	.019	.190	.850	.116	.016	.014
14	Drinking Water	-.056	.040	-.140	-1.406	.162	.070	-.117	-.101
15	A/C Facility	.096	.057	.147	1.694	.092	.245	.140	.121
16	Dust Bins	.104	.041	.238	2.521	.013	.188	.206	.180
17	Toilets Facility	-.044	.044	-.087	-.991	.323	-.032	-.083	-.071
18	Complaint and Suggestion Box	-.078	.033	-.208	-2.394	.018	-.099	-.196	-.171

Bins (X16), Toilets Facility (X17), Complaint and Suggestion Box (X18). The coefficient value 0.517 indicates that the relationship between overall service quality and the actual quality of facilities and amenities is positive.

1. **b1 = 0.005** represents the partial effect of 'Location of the Bank' on overall service quality holding other independent variables constant. The estimated positive sign implies that such effect is positive while the absolute value implies that overall service quality has direct impact of 0.05 per cent.
2. **b2 = 0.115** indicates the partial effect of 'Parking Facility' on overall service quality holding other independent variables constant. The estimated positive sign implies that such effect is positive while the absolute value implies that overall service quality has direct impact of 11.50 per cent.
3. **b3 = -0.047** represents the partial effect of 'Information about Working Hours' on overall service quality holding other independent variables constant. The estimated negative sign implies that such effect is negative while the absolute value implies that overall service quality has the inverse relation of 4.70 per cent.
4. **b4 = 0.062** represents the partial effect of 'Information about Service Timings' on overall service quality holding other independent variables constant. The estimated positive sign implies that such effect is positive while the absolute value implies that overall service quality has direct relation of 6.20 per cent.
5. **b5= 0.039** represents the partial effect of 'Availability of Personal Assistance/Guidance' on overall service quality holding other independent variables constant. The estimated positive sign implies that such effect is positive while the absolute value implies that overall service quality has the direct impact of 3.90 per cent.
6. **b6 = 0.012** represents the partial effect of display of 'Identification Boards at Counters' on overall service quality holding other independent variables constant. The estimated positive sign implies that such effect is positive while the absolute value implies that overall service quality has the direct relation of 1.20 per cent.
7. **b7 = 0.059** represents the partial effect of 'May I Help You' on overall service quality holding other independent variables constant. The estimated positive sign implies that such effect is positive while the absolute value implies that overall service quality has the direct relation of 5.90 per cent.
8. **b8 = 0.122** represents the partial effect of 'Proper Lighting' on overall service quality holding other independent variables constant.

The estimated positive sign implies that such effect is positive while the absolute value implies that overall service quality has the positive relation of 12.20 per cent.

9. **b9 = 0.047** represents the partial effect of 'Information about Available Services and Products' on overall service quality holding other independent variables constant. The estimated positive sign implies that such effect is positive while the absolute value implies that overall service quality would have the direct impact of 4.70 per cent.
10. **b10 = 0.201** represents the partial effect of 'Electronic Token Number Display and Audio Announcement System' on overall service quality holding other independent variables constant. The estimated positive sign implies that such effect is positive while the absolute value implies that overall service quality has direct relation of 20.10 per cent.
11. **b11 = -0.036** represents the partial effect of 'Waiting Room/Place' on overall service quality holding other independent variables constant. The estimated negative sign implies that such effect is negative while the absolute value implies that overall service quality would decrease by 3.60 per cent.
12. **b12 = 0.039** represents the partial effect of 'ATM Facility at Bank' on overall service quality holding other independent variables constant. The estimated positive sign implies that such effect is positive while the absolute value implies that overall service quality has the direct relation of 3.90 per cent.
13. **b13 = 0.020** represents the partial effect of 'Attractive Flooring' on overall service quality holding other independent variables constant. The estimated positive sign implies that such effect is positive while the absolute value implies that overall service quality has the direct relation of 2.00 per cent.
14. **b14 = -0.056** represents the partial effect of 'Drinking Water Facility' on overall service quality holding other independent variables constant. The estimated negative sign implies that such effect is negative while the absolute value implies that overall service quality would decrease by 5.60 per cent.
15. **b15 = 0.096** represents the partial effect of 'A/C Facility' on overall service quality holding other independent variables constant. The estimated positive sign implies that such effect is positive while the absolute value implies that overall service quality has the direct impact of 9.60 per cent.

16. **b16 = 0.104** represents the partial effect of 'Dustbins' on overall service quality holding other independent variables constant. The estimated positive sign implies that such effect is positive while the absolute value implies that overall service quality would increase by 10.40 per cent.
17. **b17 = -0.044** represents the partial effect of 'Toilets Facility' on overall service quality holding other independent variables constant. The estimated negative sign implies that such effect is negative while the absolute value implies that overall service quality has the inverse relation of 4.40 per cent.
18. **b18 = -0.078** represents the partial effect of 'Complaint and Suggestion Box' on overall service quality holding other independent variables constant. The estimated negative sign implies that such effect is negative while the absolute value implies that overall service quality would decrease by 7.80 per cent.

Since the significant value is less than 0.05 in b2 'Parking Facility' (0.004), b10 'Electronic Token Number Display and Announcement System' (0.030), b16 'Dust Bins' (0.013), and b18 'complaint and suggestion box' (0.018). The Linear regression analysis reveals that a slight increase in the above said facilities and amenities may lead to influence the overall service quality.

Hypothesis

$H_{0:}$-There is no significant relation between service quality and actual facilities and amenities provided by HDFC Bank.

$H_{A:}$-There is significant relation between service quality and actual facilities and amenities provided by HDFC Bank.

ANOVA[a]

Model		*Sum of Squares*	*df*	*Mean Square*	*F*	*Sig.*
1	Regression	14.074	18	.782	2.893	1.61[b]
	Residual	38.642	143	.270		
	Total	52.716	161			
a. Dependent Variable: Overall Satisfaction						
b Predictors: (Constant), Actual 1, Actual 2, Actual 3, Actual 4, Actual 5, Actual 6, Actual 7, Actual 8, Actual 9, Actual 10, Actual 11, Actual 12, Actual 13, Actual 14, Actual 15, Actual 16, Actual 17, Actual 18						

The above ANOVA table shows that the calculated value of *F* is 2.893 which is greater than the significance value at 0.05 level of significance is 1.61 with degree of freedom being $v_1 = 18$ and $v_2 = 161$. This analysis rejects the null hypothesis of no significant relation between customers' satisfactions towards service quality and actual facilities and amenities provided by HDFC bank. It is concluded that the difference in customers' satisfaction due to actual facilities and amenities provided by HDFC bank is significant and is just not a matter of chance.

5.18 Service Timings of HDFC

5.18.1 Cash Receipt

Table 5.69: Service Timing for Cash Receipt in HDFC Bank

	Mid Values	*Frequency*	*Per cent*	
0 - 15 Min.	7.5	143	88.30	**Standard Time 10-20 Min.**
15 - 30 Min.	22.5	15	9.30	
30 - 45 Min.	37.5	0	0.00	
Don't Know	-	4	2.50	
Total		**162**	**100.00**	
Mean Time (Min.)		**8.92**		**15**

Source: Primary Data.

From the above table it is inferred that, out of 162 HDFC customers, the highest numbers of customers, 143 customers informed that the cash receipt of the transaction would be completed within the 15 minutes. Following these 15 customers informed that time taking for cash receipt transaction in between 15-30 minutes by HDFC bank officials. Only one customer did not know the when the service timing of the cash receipt. The bank is providing this service (8.92 minutes) within the specified average time (15 minutes).

5.18.2 Cash Payment

Table 5.70: Service Timing for Cash Payment in HDFC Bank

	Mid Values	*Frequency*	*Per cent*	
0 - 15 Min.	7.5	116	71.60	**Standard Time 10-20 Min.**
15 - 30 Min.	22.5	22	13.60	
30 - 45 Min.	37.5	0	0.00	
Don't Know		24	14.80	
Total		**162**	**100.00**	
Mean Time (Min.)		**9.89**		**15**

Source: Primary Data.

As per the above table, the cash payment service in HDFC bank would be completed within the 15 minutes according to 116 customers of the bank.

The service timing for the cash payment is in between 15-30 minutes according to 22 customers. An average of 9.89 minutes is taking by TGB to pay the cash to customers against standard average time 15 minutes.

5.18.3 Issue of Draft

Table 5.71: Service Timing for Issue of Draft in HDFC Bank

Minutes	*Mid Values*	*Frequency*	*Per cent*	
0 - 15 Min.	7.5	29	17.90	
15 - 30 Min.	22.5	43	26.54	**Standard**
30 - 45 Min.	37.5	1	0.62	**Time 15-25**
Don't Know		89	54.94	**Min.**
Total		**162**	**100.00**	
Mean Time (Min.)		**16.75**		**20**

Source: Primary Data.

The details in respect of opinions of customers against service timing of issue of demand draft, 17.90 per cent of the total HDFC customers representing 29 in number stated that the service timing for the issue of DD was in between 0–15 minutes. 43 customers 26.54 per cent informed that the DD was issued by the banks within 15-30 minutes. HDFC bank is taking average time of 16.75 minutes as against standard average time 20 minutes.

5.18.4 Collection of Out Station Cheques

Table 5.72: Service Timing for Collection of Outstation Cheques in HDFC Bank

Days	*Mid Values*	*Frequency*	*Per cent*	
1 - 3 Days	2	29	17.90	
4 - 8 Days	6	35	21.60	**Standard**
8 - 12 Days	10	18	11.11	**Time 10-14**
Don't Know		80	49.38	**Days**
Total		**162**	**100.00**	
Mean Time (Days)		**5.46**		**12**

Source: Primary Data.

The data relating to the opinions of HDFC customers on collection of outstation cheques is presented in the above table. The highest number of customers does not have awareness of this service timing. 18 customers in number representing 11.11 per cent of the total customers informed that the outstation cheques were collected and credited by the banker in between

8–12 days and 21.60 per cent of the total representing 35 in number stated that the service time for this service is 4-8 days. On an average bank is collecting the outstation cheques and depositing them in customers' account in 5.46 days, against standard average time 12 days.

5.18.5 Updating Pass Book

Table 5.73: Service Timing for Updating Pass Book in HDFC Bank

	Mid Values	*Frequency*	*Per cent*	
0 - 15 Min.	7.5	16	9.88	
15 - 30 Min.	22.5	12	7.41	**Standard**
30 - 45 Min.	37.5	4	2.47	**Time 5-15**
Don' t Know		130	80.25	**Min**
Total		**162**	**100.00**	
Mean Time (Min.)		**16.88**	**16.88**	**10**

Source: Primary Data.

The data in the above table presents the details of service timing for 'updating the pass book' in HDFC. The highest number of customers indicating 80.25 per cent of the total customers does not know about the service timings. 16 customers stated that the banker update the pass book information within the 15 minutes. Twelve customers i.e. 7.41 per cent of the total customers stated that this service was done by the banker in between 15–30 minutes. Four customers stated that the time taken the banker to finish this service in between 30–45 minutes. To update the pass book HDFC is taking much time than the standard average time.

5.18.6 Issue of Cheque Book

Table 5.74: Service Timing for Issue of Cheque Book in HDFC Bank

	Mid Values	*Frequency*	*per cent*	
0 - 7 Days	3.50	22	13.60	
8 - 15 Days	11.50	61	37.70	**Standard**
16 - 21 Days	18.50	15	9.30	**Time 7-15**
Don't Know		64	39.50	**Days.**
Total		**162**	**100.00**	
Mean Time (Days)		**10.77**		**11**

Source: Primary Data.

The details of opinions of customers about the issue of cheque book were presented in the above table. Majority of the customers i.e. 39.50 per cent of the total 162 customers do not have the knowledge of the cheque book service. 15 customers indicating 9.30 per cent of the total informed that the banks are taking 16-21 days to issue the cheque book. The remaining customers stated that banks issue the cheque book within the standard time i.e. 15 days. HDFC bank is taking average time to issue the cheque book to customers.

5.19 Service Encounters

5.19.1 Service Encounters in HDFC Bank

The Table 5.75 furnishes the details about ranks based on service encounters in selected HDFC bank. It is found that the **"bank staffs are friendly with customers"** ranked first by the customers/respondents of this bank. They ranked **"bank staffs speak pleasantly with smiling face"**, **"bank staffs are informative"** and **"required suggestion, help and co-operation are provided by the bank employees"** and **"It is easy to approach or meet**

Table 5.75: Ranks Based on Service Encounters in HDFC Bank (Relationship between Bank Employees and Customers)

Sl. No.	*Statements*	*HDFC*		
		Mean	*Std. Deviation*	*Rank*
1	Front Office Employee (Receptionist) notices, welcomes and greets the customers.	4.01	1.234	12
2	Receptionist asks customer May I Help You sir.	4.01	1.249	13
3	Receptionist asks customer to be seated	4.17	1.145	11
4	Required suggestion, help and cooperation are provided by the bank employees.	4.71	0.482	4
5	Bank staff speaks pleasantly with smiling face.	4.75	0.515	2
6	Bank staffs are friendly with customers.	4.78	0.495	1
7	Bank staffs are informative.	4.73	0.628	3
8	It is easy to approach or meet Bank Manager or other superiors in the Bank.	4.65	0.718	5
9	Bank staff responds properly to the phone calls.	4.4	0.829	10
10	Bank staff shows reasonable interest in me as a customer.	4.64	0.564	6
11	Bank staff thanks me for transacting with them	3.85	1.172	14
12	Bank staff handles any problems/interruptions efficiently.	4.43	0.884	9
13	I enjoy myself dealing with the employees of this bank.	4.5	0.741	8
14	I wish to continue my relationship with this bank for long.	4.57	0.629	7

Source: Primary Data.

bank manager or other superiors in the bank" as second, third, fourth and fifth ranks respectively. Sixth, seventh, eighth and ninth ranks given to, **"bank staffs show reasonable interest in me as a customer", "I wish to continue my relationship with this bank for long", "I enjoy myself dealing with the staffs of this bank"** and **"bank staffs handle any problem or interruptions efficiently"** respectively.

Statements **"bank staffs respond properly to the phone calls", "receptionist asks customer to be seated"** and **"front office employee notices, welcomes and greets the customers"** ranked as tenth, eleventh and twelfth respectively. Thirteenth rank was posted to **"receptionist asks customer May I Help you sir"** and statement **"bank staffs thanks me for transacting with them"** was ranked fourteen.

The variables i.e. statements relating to the service encounter of HDFC bank under study were measured with the help of statistical tool 'Factor Analysis'. The statements were arranged as per their loading according to factor analysis. The results of the factor analysis are presented in the following table.

Table–5.76 Factor Analysis of Service Encounters in HDFC Banks (Relationship between Bank Employees and Customers)

Sl. No.	*Statements*	*Factor Loading*	*Factors*	*Eigen Values*		*Individual Variance*	*Cumulative Variance*
1	Receptionist asks customer May I Help You sir.	0.892		1.888			
2	Front Office Employee (Receptionist) notices, welcomes and greets the customers.	0.881		6.218			
3	Receptionist asks customer to be seated.	0.880		1.194			
4	I wish to continue my relationship with this bank for long.	0.831	Significant	0.070	10.796	77.56	
5	Bank Staffs are informative.	0.814		0.512			
6	I enjoy myself dealing with the employees of this bank.	0.789		0.109			
7	It is easy to approach or meet Bank Manager or other superiors in the Bank.	0.7768		0.470			98.664
8	Bank Staff responds properly to the phone calls.	0.713		0.398			
9	Bank staff handles any problems/interruptions efficiently.	0.683		0.155			
10	Required suggestion, help and cooperation are provided by the bank employees.	0.644		1.013			
11	Bank staffs speak pleasantly with smiling face.	0.621	Low Significant	0.966	2.955	21.104	
12	Bank Staff shows reasonable interest in me as a customer.	0.616		0.287			
13	Bank staffs are friendly with customers.	0.568		0.534			
14	Bank Staff thanks me for transacting with them.	Not Significant					

5.19.2 Factor Analysis of Service Encounters in HDFC Banks

The application of the factor analysis reduced thirteen variables of service encounter into three predominant factors based on their factor loading. Factor loadings to the variables are considered on the basis of the 'rotated component matrix'. The first factor includes of eight variables like 'front office employee asks the customer May I Help You sir', 'receptionist notices, welcomes and greets the customer', 'receptionist asks the customer to be seated', 'I wish to continue my relationship with this bank for long', 'bank employees are informative', 'I enjoy myself dealing with the staffs of this bank', 'it is easy to approach or meet bank manager or other superiors in the bank' and Bank staffs responds properly to the phone calls have the factor loading between 0.7 – 0.8. These are treated as **significant** factors.

'Bank staffs handles any problems/interruptions efficiently', 'Required suggestion, help and cooperation are provided by the bank staffs', 'Bank staffs speak pleasantly with smiling face', 'Bank staffs shows reasonable interest in me as a customer' and 'Bank staffs are friendly with customers' are having the factor loading of less than 0.7, and fall under the category of **low significant.**

The remaining one variable i.e. 'bank employees thanks me for transacting with them' is **not significant** in factor analysis because component matrix not given the any loading to this variable. That means this variable is not correlating with other variables in the factor analysis.

Hypothesis

H_0:-Service Encounter variables do not vary in importance significantly in respect of HDFC bank.

H_A:-Service Encounter variables do vary in importance significantly in respect of HDFC bank.

For the present data the value of KMO Measure of sampling adequacy is 0.814, which falls into the range of being great: so it is said that, it should be confident that factor analysis is appropriate for this data, and the Bartlett's test also highly significant (p = 0.000), and therefore factor analysis is appropriate.

Table 5.77: KMO and Bartlett's Test

Kaiser-Meyer-Olkin Measure of Sampling Adequacy.		.814
Bartlett's Test of Sphericity	Approx. Chi-Square	1558.849
	Df	91
	Sig.	0.000

With this analysis it said that the null hypothesis is rejected and proved that there is some relationship among the service encounter variables of HDFC Bank.

5.20 Evaluation of Service Quality in HDFC Bank

Table 5.78: Assessment of Service Quality in HDFC

Sl. No.	*Expected Quality (E)*	*Mean*	*Perceived Quality (P)*	*Mean*	*Gap (E-P)*	*Per cent Gap*
		A. TANGIBLES				
1	The Bank must possess the sophisticated and good looking infrastructure.	4.92	My Bank has the sophisticated and good looking infrastructure.	4.03	0.90	18.00
2	Physical facilities at banks should be visual and attractive.	4.90	Physical facilities at my banks are visual and attractive.	4.03	0.87	17.40
3	Bank employees have to be in neat dress and appear dignified.	4.90	My Bank employees are in neat dress and appearing dignified.	4.29	0.62	13.40
4	Materials (statements or passbook) with bank should be visual and excellent.	4.88	Materials (statements or passbook) with my bank are visual and excellent.	4.03	0.84	16.80
	Total	**19.60**	**Total**	**16.38**	3.22	
	Average (19.60/4)	**4.90**		**4.09**	0.81	16.20
		B. RELIABILITY				
5	If the bank promises something, it will do.	4.87	If my bank promises something, it will certainly do.	3.91	0.96	19.20
6	If customers have problems, the bank has to show sincere interest in solving them.	4.88	If customers have problems, my bank will show sincere interest in solving it.	4.02	0.86	17.20
7	The bank ought to perform the services at right time.	4.90	My bank performs the services at right time. As per time mentioned.	4.00	0.91	18.20
8	The bank should provide service at the time it promises to do so.	4.88	My Bank provides service at the time it promises to do so.	3.95	0.93	18.60
9	The Bank should keep accurate/error-free records.	4.88	My Bank keeps accurate/error-free	4.25	0.63	12.60
	Total	**24.42**	**Total**	**20.13**	**4.29**	
	Average (24.42/5)	**4.88**		**4.03**	**0.86**	**17.20**

(*Contd...*)

C. RESPONSIVENESS						
10	Employees of the bank ought to inform customers exactly when service will be performed.	4.87	Employees of my bank inform customers exactly when service will be performed.	3.61	1.26	25.20
11	The Bank employees ought to give excellent service to its customers	4.87	My Bank employees give excellent service to its customers	4.03	0.84	16.80
12	The Bank employees must be willing to help the customers.	4.87	My Bank employees are always willing to help customers.	4.02	0.85	17.00
13	The Bank employees should be always ready to respond to customers' requests.	4.87	Bank employees always ready to respond to customers' requests.	4.04	0.83	16.60
	Total	**19.60**	**Total**	**15.70**	**3.90**	
	Average (19.60/4)	**4.90**		**3.92**	**0.98**	17.60
D. ASSURANCE						
14	The Bank employees should always try to infuse confidence in the customers.	4.87	My Bank employees always try to instill confidence in customers.	4.02	0.85	17.00
15	Customers (you) have to feel safe in transactions with the Bank's employees.	4.87	Customers (me) always feel safe in transactions with my bank's employees.	4.15	0.72	14.40
16	The Bank employees always ought to be courteous and polite with customers.	4.87	My Bank employees always courteous and polite with customers.	4.13	0.74	14.80
17	The Bank must possess employees have complete knowledge to answer queries of customers.	4.87	My Bank employees have complete knowledge to answer queries of customers.	4.09	0.78	15.60
	Total	**19.60**	**Total**	**16.40**	**3.20**	
	Average (19.60/4)	**4.90**		**4.10**	**0.80**	16.00
E. EMPATHY						
18	The Bank has to give individual attention to customers.	4.87	My Bank gives individual attention to customers.	3.72	1.15	23.00
19	The Bank operating hours must be convenient to all customers.	4.87	My Bank operating hours is convenient to all the customers.	4.35	0.52	10.40
20	Bank employees ought to understand the specific needs of their customers.	4.87	Bank employees understand the specific needs of customers.	3.91	0.96	19.20
	Total	**14.70**	**Total**	**11.99**	**2.71**	
	Average (14.70)	**4.90**		**4.00**	**0.90**	18.00

5.20.2 Paired Sample Test

Table 5.80: Paired Samples Test

		Paired Differences					*t*	*df*	*Sig. (2-tailed)*
		Mean	*Std. Deviation*	*Std. Error Mean*	*95 per cent Confidence Interval of the Difference*				
					Lower	*Upper*			
TANGIBLES									
Pair 1	EQ1 - PQ1	.500	.662	.052	.397	.603	9.617	161	.000
Pair 2	EQ2 - PQ2	.568	.609	.048	.473	.662	11.865	161	.000
Pair 3	EQ3 - PQ3	.309	.514	.040	.229	.388	7.640	161	.000
Pair 4	EQ4 - PQ4	.321	.693	.054	.213	.429	5.896	161	.000
RELIABILITY									
Pair 1	EQ5 - PQ5	.586	.889	.070	.448	.724	8.394	161	.000
Pair 2	EQ6 - PQ6	.451	.740	.058	.336	.565	7.753	161	.000
Pair 3	EQ7 - PQ7	.352	.645	.051	.252	.452	6.945	161	.000
Pair 4	EQ8 - PQ8	.395	.653	.051	.294	.496	7.697	161	.000
Pair 5	EQ9 - PQ9	.296	.649	.051	.196	.397	5.812	161	.000
RESPONSIVENESS									
Pair 1	EQ10 - PQ10	.512	.790	.062	.390	.635	8.255	161	.000
Pair 2	EQ11 - PQ11	.216	.507	.040	.137	.295	5.420	161	.000
Pair 3	EQ12 - PQ12	.222	.535	.042	.139	.305	5.292	161	.000
Pair 4	EQ13 - PQ13	.210	.551	.043	.124	.295	4.849	161	.000
ASSURNACE									
Pair 1	EQ14 - PQ14	.259	.505	.040	.181	.338	6.530	161	.000
Pair 2	EQ15 - PQ15	.253	.477	.037	.179	.327	6.754	161	.000
Pair 3	EQ16 - PQ16	.191	.505	.040	.113	.270	4.822	161	.000
Pair 4	EQ17 - PQ17	.333	.610	.048	.239	.428	6.950	161	.000
EMPATHY									
Pair 1	EQ18 - PQ18	.531	.973	.076	.380	.682	6.946	161	.000
Pair 2	EQ19 - PQ19	.426	.787	.062	.304	.548	6.892	161	.000
Pair 3	EQ20 - PQ20	.605	.783	.062	.483	.726	9.833	161	.000

Hypothesis

H_0 =There is no significant difference between opinions of customers of HDFC Bank in respect of expected and perceived quality.

H_A =There is significant difference between opinions of customers of HDFC Bank in respect of expected and perceived quality.

At the a = 0.05 level of significance, there exists enough evidence to conclude that there is a difference between expected and perceived service quality variable and dimensions that are 'Tangibles", 'Reliability', Responsiveness', 'Assurance' and 'Empathy'. It is clearly establishes the significant difference between expected and perceived service quality dimensions of HDFC bank.

It is clear that there is difference in customers' opinions of HDFC in respect of the service quality. It requires the bank officials should more responsive and respond immediately to the queries and provide the needed information to the customers. Therefore it is needed proper attention of bank officials on adjusting the bank operating timings that is convenient to all type of customers particularly employees and make a focus on the needs of customers to reduce the service quality gap which lead to increase the satisfaction level of customers.

5.21 Interpretation of Overall Service Quality

5.21.1 Overall Service Quality of HDFC Bank

Table 5.81: Overall Service Quality of HDFC Bank

Particulars	*Frequency*	*Per cent*	*Mean*	*SD*
Very Poor	0	0	4.40	0.572
Poor	0	0		
Average	7	4.3		
Good	84	51.9		
Very Good	71	43.8		
Total	**162**	**100.0**		

Source: Primary Data.

The above tables reveals that the opinions of the customers on overall service quality of HDFC bank in Karimnagar district. The opinions are rated with the help of '5 point Liker Scale' ranging 1–5 points indicating 'Very Poor–Very Good'. Repondents of HDFC bank rated the Overall Service Quality between 4–5 implies 'Good to Very Good' for the services provided by the bank. The highest number of respondents representing 51.90 per cent of the total had expressed that the service quality of the bank as 'good' and following 43.80 per cent indicating 71 in number rated as 'very good'. Customer opined overall service quality as 'average' by 7 in number representing 4.30 per cent. No customer rated the service quality as 'poor and very poor'.

Paired Samples Test

		Paired Differences					*t*	*df*	*Sig. (2-tailed)*
		Mean	*Std. Deviation*	*Std. Error Mean*	*95 per cent Confidence Interval of the Difference*				
					Lower	*Upper*			
Pair 1	Area of Bank - Overall SQ	-.667	1.858	.146	-.955	-.378	-4.566	161	.000
Pair 2	gender - Overall SQ	- 3.377	.590	.046	-3.468	-3.285	-72.850	161	.000
Pair 3	Age - Overall SQ	- 1.389	1.035	.081	-1.549	-1.228	-17.078	161	.000
Pair 4	Qualification - Overall SQ	- 1.222	1.576	.124	-1.467	-.978	-9.869	161	.000
Pair 5	Occupation - Overall SQ	- 2.284	1.006	.079	-2.440	-2.128	-28.897	161	.000
Pair 6	Annual Income - Overall SQ	- 1.494	.858	.067	-1.627	-1.361	-22.163	161	.000
Pair 7	Marital Status - Overall SQ	- 3.309	.653	.051	-3.410	-3.207	-64.530	161	.000

It is tested to prove the relation between service quality (dependent variable) and demographical details of respondents (independent variables) of HDFC bank through paired sample t-test.

H_0 – There is no significant relation between service quality and bank type, area of the bank, age, gender, qualification, occupation, annual income and marital status of the respondents of HDFC bank.

H_1– There is significant relation between service quality and bank type, area of the bank, age, gender, qualification, occupation, annual income and marital status of the respondents of HDFC bank.

5.21.2 Service Quality Meeting Needs of the Customers

Table 5.82: Service Quality Meeting Needs of the Customers

Particulars	*Frequency*	*Per cent*	*Mean*	*SD*
Strongly Disagree	0	0	4.27	0.714
Disagree	6	3.70		
Neutral	7	4.30		
Agree	86	53.10		
Strongly Agree	63	38.90		
Total	**162**	**100.0**		

Source: Primary Data.

The significance value at 0.05 is zero, hence it is rejected the null hypothesis and concluded that the difference in opinions of customers about service quality due to bank type, area of the bank, age, gender, educational qualification, occupation, annual income and marital status of respondents is significant and is just not a matter of chance.

Every person opens an account in the bank to meet his personal or business financial needs. The above table furnishes the details of the opinions of the respondents that whether the services provided by the bank were meeting their needs. The opinions are rated with the help of '5 point Liker Scale' ranging 1 – 5 points indiciating 'Strongly Disagree – Strongly Agree'. Respondents of HDFC bank were rated the Service Quality Meeting their Financial Needs in between 4 – 5 implies 'agree to strongly agree' for the services provided by the bank. The highest number of respondents representing 53.10 per cent of the total had expressed that the service quality of the bank as 'agree' and following 38.90 per cent indicating 63 in number rated as 'strongly agree' and meeting their needs. Seven customers were maintained neutral position and six customers were disagree that the overall service quality meeting their needs. No customer expressed his opinion as 'strongly disagree'.

5.21.3 Overall Satisfaction against the Service Quality

After studying the responses of respondents of HDFC bank against various aspects of service quality, an attempt is made to know their satisfaction level and furnished in the above table. The opinions are rated with the help of 5 point Liker Scale' ranging 1–5 points indiciating 'Very Dissatisfied–Very Satisfied'.

Table 5.83: Overall Satisfaction Against the Service Quality

Particulars	*Frequency*	*Per cent*	*Mean*	*SD*
Strongly Dissatisfied	0	0	4.51	0.514
Dissatisfied	0	0		
Neutral	1	.6		
Satisfied	77	47.5		
Very Satisfied	84	51.9		
Total	**162**	**100.0**		

Source: Primary Data.

The average of satisfaction level of repondents of HDFC Bank lied between 4–5 implies 'satisfied to very satisfied' for the services provided by the bank. The highest number of respondents representing 51.90 per cent of the total were very satisfied and following 47.50 per cent indicating 77 in number were satisfied. Only one customer who was neutral either satisfied or dissatisfied in respect of satisfaction level. No customer was dissatisfied with the services of HDFC bank.

Paired Samples Test

		Paired Differences					*t*	*df*	*Sig. (2-tailed)*
		Mean	*Std. Devi-ation*	*Std. Error Mean*	*95 per cent Confidence Interval of the Difference*				
					Lower	*Upper*			
Pair 1	Area of Bank - Overall Satisfaction	-.784	1.733	.136	-1.053	-.515	-5.758	161	.000
Pair 2	gender - Overall Satisfaction	-3.494	.549	.043	-3.579	-3.409	-81.027	161	.000
Pair 3	Age - Overall Satisfaction	-1.506	1.011	.079	-1.663	-1.349	-18.966	161	.000
Pair 4	Qualification - Overall Satisfaction	-1.340	1.631	.128	-1.593	-1.086	-10.453	161	.000
Pair 5	Occupation - Overall Satisfaction	-2.401	.929	.073	-2.545	-2.257	-32.902	161	.000
Pair 6	Annual Income - Overall Satisfaction	-1.611	.858	.067	-1.744	-1.478	-23.902	161	.000
Pair 7	Marital Status - Overall Satisfaction	-3.426	.588	.046	-3.517	-3.335	-74.194	161	.000

It is also tested to prove the relation between customers' overall satisfaction towards service quality (dependent variable) and demographical details of respondents (independent variables) of HDFC bank through paired sample t-test.

H_0 – Customers' satisfaction does not vary in respect of bank type, area of the bank, age, gender, qualification, occupation, annual income and marital status of the respondents HDFC bank.

H_1 – Customers' satisfaction varies in respect of bank type, area of the bank, age, gender, qualification, occupation, annual income and marital status of the respondents HDFC bank.

The significance value at 0.05 is zero, hence it is rejected the null hypothesis and concluded that the difference in customers' satisfaction towards service quality due to bank type, area of the bank, age, gender, educational qualification, occupation, annual income and marital status of respondents is significant and is just not a matter of chance.

5.21.4 Loyalty towards Bank

Table 5.84: Loyalty Towards Bank

Particulars	*Frequency*	*Per cent*	*Mean*	*SD*
Very Less Probability				
Low Probability	3	1.90		
Neutral	7	4.30	4.45	0.842

Probability	50	30.90		
Very High Probability	102	63.00		
Total	**162**	**100.00**		

Source: Primary Data.

Customers were tested to know whether they remain loyal towards the bank and continue with bank in future also. It is fact that satisfied customers definitely loyal towards the banks and also continue their fianancial transactions with the bank in the future. For the same opinions of respondents were collected and presented in the above table. The opinions were rated with the help of '5 point Liker Scale' ranging 1–5 points indicating 'Very Low Probability–Very High Probability'. Repondents of HDFC bank expressed their opinion averagely in between 4–5 implies 'Probability to Very High Probability' to continue with the bank in the future. The highest number of respondents representing strongly agreed and expressed positive opinion that definitely loyal to the bank and continue in the future with the bank. Again, with this, it is proved that that the highest number of customers were very satisfied with services of the bank.

5.21.5 Recommendations to Relatives and Friends

Table 5.85: Recommendations

Particulars	*Frequency*	*Per cent*	*Mean*	*SD*
Very Low Probability	2	1.2		
Low Probability	6	3.7		
Neutral	7	4.3	4.45	0.842
Probability	49	30.2		
Very High Probability	98	60.5		
Total	**162**	**100.00**		

Source: Primary Data.

Again it is tried to know whether satisfied customer recommend his friends, relatives to open an account in the bank and utilise the services. Opinions of the same were collected and presented in the above table. The opinions were rated with the help of '5 point Liker Scale' ranging 1–5 points indicating 'Very Less Probability–Very High Probability'. Repondents of HDFC bank expressed their opinion averagely in between 4–5 implies 'Probability to Very High Probability' to suggest others to open account in the bank. The highest number of respondents representing 147 in number agreed that they definitely suggest their friends and relatives to use the services of the bank. This indicates that the highest number of customers were very satisfied with services of the bank. Very less per cent of the total respondents i.e. 1.20 per cent indicate

and vice versa. That means lower the gap score higher the quality level and higher the gap score lower the quality level.

Variable 1: Location of any business firm is an important factor that attracts customers and improves the business of the firm. This is not an exception to banking institutions. The overall average gap score of all selected banks in the study area is 0.19. The gap score of SBH is negative against the average gap score indicates that the bank was better located and very convenient to all types of customers. The similar opinion expressed by the customers of TGB also. The gap score of HDFC bank shows that the bank was poorly located.

- HDFC bank officials should to focus on the issue of location while they selected the place to establish bank branches.

Variable 2: 'Parking facility' is another important variable which influences the customers' satisfaction. TGB is providing better parking facility as compared to SBH and HDFC bank. The gap score of TGB Bank is 1.61 against the overall average gap score 1.84.

- The officials of SBH and HDFC banks have to take needed steps to provide suitable parking place nearby bank branches to enhance the customers' satisfaction level.

Variable 3 and 4: 'Information about working hours and information about service timings' are other important factors required to customers, i.e. timings of bank. In this regard HDFC has the lowest gap score followed by TGB which means that both the banks keep their customers well informed about these variables.

- SBH needs to improve the visibility of the working hours by adopting good display systems.

Variable 5: Another important variable that impacts the satisfaction level of customers is 'personal assisting/guidance to customers'. In this regard TGB and HDFC banks are providing better services to their customers by having gap score of 0.78 and 0.85 respectively against overall average gap score of 1.12 compared to SBH bank.

- Different types of customers visit the bank for their financial needs in general but in particular, illiterates like farmers, self-help groups (SHGs) and artisans also visit the bank particularly in rural areas to receive government benefits. They require suitable guidelines in getting the bank and government benefits. Authorities should appoint an employee to assist them. This will reduce the time and work of other employees in the bank. If not, they give trouble and disturb the employees which reduces the speed and quality of work.

Variable 6: Display of identification boards at counters help customers to approach directly to concerned employee for the purpose they visit the bank. This facility is very poor at SBH and TGB and god at HDFC bank. The gap score of these banks are 1.73, 2.15 and 0.67 respectively against 1.61 average gap score.

- Customers may confuse in identifying the right person to approach to avail bank service, if identification boards are not attached before the concerned employee. It is essential to SBH and TGB to focus in fixing the identification boards before the concerned employee.

Variable 7: 'May I Help You Counter' is the most important and compulsory service in modern corporate world. It is not exception to the rural areas. This service helps the customer in finding out the information about the services and products that are offering by the bank. This service is very good at HDFC bank showing gap score of 1.25 against 2.83 average gaps and very poor at SBH (gap score 3.43) and TGB (gap score 3.33) banks.

- The proper action is required by public sector banks i.e. SBH and TGB to set up the 'May I Help You Counter' in branches to bring the corporate culture in rural areas.

Variable 8: 'Proper Lighting' in the office improves the work efficiency, increases employee performance, and enables to utilise the available resources effectively. This facility is very good at HDFC bank by having gap score of 0.11 against average gap score of 0.30.

- Public sector banks (SBH and TGB) have to concentrate to improve the lighting facility in the banks to get the benefits of proper lighting which leads to enhance to cordial relationship among employees and in between employees and customers also.

Variable 9: 'Display of information about available services and products' in the banks gives the awareness to customers that type of services offer by the bank. With this information they approach the bank to avail the required service. In displaying this information HDFC (1.15) and TGB (1.32) banks stood in better position by having less than average gap score 1.49 against SBH bank (1.88).

- SBH bank is required to take the measures to display the information about services and products those are available in the bank which visible to all customers.

Variable 10: SBH bank (gap score of 2.11 against average gap score 2.99) stood better in providing the facility of 'electronic token number display and audio announcement system' against other bank under study.

- Electronic token number display and audio announcement system reduces the burden of bank clerk in withdrawal counter and long 'Q' before the counter and increase safely. Customers may feel relax in getting cash from the counter.

Variable 11: In busy days and busy hours customers visit the bank for their needs in large number. Sufficient place is required for waiting. In this regard public sector banks TGB (gap score of 1.11) and SBH (gap score of 1.13), against average gap score of 1.49, are providing better facility against their counterpart HDFC.

- Time will be taken by the bank employees to perform the service. Customers are required to wait for some time to get the service from the employees. Customers feel convenient if sufficient place is available to wait for service. Authorities of HDFC bank have to provide sufficient space for waiting purpose.

Variable 12: An automated teller machine or automatic teller machine (ATM) is one of the advanced services of a bank. It enables the customers of a bank to perform financial transactions without the need of a human cashier, clerk or bank teller. This machine reduces the customers to the bank who visit for withdrawal of money, balance verification, payment of bills etc., and reduces the work of the bank employees. In providing this service HDFC and SBH bank stood better position, by having gap score of 0.32 and 1.29 respectively against the average gap score of 1.83, against TGB.

- Installation of ATMs enables by the bank customer to withdraw the cash anytime and anywhere and reduces number of customers visit to the bank. It is needed to TGB officials to consider installing the ATMs, to make convenience to the customers, which enhance the service and quality and customers' satisfaction.

Variable 13: Attractive flooring shows the cleanness the bank premises and work place. Clean work place increases the work efficiency of the employees and attracts the number of customers. HDFC and SBH banks are maintaining clean and attractive flooring by having gap score of 0.12 and 0.13 against the average gap score of 0.32, according to the opinions of the customers.

- It is very essential to TGB, highest gap score against average gap score, to maintain clean and attractive flooring which is also part of customers' satisfaction.

Variable 14: Clean drinking water needs to be provided for customers, at all times who thirsty and come to bank office for their transactions in hot times. This amenity rightly provided by SBH (gap score 0.76) and HDFC bank (gap score 1.00) than TGB.

- Action required by the authorities of TGB in providing adequate supply of clean drinking water. There must be one drinking water point which is easily accessible by all.

Variable 15: A bank shall ensure that, during working hours, the temperature in bank offices is appropriate for customers to remove a feeling of discomfort and rise a feeling of comfortable. Secondly for dynamic office work, a minimum temperature of 17.5° C, as far as is reasonably practicable to achieve work efficiency. Thirdly, already all bank branches installed computers for operations; it is mandate to install A.C. machines to protect the computers. Except HDFC bank, having very lowest gap score 0.25 against average gap score 2.32, other banks do not providing this facility.

- It is mandate to SBH and TGB to provide the A.C. facility in their bank branches.

Variable 16: Banks should ensure that the bank premises is kept in a clean condition, free from refuse, waste, rubbish or any and free from any smell. Proper dust bins are to be provided to maintain the cleanness in the office premises. Except HDFC bank, other banks are not maintaining the dust bins. The gap score of this bank is 1.06 against the average gap score of 2.21.

- SBH and HDFC banks are need to provided needed dust bins in the bank offices to maintain the branch office clean and safe.

Variable 17: For customers' convenience, an appropriate number of sanitary conveniences (toilets facility) must be provided, and should be adequately ventilated, lit and kept clean, separately for male and females. No bank is providing this amenity to its customers.

- No bank is providing this amenity to its customers. Bank officials should focus on this issue and adequate toilets and washing facilities for their customers.

Variable 18: The suggestion box is part of a culture of organisational feedback. Strong leaders and forward thinking organisations should welcome feedback and suggestions from their customers. It enhances relationship with customers. By having lowest gaps score i.e. 1.48 against the average gap score 2.44, only HDFC bank arranged the complaint and suggestion box to receive the feedback from its customers.

- SBH and TGB are required to arrange the complaint and suggestion box, for customers, which is visible and accessible by all customers to improve the customer relationship.

Hypothesis

H_0 –There is no significant relation between customers' satisfactions towards service quality and actual facilities and amenities provided by the selected bank.

H_1 –There is significant relation between customers' satisfactions towards service quality and actual facilities and amenities provided by the selected bank.

ANOVA[a]

Model		Sum of Squares	df	Mean Square	F	Sig.
1	Regression	84.763	18	4.709	12.271	.000[b]
	Residual	234.469	611	0.384		
	Total	319.232	629			

a. Dependent Variable: Overall Satisfaction

b. Predictors: (Constant), Actual, Actual, Actual, Actual, Actual, Actual, Actual, Actual, Actual, Actual, Actual, Actual, Actual, Actual, Actual, Actual, Actual, Actual

The above ANOVA table shows that the calculated value of *F* is 12.271 which is greater than the significance value at 0.05 level of significance is .000 with degree of freedom being $v_1 = 18$ and $v_2 = 611$. This analysis rejects the null hypothesis of no significant relation between customers' satisfactions towards service quality and actual facilities and amenities provided by the selected bank. Therefore, it may conclude that the difference in customers' satisfaction due to actual facilities and amenities provided by the selected bank is significant and is just not a matter of chance.

5.22.2 Comparison of Service Timings

Compared to selected three banks (SBH, TGB and HDFC bank), average mean time is considered, in respect of cash receipt HDFC bank (8.92 minutes) and TGB (14.37 minutes) banks are providing this service within the specified average (15 minutes).

Table 5.87: Comparison of Service Timings

Particulars	Standard Time	SBH	TGB	HDFC
Cash Receipt (in Min.)	15	23.56	14.37	8.92
Cash Payment (in Min.)	15	26.12	18.75	9.89
Issue of Draft (in Min.)	20	32.65	28.67	16.75
Collection of Out Station Cheque (in Days)	12	8.88	7.41	5.46
Updating Pass Book (in Min.)	10	20.58	16.73	16.88
Issue of Cheque Book (in Days)	11	13.70	13.33	10.77

In respect of cash payment, average mean time is considered; HDFC bank (9.89 minutes) is providing this service within the specified average time (15 minutes).

Among three selected three banks average mean time is considered, HDFC bank (16.75 minutes) issuing demand draft to its customers within the specified average (20 minutes).

All selected banks in the study area are collecting and depositing out-station cheques within the specified average number of days (12 days).

All the selected banks are updating pass book of their customers above the standard average time. Though all banks were computerised, updating the cash book above the average standard time is a worth noting one. Banks should look in to the matter and try to minimise the time by opening a separate counter for recording the pass book transactions.

By comparison, selected three banks, it is found that HDFC bank (10.77 days) is issuing the cheque book within the specified average time (11 days).

From the above analysis it is inferred that, comparatively, service timings of HDFC bank was very less. This is because the bank is well appointed sufficient no. of employees members and installed the right number of computers and other electronic equipments with high configuration.

SBH and TGB banks should try to minimise the service timing for the issue of the and save the time of business people in particular and all customers in general.

5.22.3 Bank-wise Variance in Service Encounters

ANOVA					
Service Encounters					
	Sum of Squares	***df***	***Mean Square***	***F***	***Sig.***
Between Groups	26359.006	2	13179.503	264.181	0.03
Within Groups	31279.921	627	49.888		
Total	**57638.927**	**629**			

Table 5.88: Multiple Comparisons Dependent Variable: Service Encounter

Bank Type (I)		***Bank Type (J)***	***Mean Difference (I-J)***	***Std. Error***	***Sig.***	***95 per cent Confidence Interval***	
						Lower Bound	***Upper Bound***
Tukey HSD	SBH	TGB	-7.42368*	.65320	.000	-8.9582	-5.8891
		HDFC	-16.48086*	.71821	.000	-18.1681	-14.7936
	TGB	SBH	7.42368*	.65320	.000	5.8891	8.9582
		HDFC	-9.05718*	.72578	.000	-10.7623	-7.3521
	HDFC	**SBH**	**16.48086***	**.71821**	**.000**	**14.7936**	**18.1681**
		TGB	**9.05718***	**.72578**	**.000**	**7.3521**	**10.7623**
Tamhane	SBH	TGB	-7.42368*	.62895	0.000	-8.9316	-5.9158
		HDFC	-16.48086*	.79363	0.000	-18.3847	-14.5770
	TGB	SBH	7.42368*	.62895	0.000	5.9158	8.9316
		HDFC	-9.05718*	.69021	0.000	-10.7156	-7.3988
	HDFC	**SBH**	**16.48086***	**.79363**	**0.000**	**14.5770**	**18.3847**
		TGB	**9.05718***	**.69021**	**0.000**	**7.3988**	**10.7156**

Hypothesis

H_0:-Service Encounter variables do not vary in importance significantly in respect of selected banks.

H_A:-Service Encounter variables vary in importance significantly in respect of selected banks.

ANOVA test was conducted to test the Homogeneity of Variances of service encounters of the selected banks i.e. SBH, TGB and HDFC banks. It is found that the null hypothesis i.e. ***no variance among the service encounters of selected banks*** is rejected and proved that there is some variance among the service encounter variables of selected banks. Further, ANOVA Post Hoc (Tukey's and Tamhane's) test also carried out and proved that the service encounters vary among the banks and HDFC is the highest scoring bank in regards to service encounters.

As HDFC bank is a new generation private sector bank appoints right number of employees and trains them how to behave with the customers. The bank employees give high importance to the needs of customers and attract them with polite behaviour. They welcome the customers when they enter the bank and ask them to sit. This increases the cordial relation between the employee and the customer. The same is also proved with help of ANOVA Post Hoc Test.

Area-wise Variance in Service Encounters

ANOVA

Service Encounter					
	Sum of Squares	***df***	***Mean Square***	***F***	***Sig.***
Between Groups	1796.25	5	359.25	4.014	0.21
Within Groups	55842.677	624	89.491		
Total	**57638.927**	**629**			

Table 5.89: Multiple Comparisons Dependent Variable: Service Encounter (Area-wise)

Area of Bank (I)	***Area of Bank (J)***	***Mean Difference (I-J)***	***Std. Error***	***Sig.***	***95 per cent Confidence Interval Lower Bound***	***Upper Bound***
	Huzurabad	**5.53961***	**1.33127**	**.001**	**1.7340**	**9.3452**
	Jagitital	**4.14727***	**1.30709**	**.020**	**.4108**	**7.8837**
Siricilla	**Jammikunta**	**2.75636**	**1.30709**	**.284**	**-.9801**	**6.4928**
	Sulthanabad	**2.54727**	**1.30709**	**.373**	**-1.1892**	**6.2837**
	Metpally	**2.13224**	**1.34465**	**.608**	**-1.7116**	**5.9761**

(*Contd...*)

Tukey HSD	Huzurabad	Siricilla	-5.53961*	1.33127	.001	-9.3452	-1.7340
		Jagitital	-1.39234	1.30036	.893	-5.1095	2.3249
		Jammikunta	-2.78324	1.30036	.268	-6.5004	.9339
		Sulthanabad	-2.99234	1.30036	.195	-6.7095	.7249
		Metpally	-3.40736	1.33811	.113	-7.2325	.4178
	Jagitital	Siricilla	-4.14727*	1.30709	.020	-7.8837	-.4108
		Huzurabad	1.39234	1.30036	.893	-2.3249	5.1095
		Jammikunta	-1.39091	1.27559	.885	-5.0373	2.2555
		Sulthanabad	-1.60000	1.27559	.810	-5.2464	2.0464
		Metpally	-2.01503	1.31405	.643	-5.7714	1.7413
	Jammikunta	Siricilla	-2.75636	1.30709	.284	-6.4928	.9801
		Huzurabad	2.78324	1.30036	.268	-.9339	6.5004
		Jagitital	1.39091	1.27559	.885	-2.2555	5.0373
		Sulthanabad	-.20909	1.27559	1.000	-3.8555	3.4373
		Metpally	-.62412	1.31405	.997	-4.3805	3.1322
	Sulthanabad	Siricilla	-2.54727	1.30709	.373	-6.2837	1.1892
		Huzurabad	2.99234	1.30036	.195	-.7249	6.7095
		Jagitital	1.60000	1.27559	.810	-2.0464	5.2464
		Jammikunta	.20909	1.27559	1.000	-3.4373	3.8555
		Metpally	-.41503	1.31405	1.000	-4.1714	3.3413
	Metpally	Siricilla	-2.13224	1.34465	.608	-5.9761	1.7116
		Huzurabad	3.40736	1.33811	.113	-.4178	7.2325
		Jagitital	2.01503	1.31405	.643	-1.7413	5.7714
		Jammikunta	.62412	1.31405	.997	-3.1322	4.3805
		Sulthanabad	.41503	1.31405	1.000	-3.3413	4.1714
Tamhane	**Siricilla**	**Huzurabad**	**5.53961***	**1.45772**	**.003**	**1.2136**	**9.8656**
		Jagitital	**4.14727***	**1.03949**	**.001**	**1.0652**	**7.2293**
		Jammikunta	**2.75636**	**1.27809**	**.388**	**-1.0298**	**6.5425**
		Sulthanabad	**2.54727**	**1.14601**	**.340**	**-.8473**	**5.9418**
		Metpally	**2.13224**	**1.32645**	**.825**	**-1.8021**	**6.0666**
	Huzurabad	Siricilla	-5.53961*	1.45772	.003	-9.8656	-1.2136
		Jagitital	-1.39234	1.36064	.996	-5.4388	2.6541
		Jammikunta	-2.78324	1.55059	.685	-7.3784	1.8120
		Sulthanabad	-2.99234	1.44366	.455	-7.2768	1.2921
		Metpally	-3.40736	1.59068	.399	-8.1224	1.3076
	Jagitital	Siricilla	-4.14727*	1.03949	.001	-7.2293	-1.0652
		Huzurabad	1.39234	1.36064	.996	-2.6541	5.4388
		Jammikunta	-1.39091	1.16616	.982	-4.8494	2.0676
		Sulthanabad	-1.60000	1.01968	.848	-4.6202	1.4202
		Metpally	-2.01503	1.21897	.795	-5.6371	1.6071
	Jammikunta	Siricilla	-2.75636	1.27809	.388	-6.5425	1.0298
		Huzurabad	2.78324	1.55059	.685	-1.8120	7.3784
		Jagitital	1.39091	1.16616	.982	-2.0676	4.8494
		Sulthanabad	-.20909	1.26203	1.000	-3.9467	3.5285
		Metpally	-.62412	1.42788	1.000	-4.8545	3.6062
	Sulthanabad	Siricilla	-2.54727	1.14601	.340	-5.9418	.8473
		Huzurabad	2.99234	1.44366	.455	-1.2921	7.2768
		Jagitital	1.60000	1.01968	.848	-1.4202	4.6202
		Jammikunta	.20909	1.26203	1.000	-3.5285	3.9467
		Metpally	-.41503	1.31098	1.000	-4.3030	3.4730
	Metpally	Siricilla	-2.13224	1.32645	.825	-6.0666	1.8021
		Huzurabad	3.40736	1.59068	.399	-1.3076	8.1224
		Jagitital	2.01503	1.21897	.795	-1.6071	5.6371
		Jammikunta	.62412	1.42788	1.000	-3.6062	4.8545
		Sulthanabad	.41503	1.31098	1.000	-3.4730	4.3030

*. The mean difference is significant at the 0.05 level.

Hypothesis

H_0:-Service Encounter variables do not vary in importance significantly in respect of selected mandals.

H_A:-Service Encounter variables vary in importance significantly in respect of selected mandals.

Area-wise ANOVA test was conducted to test the Homogeneity of Variances of service encounters in the selected mandal areas i.e. Siricilla, Huzurabad, Jagitial, Metpaaly, Jammikunta and Sulthanabad of SBH, TGB and HDFC banks. It is found that the null hypothesis i.e. ***no equal variance among the service encounters of selected banks in selected areas*** is rejected and proved that there is some variance among the service encounter variables of selected banks in selected madals. Further, ANOVA PostHoc (Tukey's and Tamhane's) test also carried out and proved that the service encounters vary among the banks of various madals and Siricilla had the highest influencing area with regard to service encounters.

With this analysis, study on Service Encounters of Selected banks in Karimnagar District, it is found that high significant variables were more in number i.e. six and low significant variables were less in number (two) in case of SBH. The high significant variables were five in number and low significant variables were also five in number in case of TGB. In case of HDFC bank, there were no high significant variables. It had low significant variables six in number. The 'highly significant and significant indicate the desirability of the factors expected by customers. In this context it can be seen that service encounters as compared to HDFC bank, the highly significant and significant variables are more in number in case of SBH and TGB. The same is confirmed by the means given in the table.

The Bank officials of SBH and TGB need to focus much attention on highly significant and significant variables which play vital role in satisfying the customers.

5.22.4 Comparative Evaluation of Service Quality of Selected Banks

Table 5.90: Average Gap Score of Service Quality Factors

		SBH			*TGB*			*HDFC*		
Sl. No.	*Categories*	*Expected SQ(E)*	*Actual SQ (P)*	*SQ Gap (E-P)*	*Expected SQ(E)*	*Actual SQ (P)*	*SQ Gap (E-P)*	*Expected SQ(E)*	*Actual SQ (P)*	*SQ Gap (E-P)*
1	Tangibles	4.90	4.09	0.81	4.83	4.02	0.81	4.90	4.09	0.81
2	Reliability	4.88	4.02	0.86	4.83	4.5	0.33	4.88	4.03	0.85
3	Responsiveness	4.88	3.92	0.96	4.79	4.46	0.33	4.90	3.92	0.98
4	Assurance	4.90	4.10	0.80	4.82	4.65	0.17	4.90	4.10	0.80
5	Empathy	4.89	4.00	0.89	4.77	4.41	0.36	4.90	4.00	0.90
	Total	**24.45**	**20.13**	**4.32**	**24.04**	**22.04**	**2**	**24.48**	**20.14**	**4.34**
	Average	**4.89**	**4.03**	**0.86**	**4.808**	**4.408**	**0.4**	**4.90**	**4.03**	**0.87**

An attempt was also made to find out the service quality level in the selected banksunder study. A comparative statement is prepared with the gap scores of selected banks and compared with the overall average gap score to know the quality level in the selected three banks. Lower gap score against the overall average gap score indicates higher quality level and vice versa. That means lower the gap score higher the quality level and higher the gap score lower the quality level.

Table 5.91: Comparative Assessment of Service Quality of Selected Banks

Sl. No.	*Gap Score of Service Quality (E - P)*	*SBH*	*TGB*	*HDFC*	*Total*
	A. TANGIBLES				
1	My Bank has the sophisticated and good looking infrastructure.	0.89	1.04	0.90	0.85
2	Physical facilities at my banks are visual and attractive.	0.87	0.89	0.87	0.80
3	My Bank employees are in neat dress and appearing dignified.	0.62	0.56	0.62	0.52
4	Materials (statements or passbook) with my bank are visual and excellent.	0.84	0.74	0.84	0.67
	Total	**3.22**	**3.24**	**3.22**	**2.83**
	Average	0.81	0.81	0.81	0.71
	B. RELIABILITY				
5	If my bank promises something, it will certainly do.	0.96	0.38	0.96	0.65
6	If customers have problems, my bank will show sincere interest in solving it.	0.86	0.32	0.86	0.56
7	My bank performs the services at right time. As per time mentioned.	0.91	0.36	0.91	0.57
8	My Bank provides service at the time it promises to do so.	0.93	0.43	0.93	0.61
9	My Bank keeps accurate/error-free records.	0.63	0.19	0.63	0.38
	Total	**4.29**	**1.68**	**4.29**	**2.78**
	Average	0.86	0.34	0.86	0.56
	C. RESPONSIVENESS				
10	Employees of my bank inform customers exactly when service will be performed.	1.26	0.68	1.26	0.86
11	My Bank employees give excellent service to its customers	0.85	0.19	0.84	0.45
12	My Bank employees are always willing to help customers.	0.85	0.18	0.85	0.45
13	Bank employees always ready to respond to customers' requests.	0.86	0.26	0.83	0.48
	Total	**3.82**	**1.31**	**3.90**	**2.23**
	Average	0.96	0.33	0.98	0.56
	D. ASSURANCE				
14	My Bank employees always try to instill confidence in customers.	0.86	0.11	0.85	0.43
15	Customers (me) always feel safe in transactions with my bank's employees.	0.75	0.13	0.72	0.40
16	My Bank employees always courteous and polite with customers.	0.75	0.11	0.74	0.37
17	My Bank employees have complete knowledge to answer queries of customers.	0.82	0.36	0.78	0.53
	Total	**3.18**	**0.71**	**3.20**	**1.73**
	Average	0.80	0.18	0.80	0.43
	E. EMPATHY				
18	My Bank gives individual attention to customers.	1.17	0.46	1.15	0.75
19	My Bank operating hours is convenient to all the customers.	0.55	0.18	0.52	0.38
20	Bank employees understand the specific needs of customers.	0.97	0.43	0.96	0.68
	Total	**2.68**	**1.07**	**2.71**	**1.81**
	Average	0.89	0.36	0.90	0.60

Table 5.92: Gap Score of Selected Banks in Karimnagar

Sl. No.	*Categories*	*SBH*	*TGB*	*HDFC*	*Total*
1	Tangibles	0.81	0.81	0.81	0.71
2	Reliability	0.86	0.33	0.85	0.56
3	Responsiveness	0.96	0.33	0.98	0.56
4	Assurance	0.80	0.18	0.80	0.43
5	Empathy	0.89	0.36	0.90	0.6
	Total	**4.32**	**2.00**	**4.34**	**2.86**
	Average	**0.86**	**0.40**	**0.87**	**0.572**

The Tables 5.91 and 5.92 show the gap score of service quality for selected three types of banks in six mandals in Karimnagar district. Overall gap score of these three selected banks stood at 0.572. The gap score of TGB (0.40) was low compared to SBH (0.86) and HDFC bank (0.87). This indicates that customers rated high and were satisfied with the service quality given by TGB against SBH and HDFC bank. Individual factors' gap score is concerned, TGB has low gap score, against the other two banks under study, for four factors namely 'Reliability', 'Responsiveness', 'Assurance' and 'Empathy'. In the 'Tangibles' all the three banks have the high gap score (0.81) than the average gap score (0.71).

Proper attention is required by the officials of SBH and HDFC bank to improve the bank service quality, in respect of the Tangibles, Reliability and Responsiveness, Assurance and Empathy factors, to satisfy the customers.

5.22.5 Comparative Interpretation of Overall Service Quality

Table 5.93: Comparative Statement of Overall Service Quality

Variables	SBH		TGB		HDFC		TOTAL	
	Mean	SD	Mean	SD	Mean	SD	Mean	SD
Overall Service Quality	3.97	0.830	4.4	0.567	4.4	0.572	4.23	0.712
SQ Meeting Needs of Customers	4.07	0.837	4.45	0.557	4.27	0.714	4.25	0.733
Overall Satisfaction	4.04	0.886	4.53	0.534	4.51	0.514	4.34	0.724
Loyalty towards the Bank	4.2	0.952	4.61	0.579	4.45	0.842	4.41	0.824
Recommendations To Relatives and Friends	4.35	0.897	4.65	0.504	4.45	0.842	4.51	0.728
Average	**4.13**	**0.88**	**4.53**	**0.55**	**4.42**	**0.70**	**4.35**	**0.74**
CV (SD/Mean*100)	**21.31**		**12.14**		**15.84**		**17.01**	

Having discussed the opinions of respondents from the selected banks individually on overall service quality, SQ meeting the needs of the customers overall satisfaction, loyalty and making recommendation to relatives and friends, an attempt is made to compare the opinions of selected bank customers. The comparative analysis is made and presented in the following paragraphs.

Table 5.94: ANOVA–Overall Service Quality

		Sum of Squares	*df*	*Mean Square*	*F*	*Sig. (0.05)*
Overall Service Quality	Between Groups	27.905	2	13.953	30.029	.000
	Within Groups	291.327	627	.465		
	Total	**319.232**	**629**			
Overall SQ Meet the Needs of the Customer	Between Groups	18.557	2	9.278	18.190	.000
	Within Groups	319.818	627	.510		
	Total	**338.375**	**629**			
Overall Satisfaction	Between Groups	34.464	2	17.232	36.645	.000
	Within Groups	294.844	627	.470		
	Total	**329.308**	**629**			
Customers Loyalty toward the Bank	Between Groups	20.331	2	10.166	15.678	.000
	Within Groups	406.540	627	.648		
	Total	**426.871**	**629**			
Customers' Recommendations to Others	Between Groups	11.415	2	5.707	11.113	.000
	Within Groups	322.028	627	.514		
	Total	**333.443**	**629**			

Table 5.95: ANOVA-Total

	Overall Service Quality Total				
	Sum of Squares	*df*	*Mean Square*	*F*	*Sig.(0.05)*
Between Groups	529.240	2	264.620	27.703	.000
Within Groups	5989.134	627	9.552		
Total	**6518.375**	**629**			

Hypothesis

Ho: There is no significant difference among SBH, TGB and HDFC Banks with respect to customers' overall satisfaction of service quality.

H_A: There is a significant difference among SBH, TGB and HDFC Banks with respect to customers' overall satisfaction of service quality.

The above table shows the comparison among selected banks (SBH, TGB and HDFC) in respect to overall satisfaction variables. Mean and standard deviation of variables are considered for comparison. Co-efficient of Variance is applied and tested the significance relation of overall satisfaction variables among selected banks. The average SD of TGB (0.55) and HDFC bank (0.70) is less than overall standard deviation (0.74). The CV of the said banks (12.14 and 15.84 respectively) is also less than the overall CV (17.01). The standard deviation and co-efficient of variance of SBH are greater than the overall average SD and CV.

ANOVA test is also applied and tested the significance among the overall satisfaction of service quality variables. At five per cent significance level calculated F value is greater than the F critical.

Hence, it is found that the null hypothesis is rejected and proved that there is significant difference among SBH, TGB and HDFC banks with respect to the overall satisfaction of service quality variables.

5.22.6 Overall Service Quality–Profile of Respondents

Table 5.96: Paired Samples Test

		Paired Differences					*t*	*df*	*Sig. (2-tailed)*
		Mean	*Std. Deviation*	*Std. Error Mean*	*95 per cent Confidence Interval of the Difference*				
					Lower	*Upper*			
Pair 1	Bank Type – Overall SQ	-2.359	.919	.037	-2.431	-2.287	-64.440	629	.000
Pair 2	Area of Bank – Overall SQ	-.724	1.916	.076	-.874	-.574	-9.484	629	.000
Pair 3	gender – Overall SQ	-3.017	.831	.033	-3.083	-2.952	-91.094	629	0.000
Pair 4	Qualification – Overall SQ	-.306	1.961	.078	-.460	-.153	-3.920	629	0.000
Pair 5	Occupation – Overall SQ	-1.835	1.294	.052	-1.936	-1.734	-35.599	629	.000
Pair 6	Annual – Overall SQ	-1.897	1.135	.045	-1.986	-1.808	-41.947	629	.000
Pair 7	Marital Status – Overall SQ	-3.183	.742	.030	-3.241	-3.125	-107.703	629	0.000

It is tested to prove the relation between service quality (dependent variable) and demographical details of respondents (independent variables) of selected banks through paired sample t- test.

H_0– There is no significant relation between service quality and bank type, area of the bank, age, gender, qualification, occupation, annual income and marital status of the respondents.

H_1– There is significant relation between service quality and bank type, area of the bank, age, gender, qualification, occupation, annual income and marital status of the respondents.

The significance value at 0.05 is zero, hence it is rejected the null hypothesis and concluded that the difference in opinions of customers about service quality due to bank type, area of the bank, age, gender, educational qualification, occupation, annual income and marital status of respondents is significant and is just not a matter of chance.

5.22.7 Overall Satisfaction–Profile of Respondents

Table 5.97: Paired Samples Test

		Paired Differences					*t*	*df*	*Sig. (2-tailed)*
		Mean	*Std. Deviation*	*Std. Error Mean*	*95 per cent Confidence Interval of the Difference*				
					Lower	*Upper*			
Pair 1	Bank Type Overall Satisfaction	-2.463	.912	.036	-2.535	-2.392	-67.832	629	0.000
Pair 2	Area of Bank Overall Satisfaction	-.829	1.889	.075	-.976	-.681	-11.007	629	0.000
Pair 3	gender Overall Satisfaction	-3.122	.853	.034	-3.189	-3.055	-91.880	629	0.000
Pair 4	Qualification Overall Satisfaction	-.411	1.992	.079	-.567	-.255	-5.179	629	0.000
Pair 5	Occupation Overall Satisfaction	-1.940	1.299	.052	-2.041	-1.838	-37.473	629	0.000
Pair 6	Annual Income Overall Satisfaction	-2.002	1.138	.045	-2.091	-1.913	-44.136	629	0.000
Pair 7	Marital Status Overall Satisfaction	-3.287	.749	.030	-3.346	-3.229	-110.141	629	0.000

It is also tested to prove the relation between customers' overall satisfaction towards service quality (dependent variable) and demographical details of respondents (independent variables) of selected banks through paired sample t- test.

H_0 – Customers' satisfaction does not vary in respect of bank type, area of the bank, age, gender, qualification, occupation, annual income and marital status of the respondents selected bank.

H_1 – Customers' satisfaction varies in respect of bank type, area of the bank, age, gender, qualification, occupation, annual income and marital status of the respondents selected bank.

The significance value at 0.05 is zero, hence it is rejected the null hypothesis and concluded that the difference in customers' satisfaction towards service quality due to bank type, area of the bank, age, gender, educational qualification, occupation, annual income and marital status of respondents is significant and is just not a matter of chance.

Chapter - 6

Summary of Findings, Suggestions and Conclusions

6.1. Introduction

Business concern directly depends on its customers to earn revenues. Attracting customers, maintaining and retaining them are the most important means for success of the business firm. Banking institutions in service sector are not exception to this. Because of globalisation and privatisation, private and foreign banks with innovative service have emerged in the market. Advancement in technology and revolution in the economic environment have changed the expectations of bank customers and it has become very difficult to, traditional banks particularly in public sector, meet the needs of the customers with just traditional and outdated products and services. Banks should be innovative to cater to the requirements of the customers in the highly competitive market place.

Customers are newly familiarised to such services and facilities being offered by the services sector industries. Customers' expectations, from banks in particular and service sector in general, before and after sales service have increased. A customer starts the relation with bank and continues only as long as he reaches or exceeds his changing expectations and requirements. Once customers attain a comfortable relationship with the banker, they continue the relationship and stop if they encounter major dissatisfaction. When customers are delighted with the quality of service delivery by the employees they give high rating to the banks on overall satisfaction. Hence, the service quality by the bank and customers satisfaction are inter dependent and play crucial role in banking sector.

This chapter presents the summary of study findings from the analysis of data collected so far, and necessary suggestions and sum up the conclusions and directions for future research are also stated for the purpose of helping the future researchers.

6.2. Objectives of the Study

The following are the objectives of the study:

1. To examine the growth and development of banking sector in India
2. To present the profile of selected banks in Karimnagar district.
3. To study the customers' expectations of banking services in the rural context.
4. To analyse the customers' satisfaction on service quality of banks in rural areas.
5. To study the bankers' perceptions towards service delivery mechanism.

6.3 Methodology and Data Base

The study is primarily a descriptive study of the impact of banking services in the rural areas. One public sector bank, one private sector bank and one rural bank was selected as target banks for the study. SBH from public sector, HDFC from private sector and TGB (earlier DGB) from rural banks for identifying as the target banks.

6.4 Data Collection

The required data was collected from two sources namely, Primary Data and Secondary Data. Primary data was collected through two structured questionnaires. While one questionnaire was intended for the bank officials and another one was meant for the bank customers. Secondary data was collected from RBI bulletins, NCAER, IBA, District Statistical Reports, Reports of Institutions and Agencies etc., which are engaged in development of banking sector and other published reports.

6.5 Sample Unit

The sample unit consisted of customers of the public sector (SBH), the private sector banks (HDFC) and RRBs (TGB) of rural areas in Karimnagar district of Telangana State. The respondents were farmers, teachers, business people and professionals in the age group of 25–60 years.

6.6 Reason for Selecting Karimnagar District

Karimnagar district is a predominantly an agrarian district. The availability of Lower Manair Dam (LMD) and water resources led to prospective farming due to which the district has become a leading producer of agricultural products. Since the independence rural credit in the form of PACS was the leading provider of finance for the agriculture and allied activities.

The progress in the agriculture piloted the prosperity in the rural Karimnagar which in term showed the way to growth and development of other economic activities such as trade, healthcare, education and business... The district is also endowed with rich mining resources such as coal, limestone and granite. These directed to the booming demand for credit which is mainly providing by commercial banks, regional rural banks (RRBs) apart from the primary agricultural credit societies (PACS).

Hence, the district of Karimnagar was selected as the area of study for the research topic.

6.7 Reason for Selecting Mandals

For the present study six mandals i.e. Siricilla, Jagitial, Huzurabad, Jammikunta, Metpally and Sultanabad in Karimnagar district were selected purposefully. Selected three banks (SBH, TGB and HDFC bank) were located and functioning in these six mandals only. Hence, these mandals were selected for the study.

6.8 Sample Size

For the study judgment sampling is used. The following is the sample distribution.

Table 1.10: Sample Size

Particulars	***No.***
No. of Mandals Selected for the study (10 per cent of the Total 57 Mandals in the District)	6
No. of Banks Selected (SBH, DGB and HDFC)	3
Target Groups (Farmers, Employees, Business People and SHGs)	4
No. of Respondents from each group	10
Total Sample Size (For SBH and DGB - 6*2*4*10) + (For HDFC - 6*3*10)	**660**
No. of Respondents	**630**
Per cent of Response	**95.45%**

Note: As a private bank HDFC bank is not offering SHG Scheme.

6.9 Tools of Data Analysis

So, collected data was analysed with the help of statistical techniques like tables, averages, percentages and bar diagrams. Graphs are presented wherever necessary. The results are interpreted with the help of percentages in a meaningful manner. Based on the need, the statistical techniques like, factor analysis, paired sample test, multi-variable analysis, correlation, ANOVA, etc., are employed to arrive logical conclusions.

6.10 Scope of the Study

The study is restricted to Karimnagar district only. The district is one of the developed districts in Telangana state. So the district is selected purposefully to understand the process of service delivery by selected banks in the rural areas of the district.

6.11 Organisation of the Study

The present study is structured into seven chapters organised to present the study from a basic introduction to findings and conclusions. The following table displays the scheme of Chapterisation of the study.

Table 1.13: Organisation of the Study

Chapter – I	Introduction
Chapter – II	Growth and Development of Banking Sector in India
Chapter – III	Profile of Selected Banks in Karimnagar District.
Chapter – IV	Customers' Expectations of Banking Services
Chapter – V	Customers' Satisfaction of Service Quality
Chapter – VI	Summary of Conclusions, Findings and Suggestions

Chapter–I Introduction

This chapter introduces the study and states about Conceptual Framework, Need for the study, Objectives of the study, Statement of the Problem, Research Methodology, Scope of the study, Limitations of the Study and Scheme of Chapterisation.

Chapter–II Growth and Development of Banking Sector in India

This chapter starts from the meaning, evolution, origin of banking in India, Indian banking system and its growth and classification of banks.

Chapter–III Profile of Selected Banks in Karimnagar District

This chapter deals with the brief profile of the selected banks for the study i.e. public sector bank (SBH), private sector bank (HDFC) and rural bank (TGB) and profile of the selected district.

Chapter–IV Customers' Expectations of Banking Services

This chapter states the demographic profile of the respondents in the selected study area. It includes the analysis of the opinions of the respondents on availability of banking services.

Chapter–V Customers' Satisfaction of Service Quality

This chapter deals with the data collected from the bankers in the rural areas of Karimnagar.

Chapter–VI Summary of Conclusions, Findings and Suggestions

In this chapter, the introduction, objectives and summary of findings of the research study are presented one by one, based on findings necessary suggestions are offered. It concludes by setting out the study's contribution to knowledge and scope for future research is also stated for the benefit of future researchers.

6.12 Summary of Findings

The summary of findings from the study is presented in the following paragraphs.

The analysis related to the profile of the respondents under the study area reveals the following findings. The study finds that 38.10 per cent of the total 630 respondents belonged to public sector bank and 36.19 per cent of the total belonged to rural bank and remaining 25.71 per cent of respondents belonged to private sector bank. Area-wise analysis shows that the 17.46 per cent of the total respondents are in each of three mandals i.e. Jagitial (JGTL), Jammikunta (JMKT) and Sultanabad (SLTBD) representing 110 respondents in each. In Huzurabad (HZB) 102 respondents, 100 respondents in Siricilla (SRSL) and 98 respondents in Metpalli (MTPL) representing 16.19 per cent, 15.87 per cent and 15.56 per cent respectively. The gender-wise distribution of respondents also clearly indicates that majority of them are male (78.25 per cent) from SBH, TGB and HDFC banks. The study further reveals that most of the potential customers are in the age group of 31–40 years of age.

The analysis relating to the marital status of the respondents also implies that married customers in SBH, TGB and HDFC banks are mostly using the banking services. It is also noted that the customer's qualified up to under graduation (29.58 per cent) in SBH and 38.27 per cent in HDFC, secondary school education and under graduation (21.05 per cent) in TGB are of high percentage. The study further identified that majority of the customers 26.32 per cent and 37.04 per cent in TGB and HDFC banks are belong to Business class and in SBH customers are equally spread as farmers, business, employees and SHGs category. Annual income categories of Rupees one lakh to five lakh are of 34.58 per cent in SBH, 39.03 per cent in TGB and 60.49 per cent in HDFC banks are of high percentage. Customers are mostly using the banks for operating saving bank account rather than other purposes. The highest numbers of customers 62.92 per cent in SBH, 41.23 per cent in TGB are using the bank more than five years and 56.17 per cent in HDFC are using the bank for the past three years. Majority of the customers are transacting with SBH and TGB banks for one time in a month and in HDFC bank for two to four times in a month that too mostly for the purpose of operating saving bank account. The customers have chosen the bank for variety of reasons, but the major reasons for choosing the public sector (SBH and TGB) banks were of the prompt services, qualitative services, location of the bank, benefits from the government schemes etc., and private sector bank (HDFC) was chosen because of the convenient business hours and speed services.

6.13 Overall Findings

6.14.1 Awareness of Customers on Availability of Products and Services

The study disclosed that the majority of customers do not have the knowledge about the most of the banking services or products like credit card, commercial vehicles loans, internet banking, telephone banking, mobile banking in SBH and TGB banks. In, HDFC bank, private sector bank, also the highest number of customers do not know about the services offered by the bank.

6.13.2 Facilities and Amenities Provided by the Banks.

Convenience facilities and amenities in the banks are considered the most important variables for evaluating the service quality. So, customers transact with the banks in a comfort environment. The present study finds the expectations of customers under study area are higher regarding the information about working hours, information about service timings, Proper Lighting, information about available services and products, and availability of personal assistance/guidance and Complaint and Suggestion Box.

6.13.3 Service Encounters (Relationship between Bank Employee and Customers)

Service encounter is the one of the most important service quality factors, to measure the service quality of bank. The environment in which the customer directly interacts with the bank employees during the period of time is also studied. It has been found that the SD and CV values of TGB and HDFC are lower than SBH bank. This implies that TGB and HDFC banks are maintaining effective customer relationships during the banking transactions.

6.13.4 Service Quality Dimensions

The study used the five dimensions of SERVQUAL scale for enquiring the service quality of banks in the study area. Variables which are having low gap score in the scale are treated as highly preferable variables. The study ranked the most preferred variables of banking service quality in the SERVQUAL scale like 'employees are in neat dress and appearing dignified' (out of four variables of Tangibles), 'bank keeps accurate and error free records' (out of five variables of Reliability), 'bank employees give 'excellent service to its customers' and 'bank employees are always willing to help customers' (out of four variables of Responsiveness), 'bank employees always courteous and polite with customers' out of four variables of Assurance and 'bank operating hours are convenient to all customers' out of three variables of Empathy in selected banks in the Karimnagar district. Out of five dimensions of SERVQUAL, dimension 'assurance' has the low overall average gap score in selected three banks.

6.13.5 Gap Analysis

The gap score is very less in 'Assurance' reveals that customers were highly satisfied with the assurance aspects associated with the service. Tangibles and empathy dimensions have the greater average gap score than other dimensions, implying dissatisfaction of customers towards these dimensions.

6.14 Findings-SBH Bank

6.14.1 Awareness of Customers on Availability of Products and Services

The study disclosed that the majority of customers do not have the knowledge about the most of the banking services or products like credit card, commercial vehicles loans, internet banking, telephone banking, mobile banking in SBH.

6.14.2 Facilities and Amenities Provided by the Banks

Convenience facilities and amenities in the banks are considered the most important variables for evaluating the service quality. So, customers transact with the banks in a comfort environment. The present study finds SBH customers' expectations are higher regarding the availability of personal assistance/guidance, information about service timings, information about available services and products, information about working hours and complaint and suggestion box, proper lighting and personal assistance/ guidance etc

The study also finds the actual quality of facilities and amenities provided by the banks. SBH bank provides high quality of the facilities and amenities like location of the bank, proper lighting, attractive flooring, drinking water, waiting room/place etc.

6.14.3 Service Encounters (Relationship between Bank Employee and Customers)

Service encounter is the one of the most important service quality factors, to measure the service quality of bank. The environment in which the customer directly interacts with the bank employees during the period of time is also studied. It has been found that the SD and CV values of SBH bank are high as compared to the other banks under study. This implies that SBH bank is maintaining ineffective customers' relationships during the banking transactions comparing to TGB and HDFC banks.

6.14.4 Service Quality Dimensions

The study used the five dimensions of SERVQUAL scale for enquiring the service quality of banks in the study area. Variables which are having low gap score in the scale are treated as highly preferable variables.

Variables were ranked as the most preferred variables of banking service quality in the SERVQUAL scale like 'employees are in neat dress and appearing dignified' (out of four variables of Tangibles), 'bank keeps accurate and error free records' (out of five variables of Reliability), 'bank employees give 'excellent service to its customers' (out of four variables of Responsiveness), 'customers always feel safe in transacting with the bank employees' and 'bank employees always courteous and polite with customers' out of four variables of Assurance and 'bank operating hours are convenient to all customers' out three variables of Empathy in SBH bank.

6.14.5 Gap Analysis

The gap score is less in 'Assurance and Tangible, which are less than the overall average reveal that customers were much satisfied with the 'Assurance and Tangibles' aspects. Responsiveness and Empathy have the greater average gap score implying high dissatifaction of customers towards these factors.

6.15 Findings-TGB

6.15.1 Awareness of Customers on Availability of Products and Services

The study disclosed that the majority of customers do not have the knowledge about most of the banking services or products like credit card, ATM/debit card commercial vehicles loans, internet banking, telephone banking, EFT, mobile banking in TGB.

6.15.2 Facilities and Amenities Provided by the Banks.

The present study found TGB customers' expectations are higher regarding the availability of personal assistance/guidance, information about service timings, information about available services and products, information about working hours and complaint and suggestion box, proper lighting and personal assistance/guidance etc.

The study also found the actual quality of facilities and amenities provided by the banks. TGB bank provides the good quality of facilities and amenities like Location of the Bank, Proper Lighting, personal assistance/guidance, Information about working hours, Attractive Flooring Waiting Room/Place etc.

6.15.3 Service Encounters (Relationship between Bank Employee and Customers)

Service encounter is the one of the most important service quality factors, to measure the service quality of bank. The environment in which the customer directly interacts with the bank employees during the period of time is also studied. It has been found that the SD and CV values of HDFC bank are low as compared to SBH bank under study. This implies that HDFC bank is maintaining effective customers' relationships during the banking transactions as compared to SBH bank.

6.15.4 Service Quality Dimensions

The study used the five dimensions of SERVQUAL scale for enquiring the service quality of banks in the study area. Variables which are having low gap score in the scale are treated as highly preferable variables.

Variables were ranked as the most preferable like 'employees are in neat dress and appearing dignified' (out of four variables of Tangibles), 'bank keeps accurate and error free records' (out of five variables of Reliability), 'bank employees are always willing to help customers' out of four variables of Responsiveness, 'bank employees always try to instill confidence in customers' and 'bank employees always courteous and polite with customers' out of four variables of Assurance, and 'bank operating hours are convenient to all customers' out of three variables of Empathy in TGB bank.

6.15.5 Gap Analysis

The gap score is very less in 'Assurance' reveals that customers are highly satisfied with the assurance aspects associated with the service. Tangibles have the greater average gap score than others dimensions, implying dissatifaction of customers.

6.16 Findings–HDFC Bank

6.16.1 Awareness of Customers on Availability of Products and Services–HDFC Bank

The study disclosed that the majority of customers in HDFC bank do not have the knowledge about the most of the banking services or products like education loan, land mortgage loan, loans for livestocks, commercial vehicles loans, in HDFC bank.

6.16.2 Facilities and Amenities Provided by the Banks.

The present study found HDFC bank customers' expectations are high with respect to the facilities and amenities like information about service timings, information about working hours, personal assistance/guidance, proper lighting and waiting room/place etc.

The study also found the actual quality of facilities and amenities provided by the banks. HDFC Bank provides high quality of facilities and amenities like Proper Lighting, Attractive Flooring, ATM facility at the branch, A/C Facility, Display of identification boards at counters, location of the branch, personal assistance/guidance etc.

6.16.3 Service Encounters (Relationship between Bank Employee and Customers)

Service encounter is the one of the most important service quality factors, to measure the service quality of bank. The environment in which the customer directly interacts with the bank employees during the period of time is also studied. It has been found that the SD and CV values of HDFC bank are low as compared to SBH bank under study. This implies that HDFC bank is maintaining effective customers' relationships during the banking transactions as compared to SBH.

6.16.4 Service Quality Dimensions

The study used the five dimensions of SERVQUAL scale for enquire the service quality of banks in the study area. Variables which are having low gap score in the scale are treated as highly preferable variables.

Variables were ranked as the most preferable like 'employees are in neat dress and appearing dignified' (out of four variables of Tangibles), 'bank keeps accurate and error free records' (out of five variables of Reliability), 'bank employees are always ready to respond to customers' requests' out of four variables of Responsiveness, 'customers always feel safe in transacting with the bank employees' out of four variables of Assurance, and 'bank employees give individual attention to customers' out of three variables of Empathy in HDFC bank.

6.16.5 Gap Analysis

The gap score is very less in 'Assurance' reveals that customers are highly satisfied with the assurance aspects associated with the service. Responsiveness and Empthy factors have the greater average gap score implies dissatifaction of customers in respect to these factors.

6.17. A Comparison of SBH, TGB and HDFC Banks

Required statistical techniques were used and necessary hypothesis are established to find the significant different among selected banks SBH, TGB and HDFC banks with respect of services and products offered, expected and actual facilities and amenities provided by the banks, service encounters and service quality dimensions. The results are presented in the following paragraphs.

6.17.1 Awareness of Customers on Availability of Products and Services

By comparison it is inferred that SBH bank should strengthen the perceptions of customers in respect of the banking services or products like credit card, commercial vehicles loans, internet banking, telephone banking, mobile banking etc. TGB bank should also create the awareness about the banking services or products like credit card, ATM/debit card commercial vehicles loans, internet banking, telephone banking, EFT, mobile banking etc. HDFC bank must intensify the perceptions of customers against the services or products like education loan, land mortgage loan, loans for livestocks, commercial vehicles loans, in HDFC bank.

On the whole it is concluded that service quality and customers' satisfaction are decided by various perceptions of customers regarding the awareness about availability of services or products in the banks.

6.17.2 Facilities and Amenities Provided by the Banks

A comparative analysis is made among three selected banks with respect to expected and actual facilities and amenities provided. Gap score between expectations of customers with respect to facilities and amenities and actual facilities and amenities provided by the banks is considered. Average gap score of HDFC bank is very less than the overall average gap score. It is concluded that HDFC bank is providing excellent facilities and amenities to its customers compared to SBH and TGB under the study. HDFC bank is a new generation private sector bank and established with all sophisticated infrastructure facilities and providing high quality services to its customers.

With the help of multivariate analysis, it is found that three significant difference between expected quality and actual quality of facilities and amenities are provided by the selected banks.

6.17.3 Service Encounters

A comparison is made among SBH, TGB and HDFC banks with respect of service encounters. Bank-wise ANOVA and ANOVA PostHoc (Tukey's and Tamhane's) test also carried out and proved that the service encounters vary among the banks and HDFC is the highest influencing bank with regard to service encounters.

Area-wise ANOVA test and ANOVA PostHoc (Tukey's and Tamhane's) are conducted to test the Homogeneity of Variances of service encounters in the selected mandal areas i.e. Siricilla, Huzurabad, Jagitial, Metpally, Jammikunta and Sulthanabad of SBH TGB and HDFC banks and proved that there is some variance among the service encounter variables of selected banks in selected madals. Further, it is found that the service encounters vary among the banks of various madals and Siricilla mandal is the highest influencing area with regard to service encounters.

6.17.4 Service Quality Dimensions

The comparative analysis of the service quality found that the average gap score of TGB is low against the average gap score of SBH and HDFC bank. This indicates that customers rated high and are satisfied with the service quality given by TGB against SBH and HDFC bank. Individual factors' gap score is concerned, TGB has low gap score, against the other two banks under study, for four factors namely 'Reliability', 'Responsiveness', 'Assurance' and 'Empathy'. In the 'Tangibles' all the three banks have the same gap score.

It is found from the comparative interpretation of overall service quality that there is significance difference among the selected three banks with respect to the overall satisfaction of service quality variables.

6.17.5 Gap Analysis

Overall gap score of these three selected banks is concerned, the gap score of TGB was low compared to SBH and HDFC bank. This indicates that customers rated high and were satisfied with the service quality given by TGB against SBH and HDFC bank. Individual factors' gap score is concerned, TGB has low gap score, against the other two banks under study, for four factors namely 'Reliability', 'Responsiveness', 'Assurance' and 'Empathy'. In the 'Tangibles' all the three banks have the high gap score than the average gap score.

7.18 Suggestions

Banks should offer excellent quality of services to their customers, irrespective of area either urban or rural, to ensure customer satisfaction and retain them for long. Satisfied customer will be loyal to the bank and recommend others to utilise the particular bank services. The present study is making the following suggestions for improvement of quality of services to enhance the customers' satisfaction.

7.18.1 SBH Bank

State Bank of Hyderabad (SBH) is a financial services provider, based in India. SBH is a nationalised bank, with headquarters at Hyderabad, Telangana. It is one of the five associate banks of State Bank of India and is one of the scheduled banks in India. It was founded in 1941 as Hyderabad State Bank. Since 1956 it has been a subsidiary of State Bank of India and now is State Bank's largest associate bank. SBH has over 1,800 branches and about 17,000 employees as on 31.03.2015. It has its presence in Telangana, Andhra Pradesh, Karnataka, Maharashtra, and among others.

The bank offers accounts and deposits, savings accounts, current accounts, term deposits, home loans, new car loan, used car loan, educational loan, gold loans, merchant banking, infrastructure bonds, depository services, and others.

It provides cheque collection policy, demat/depository services, electronic fund transfer system, new pension system, retail sale of gold coins, and safe deposit lockers services. The bank offers production credit loans, investment credit loans, internet banking, mobile banking, and other services.

Having a great reputation and wide network, the bank is also suffering from some of the weaknesses. The points observed during the study are presented in the following lines with suggestions.

Active Participation of Bank Employees

It is found that, in the most of SBH branches employees are not treating customers well and no cordial relations between employees and customers. There is an opinion in minds of customers that the bank official are giving high priority to the wealthy and high end customers.

The employees of the bank should realise and ensure that providing the right service at right time only satisfy the requirements of the customers. It is the duty of every employee working in the bank. Even, illiterate or less educated customers visit the bank, for their needs, employees should treat them with courtesy and smiling face.

May I Help You Counter

All the public sector banks have the main drawback is not having front office employee to receive customers and explain about the bank's services and right person to approach for their transactions.

Bank should open May I Help You Counter and appoint a right person who has much patience in treating illiterate rural customers. This counter reduces the burden of other employees, saves the time and encourages speedy transactions.

Bank Timings

Most of the customers particularly business and employees are facing the problem of bank timing. Present bank timings are not convenient to these people.

Bank business hours must be convenient to all type of customers. Most of the business people and employees visit the bank after 4.00 pm. So, majority of the customers are seeking extension of bank timings. Bank officials should look into the possibilities to extend the bank timings.

Well-designed Infrastructure and Products

Poor infrastructure facilities and traditional products are observed in SBH bank in rural. Old and low configured computers and outdated equipments are maintained in many branches.

Required infrastructure facilities should be well equipped in the banks in rural areas. It should look a modern and elegant and exhibit complete professionalism. The bank should install high configured computers to attend the customers immediately. In rural areas also banks should introduce online business transactions in all branches. The bank should introduce innovative and advanced services continuously as per needs of different kinds of customers like farmers, artisans, employees, business people, SHGs, students and segment the customers as age, gender, occupation, income etc., to satisfy the expectations of the customers.

Create Awareness about Services and Products offered by the Banks

Majority of SBH bank customers in the rural areas do not have sufficient knowledge about services and products that are being offered by the bank. They do not know the usage of the modern services like e-banking, mobile banking, EFT, tele banking, credit cards etc.

For this, banks should conduct awareness programmes frequently to create awareness about the services and explain the utilisation of those services and products that are offered by banks. This knowledge helps the customers to choose the product or service which satisfies their needs and to recommend their relatives and friends.

Customer Friendly System

It is also observed that there is very lengthy process to complete the transactions particularly to farmers and rural business people. 7-10 days are required to open a account in the bank. Bank is demanding many documents to open a account and to receive the benefit from the bank.

Customers in urban or rural areas do not like lengthy and complex process of transactions. This damages the goodwill of the bank. Thus, the system in the bank should be simple and customers' friendly. The bank should provide complete information to the customers in clear and in regional/local language.

Sufficient Number of Employees

The biggest problem of SBH bank is lack of sufficient number employees members. Most of the employees are unwilling to work in rural branches. Due to this reason, customers have to wait for long time. With this, bank is unable to provide the services at right time to its customers.

To fill this gap, banks should appoint right number of employees and encourage them, by offering extra benefits, to work in rural bank branches.

Facilities and Amenities in the Banks

In most of SBH bank branches, during the study period, it is found that lack of proper facilities and amenities like 'drinking water, seating arrangements, suggestion and complaint box, information about the services and working hours etc.

In the highly competitive world, banks should focus their attention on customers' satisfaction. It is the key factor to survive in the long run. Banks should provide facilities like drinking water, seating arrangements, proper lighting, sufficient floor area, proper display of boards, display of information of about the available services and service timings etc. With these facilities amenities customers feel comfort at the time of transaction.

Separate Counters

SBH bank is a public sector bank, serving for long and well known to all types of people. The government benefits are offered through this bank, particularly. It is common that customers visit this bank for their financial needs are very high in number. It is observed that there is only one counter in the bank which is not sufficient to meet the floating of customers. Customers are feeling very difficult to make transactions with the bank.

It is observed in many banks, during the first ten days of the month, customers feel very discomfort in the banks because of single counters. First ten days are busy days; the bank should open extra counters for SHGs and old people to serve the rush in time.

Illiterate Customers and Language Problem

Rural customers especially farmers and SHGs are illiterates. They do not know how to fill the vouchers and applications. It is very difficult to them to fill all the vouchers and applications. They disturb the bank employees and request them to fill the vouchers. Due to the busy work employees reject their plea. It leads to contradiction between employees and customers.

Bank officials should nominate a separate employee to assist in filling the applications. Bank should print all the vouchers and applications in regional language. With this, the problem may be reduced up to some extent.

6.18.2 Suggestions–TGB

The Bank was established by amalgamating four RRB's Sponsored by State Bank of Hyderabad, viz. (1) Sri Saraswathi Grameena Bank, Adilabad (2) Sri Satavahana Grameena Bank, Karimnagar (3) Sri Rama Grameena Bank, Nizamabad and (4) Golconda Grameena Bank, Ranga Reddy (Hyderabad) with an aggregate network of 330 branches. Branch Network is spread in the five districts of Telangana Region in the state of Telangana.

The bank offers accounts and deposits, savings accounts, current accounts, term deposits, home loans, personal and educational loan, gold loans and others. It provides cheque collection policy, electronic fund transfer system (limited), and safe deposit lockers services. The bank is providing agricultural loans particularly to rural farmers.

It is the specialised bank in providing credit to agricultural and allied activities. It is offering transparent and efficient banking services at a reasonable cost and ensuring 100 per cent financial inclusion. Its services in rural aim at empowerment of rural customers, promote Self Help Group (SHGs) movement with special emphasis on women. Thus, it is earning continuous profits by having a healthy business mix and becoming one of the leading banks among the RRBs.

Though, the banks functions are efficient, the bank suffers from some lacunas. Some of the important points observed in TGB are presented in the following paragraphs following with suggestions.

Well-designed Infrastructure and Products

Poor infrastructure facilities and traditional products are observed in TGB bank. Old furniture and low configured computers and outdated equipments are observed in many branches.

Required infrastructure facilities should be well equipped in the banks in rural areas. It should look a modern and elegant and exhibit complete professionalism. The bank should install high configured computers to attend the customers immediately. In rural areas also banks should introduce online business transactions in all branches. The bank should introduce innovative and advanced services continuously as per needs of different kinds of customers like farmers, artisans, employees, business people, SHGs, students and segment the customers as age, gender, occupation, income etc., to satisfy the expectations of the customers.

Illiterate Customers

Rural customers especially farmers and SHGs are illiterates. They do not know how to fill the vouchers and applications. It is very difficult to them to fill all the vouchers and applications. They disturb the bank employees and request them to fill the vouchers. Due to the busy work employees reject their plea. It leads to contradiction between employees and customers.

Bank officials should appoint a separate employees to assist in filling the applications. Bank should print all the vouchers and applications in regional language. With this, the problem may be reduced up to some extent.

ATMs

TGB is not offering ATM services. Most of the bank customers are demanding the ATM facility and issue debit card.

ATM is the modern and required facility to bank customers helps to withdraw the needed amount at anytime and anywhere. It reduces the customers and work burden to the bank employees. Bank officials are required to look into the issue and establish the ATMs which are more useful to both customers and bank employees.

Create Awareness about Services and Products offered in the Banks

Though official of TGB are conducting meetings with their customers, still, majority of customers do not have sufficient knowledge about services and products that are being offered by the bank. They do not know the usage of the modern services like e-banking, mobile banking, EFT, etc.

For this, bank officials should explain customers about the availability of and educate them how to utilise those services and products that are being offered by the bank. This knowledge helps the customers to choose the right product or service which satisfies their needs and to recommend their relatives and friends.

Customer Friendly System

It is also observed that there is very lengthy process to complete the transactions particularly to farmers and rural business people. Bank is demanding many documents to open a account and to receive the benefit from the bank.

Customers in urban or rural areas do not like lengthy and complex process of transactions. This damages the goodwill of the bank. Thus, the system in the bank should be simple and customers' friendly. The bank should provide complete information to the customers in clear and in regional/local language.

Sufficient Number of Employees

The biggest problem of TGB bank is lack of sufficient number employees members. Most of the employees are unwilling to work in rural branches. Due to this reason, customers have to wait for long time. With this, bank is unable to provide the services at right time to its customers.

To fill this gap, banks should appoint right number employees and encourage them, by offering extra benefits, to work in rural bank branches.

Facilities and Amenities in the Banks

In most of TGB bank branches, during the study period, it is found that lack of proper facilities and amenities like 'drinking water, toilets, seating arrangements, suggestion and complaint box, information about the services and working hours etc.

In the highly competitive world, banks should focus their attention on customers' satisfaction. It is the key factor to survive in the long run. Banks should provide facilities like drinking water, seating arrangements, proper lighting, sufficient floor area, proper display of boards, display of information of about the available services and service timings etc. With these facilities amenities customers feel comfort at the time of transaction.

Separate Counters

TGB bank is a public sector bank, serving for long and well known to all types of rural people. The government offer benefits to farmers, rural artisans and SHGs through this bank also. It is common that customers visit this bank for their financial needs are very high in number. It is observed that there is only one counter in the bank which is not sufficient to meet the floating of customers. Customers are feeling very difficult to make transactions with the bank.

It is observed in many banks, during the first ten days of the month, customers feel very discomfort in the banks because of single counters. First ten days are busy days; the bank should open extra counters for SHGs and old people to serve the rush in time.

6.18.3 Suggestions-HDFC Bank

HDFC bank is the second largest private banking sector in India located in 2171cities, having 3403 branches and 11256 ATM's as on 31st March 2014.

HDFC Bank Limited (HDFC) offers a wide range of financial and banking products and services to individuals, retail customers and corporate clients. It offers checking accounts, loans, cards, insurance, investments, private banking and forex services. The bank undertakes trading operations on the proprietary account, foreign exchange operations, and derivatives trading both on the proprietary account and customer flows.

The bank's ATM card is compatible with all domestic and international Visa/Master card, Visa Electron/ Maestro, Plus/cirus and American Express. This is one reason for HDFC cards to be the most preferred card for shopping and online transactions. HDFC bank has the high degree of customer satisfaction when compared to other banks in India.

Though the bank has the high degree of customers' satisfaction and high reputation in the banking industry, this bank also suffers from some weaknesses. The following are important observations during the study presented in the following paragraphs.

Location problem

The most important drawback of the bank is location. Bank branches are located far from the busy place. It becomes very difficult to customers to visit the bank.

Bank officials should take proper steps in deciding the location of the branch at time of starting new branches. If the bank is well located, the business of the bank highly increases and it is mostly convenient to all types of customers.

No Proper Place for Waiting

Another noteworthy point to consider that there is no proper place or sitting arrangement is available to customers who visit the bank. The bank is highly congested, and customers are feeling very discomfort while transacting.

HDFC Bank officials have to focus on the place of the bank and try to needed arrangements for customers' waiting.

The bank focuses mostly on high end (wealthy) customers

The greatest criticism, was observed during the study, on the bank is that the bank gives high priority to wealthy customers.

All type of customers visit the banks as per their financial needs and capabilities. Banks should give the equal preference to all types of customers. Higher authorities should consider the issue and instruct all the employees to treat the customers equally.

Account Opening Charges

Comparing to the public sector banks; cost of account opening is high in private sector banks. HDFC bank is not exception to this. With this rural customers are not showing much interest to open the account with the banks. So, bank doesn't have strong presence in rural areas.

In rural areas people are not so wealthy and not financially able to open an account by paying high amount. Bank officials should look into the possibilities to reduce the amount that equal to public sector banks.

No. of Bank Branches

Bank branches in rural are very less in number as compared to public sector banks. So, HDFC bank cannot enjoy the full advantage of the rural market. In general, rural people are extreme loyal in terms of banking services, if sufficient services are provided.

The bank has to try to utilise the advantages of the rural market by opening more branches in potential rural areas. Bank officials should educate the rural customers about the advanced services that are offering by the bank and explain them make use of those services for their benefit.

High Transaction Costs

Majority of the customers expressed the opinion that the transaction cost is very high and transaction includes hidden charges, as compared to the public sector banks. In general, business people and employees are the main customers of the bank. In a month, they transact with the bank above 10 times.

HDFC bank official have to reduce the transaction costs by avoiding hidden charges. With this no. of transactions will be increased and business of the bank also be expanded.

6.18.4 General Suggestions

Introduction of Plastic Money in Rural

The banks should introduce plastic currency (debit cards and credit cards) in the rural areas also for accurate transactions. With the introduction of plastic money, the work load of the bank will be reduced and all transactions will be safe and accurate. Usage of plastic money increases the revenue to the government. So, needed steps to be taken to create awareness about the usage of cards and popularise the plastic money in the rural areas also.

Security at ATMs

The most important point, during the study, is observed that majority number of bank ATMs is not properly protected. There is no proper place to transact with ATMs and there is no availability of security person at ATMs.

Officials of banks should consider the issue and provide sufficient protection at ATMs. It is highly important and immediate attention is required.

Sanitary Facilities

During the study, it is observed that no bank is providing sanitary facilities to their customers. Customers are feeling very discomfort for this. For customers' convenience, an appropriate number of sanitary conveniences (toilets facility) must be provided, and should be adequately ventilated, lit and kept clean, separately for male and females. Bank officials should focus on this issue and provide adequate toilets and washing facilities for their customers.

Customised Service

Customer is the most important person who gives the choice to serve him. Banks should offer services to him exactly what he requires. This type of customised services will increase the image of the bank. The bank should render services as per the needs of different segment of customers like age, gender, occupation, income etc., particularly in rural areas.

Receiving Complaints

The bank officials should feel that the complaint is an opportunity to recollect and rectify their mistakes. Complaint and suggestion box must be kept at visible and convenient place. Required time and free should be given to the customers to express their opinions about bank transactions. The managers welcome the complaints from the customers in positive manner. Mobile numbers of bank branch managers and concerned authorities to be displayed well, to make convenient, to the customers and invite complaints.

Grievance Handling

The bank should effectively handle the customers' queries and complaints. Managers should personally take the responsibility for redressing customers' grievances. Managers should conduct meetings once in a month with the customers and motivate employees to handle the customers' problems at most polite way.

6.19 Conclusions

Prior to the financial sector reforms, public sector banks played a dominant role and private sector and foreign banks were not so popularised. LPG (liberalisation, privatisation and globalisation) opened the banking sector doors to private and foreign banks in the economy. This has created a competitive market in the banking industry and provided customers of a bank with a wide range of services and products. Now, it becomes inevitable to all types of banks to focus on customer satisfaction by providing service quality to maintain customer base.

The efficiency of a bank is measured based upon how best it delivers the services to its customers. In order to survive in the present competitive environment, banks are now required to concentrate to introduce innovative services and improvement of service delivery by adopting advanced technology. To attract and retain the customers, banks should provide needed facilities and amenities, which play a key role in customer satisfaction, and give much priority to the factors that have been highlighted in the present study.

It can be concluded that public sector bank (SBH), private sector bank (HDFC) and rural rank (TGB) lack in creating awareness, to the rural customers, about availability services in the banks. This is the reason why rural customers are unable to utilise the services properly that are being providing by the banks. So, it is suggested that banks should conduct frequent awareness programmes on services or products that are offered by the banks.

Banks should introduce new services or products to accommodate the requirements of different category of rural customers. While launching new products the customer must be made aware about the quality of customised services.

In order to differentiate themselves in the highly competitive marketplace, banks are driving for service excellence by continuously improving their service quality. Growth and value creation have become the dominant subject matter and human interactions between banks and customers are becoming the centre of attention of value creation. Therefore, it becomes critical point on the development of customer–employee (service provider) relationships through interaction and dialogue. These relationships usually develop at the service encounter between customers and frontline employees. Interactions between customers and employees are thus central point for value creation. Due to the fact that employees' attitudes and their behaviour at the service encounter can positively or negatively influence customers' perceptions of service quality, it is important that banks should focus their employees on ensuring that such service encounters are delivered in a reliable and consistent manner. It is observed during the study that private banks and rural banks are maintaining effective customer relationships during the banking transactions. It is also suggested that the public sector banks should give needed priority to the service encounters.

Service quality is one of the most useful strategic tools to get a competitive advantage over the competitors. Because of the globalisation and entry of foreign banks, the competition in the banking industry has strengthened. 24x7 banking now become a reality. Recognition of service quality now acts as a competitive weapon. It is found that customers are dissatisfied with respect of 'tangibles' and 'empathy' dimension as the twin concept that is lacking in the banks. Analysis of average gap score reveals that, Regional Rural Bank (TGB) has the low gap score for four dimensions reliability, responsiveness, assurance and empathy as compared to SBH and HDFC banks.

It is suggested that the public sector bank (SBH) and private sector bank (HDFC) in rural should generate a strong confidence among the customers that its primary objective can be achieved through the provision of a good **Service Quality** level accurately and timely with a strong performance.

It is necessary for public and private sector banks in rural to pay more attention to development and provision of commercial services and dimensions of service quality that enables these banks to compete continuously and provide excellent services to rural people.

With this, it is concluded that banks should aim at increasing the quality of services with a strategic vision to increase the satisfaction of customers. This will not be achieved unless banks can realise the effective factors on understanding the service quality and explaining appropriate strategies for each of these factors.

6.20 Utility of the Study

The present study "Impact of Service Delivery by Banks in Rural Areas" is greatly considerable in various ways to bankers, policy-makers and researchers. To the bankers, the findings and results that will be reported in this study will provide a more reliable scientific measure and perspective for describing and evaluating the opinions of their customers towards service quality and satisfaction with the services they delivered. It provides an invaluable source of information that brings to limelight the customers' perceptions against their banks where they operate accounts. It will also serve the bankers useful information in respect of customers' awareness about the services offered by the banks. This study highlights the gaps of service quality that are offering by the banks in rural areas. The results of this study, about customers' expectations and perceptions of service quality, provide some insights on how customers rate the service quality variables of a particular bank. This study helps bankers in identifying gaps in delivery of service, and actions needed to bridge the gaps. Suggestions are mostly useful to policy-makers to improve the delivery of service quality and increase the satisfaction levels of customers, if they consider.

This study results are highly useful, as a guide, to the future researchers. This useful beckon obviously will instill confidence and show a path towards excellence in research.

6.21 Limitations of the Study

The present study like other research studies is similar and allied lines cannot claim to be a perfect one in all respects. Although every effort was made to conduct the study as rigorously as possible, certain limitations were unavoidable as indicated bellow.

1. First and foremost limitation of the study is that it has taken only three banks for deeper analysis. In view of this, it cannot claim to be a comprehensive study concerning all banks in the sector.
2. Though the analysis of selected banks is for fairly a log period of time i.e. five and half years (from June 2010 to Dec. 2015), it does not capture the whole period from their inception.
3. (A) The size of sample respondents is only 630. Hence the findings usually cannot be generalised to the populations or community. (B) This study is limited to only six mandals and does not cover entire mandals in the district.

4. Only five factors of service quality (RATER)* and 20 variables were considered. Hence it is considered another limitation.
5. Required primary data is gathered by interviewing the respondents randomly selected in rural areas. Results reflect opinions of respondents. Data may not be robust enough to explain complex issues.

   (*R-Reliability, A-Assurance, T-Tangibles, E-Empathy and R-Responsiveness)
6. It may not be totally correct to make generalisation on the basis of limited study but its findings and conclusions can be of much generalised to use.

6.22 Scope for Future Research

The present research study "Impact of Service Quality Delivery by Commercial Banks in Rural Areas" (A Comparative Study of Selected banks in Karimnagar District) by using SERVQUAL analysis is restricted to Karimnagar district in Telangana State and also to certain banks in public sector (SBH), private sector (HDFC) and regional rural bank (TGB) banks. This research provides some important insights into service quality and customer satisfaction in public sector, private sector and regional rural banks. Still there is an opportunity to extend these findings to gain more comprehensive understanding of service quality and customer satisfaction of commercial banks.

1. The similar study can also undertake as a future research by expanding to some other districts other than Karimnagar and by selecting some other or more number of commercial banks.
2. A state-wise study can be conducted on Service Quality of Public and Private Sector Banks to understand quality of banking services.
3. A study can be conducted to analyse the service delivery practices by commercial banks.
4. A study can be conducted to evaluate the association between the Service Quality and Performance of Banks.
5. A comparative study on service quality of Commercial Banks by taking old and new generation private banks.

It is expected that the future research may highlight the service quality in banking industry in total, comparative analysis on SERVQUAL and SERVPERF scores in different sectors of banking industry. It is also expected that the future research may provide required directions to analyse the reasons for variations in SERVQUAL and SERVPERF scores among customers in the banking industry.

Bibliography

Books

1. Akbar, S. A. *Bank Management - Some Issues* (Vol. 4). IOB MNR.
2. *An Overview of Banking.* (2006). Hyderabad: ICFAI University Press.
3. *Banking Services Operations.* (2006). Hyderabad: ICFAI University Press.
4. Bhattachrjee, C. (2007). *Service Sector Management.* Mumbai: Jaico Publishing House.
5. Chakrabarti, M. (2011). *Rural Banking in India.* New Delhi: New Century Publications.
6. Chrstopher Lovelock, J. W. (2005). *Services Marketing People, Technology, Strategy.* New Delhi: Pearson Education.
7. D.P. Apte. (2009). *Stattistical Tools for Managers - Using MS Excel.* New Delhi: Excel Books.
8. David, A; Aaker, V. G. (2002). *Marketing Research.* New York: John Wiley & Sons.
9. Desai, V. (2007). *The Indian Financial System and Development.* Bangalore: Himalaya Publishing House.
10. Dr S. Sahajan. (2006). *Research Methods for Management.* Mumbai: Jaico Publishing House.
11. Gomez, C. (2008). *Financial Markets, Institutions and Financial Services.* New Delhi: Prentice Hall of India.
12. Gordon, M. A. (2001). *Banking and Financial Systems* (1st ed.). Hyderabad: Himalaya Publishing House.
13. Jha, S. (2007). *Services Marketing.* Bangalore: Himalaya Publishing House.
14. Joshi, D. P. (2011). *The Finanical Inclusion Imperative and Sustainable Approaches.* New Delhi: Cambridge University Press India Private Ltd.
15. Kennenth, E. Clow, D. L. (2004). *Services Marketing Operations, Management and Strategy.* New Delhi: Biztzntra Publishers.
16. Kothari, C. (2005). *Research Methodology Methods and Techniques.* New Delhi: New Age International Publishers.
17. Kumar, R. (2006). *Services Marketing-Indian Perspective.* New Delhi: Excel Books.

18. M.Y. Khan. (2006). *Financial Services.* New Delhi: TMH Publishing Company.
19. Mishra, S. S. (2005). *Indian Banking System.* New Delhi: Mahamaya Publishing House.
20. Mishra, S. S. (2005). *Indian Publishing System.* New Delhi: Mahamaya Publishing House.
21. *Money and Banking.* (2005). Hyderabad: ICFAI University Press.
22. N. Rajsekhar. (2004). *Banking in the New Millennium.* Hyderabad: ICFAI University Press.
23. Nargundkar, R. (2004). *Services Marketing - Text and Cases.* New Delhi: Tata McGraw Hill Publishing Company.
24. Nimit Chowdhary, M. C. (2005). *Text Book of Marketing Services: The Indian Experience.* New Delhi: Macmillan India Ltd.
25. Paul, S. M. (2000). *Banking and Financial Services.* Hyderabad: Kalyani Publishers.
26. Puri, M. A. (2009). *Indian Economy* (27 ed.). New Delhi: Himalaya Publishing House.
27. R. Paneerselvam. (2005). *Research Methodology.* New Delhi: Prentice Hall India Private Ltd.
28. Rao, K. (2005). *Banking-New Challenges.* Hyderabad: The ICFAI University Press.
29. Rao, N. (2005). *Indian Financial Markets-Emerging Scenario.* Hyderabad: ICFAI University Press.
30. *Rural Banking and Micro Finance.* (2006). Hyderabad: ICFAI University Press.
31. Sarkar, V. A. (1999). *Banking Law and Practice* (18th ed.). New Delhi: Sultan Chand and Sons.
32. Sarkar, P.N., V. A. (1999). *Banking Law and Practice* (18th ed.). New Delhi: Sultan Chand and Sons.
33. Sundaram, R. D. (2010). *Indian Economy* (61st ed.). New Delhi: S.Chand.
34. Uppal, R. (2008). *Financial Sector of India - Emerging Challenges.* New Delhi: New Century Publications.
35. Zeithaml, VA, G. D. (2009). *Services Marketing.* New Delhi: Tata McGraw Hill.
36. Hand Book of Statistics, Kaimnagar District 2005, 2009 and 2011.
37. District Annual Credit Plans 2005 to 2014.

Journals

1. Ahmed*, H. U. (2008). "An Empirical Analysis of the Determinants", *Pakistan Economic and Social Review*, *46* (2), 147-160.
2. Almossawi, M. (2001). Bank Selection Criteria Employed by College Students in. *International Journal of Bank*, *3* (19), 115-25,.
3. Allred, A.T. and Addams, H.L., (2000), "Service Quality at Banks and Credit Unions: What They Do Their Custoemers Say?" *Managing Service Quality,* Vol. 10, No. 1, pp. 52-60.

4. Angur et al (1999), "Service Quality in the Banking Industry: An Assessment in Developing Economy", *International Journal of Bank Marketing*, Vol. 17, No. 3, pp. 116-123.
5. Anwar, S.A. 2003, Testing Marketing Orientation of Banks Manager in the Merging Economy of Brunei, *International Journal of Bank Marketing*, Vol. 21.
6. Asubonteng, P., Mccleary, K.J. amd Swan, J.E. (1996), "SERVQUAL Revisited: A Critical Review of Service Quality", *Journal of Service Marketing,* Vol. 10, No. 6, pp. 62-81.
7. Azouzi, D. (2009). The Adoption of Electronic Banking in Tunisia: An Exploratory Study. *Journal of Internet Banking and Commerce*, *14* (3), 1-11.
8. Babakus, E., and G.W. Boller (1992), An empirical assessment of the SERVQUAL scale, Journal of Business Research, Vol. 24, no. 3, pp. 253-268.
9. Bhatia, M. B. (2012, October). Assessment of Service Quality in Public and Private Sector Banks of India with Special Reference to Lucknow City. *International Journal of Scientific and Research Publications, 2*(10), 1-7.
10. Bhatia, M. B. (n.d.). Assessment of Service Quality in Public and Private Sector Banks of India with Special Reference to Lucknow City. *International Journal of Scientific and Research Publications, 2*(10), 1 - 7. Cicic M., B. N. (2004). Bank Selection Criteria Employed by.
11. Brown, S.W. and Bitner, M.J. (2007). Mandating a service revolution for marketing. in Lush, R.F. and Vargo, S.L.(Eds). *The Service-Dominant Logic of Marketing: Dialog, Debate and Directions* (pp. 393-405). Armonk, NY: M.E. Sharp.
12. Commercial Bank Selection. (2009). *European Journal of Economics, Finance and Administrative Sciences*, *1* (16), 263-73.
13. Cronin, J.J., and S.A. Taylor (1992), Measuring service quality: a re-examination and extension, Journal of Marketing, Vol. 56, no. 3, pp. 55-68.
14. Debasish, S.S. (2002). Service Quality in Commercial Banks: A Comparative Analysis of Selected banks in India. *Indian Journal of Marketing*, Vol. 1, No. 1, pp. 3-10.
15. Desta, T. S. (2011, November). Perceived Quality of Services Rendered by Commercial Banks: A Case Study of State Bank of. *International Journal of Research in Commerce and Management, 2*(11), 26 - 36.
16. Dhandabani, S. (2010, July-Dec.). Linkage between Service Quality and Customers Loyalty in Commercial Banks. *International Journal of Management & Strategy, 1*(1), 1-22.
17. Dr Mohmod Jasim Alsamydia, D. O. (2012). The factors Influencing consumers' satisfaction and continuity to deal with E-Banking Services in Jordan. *Global Journal of Managment and Business Research*, *12* (14), 129-141.
18. Dr Naveen Kumar and Dr V.K. Gangal (2011), held a study on Customer Satisfaction in New Generation Banks (A Case Study of HDFC Bank), International Refereed Research Journal, Vol. II, Issue 4, Oct. 2011, pp. 177–186.
19. Dr Rupa Rathee, D. A. (2014, July). To Identify Service Quality Gaps in Banking Sector: A Study of Private Banks. *International Journal of Emerging Research in Management and Technology,* 3(7), 101-106.

20. Duncan, E. and Elliot, G. (2004), "Efficiency, Customer Service and Financial Performance among Australian Financial Institutions", *The International Journal of Bank Marketing,* Vol. 22, No. 5, pp. 319-342.
21. Fatoki, C. C. (2011). Factors Influencing the Choice of Commercial Banks by *International Journal of Business and Management*, *6* (6), 66-76.
22. Gefan, D. (2002), "Customer Loyalty in e–Commerce", *Journal of the Association of Information System,* Vol. 3, No. 1, pp. 27-51.
23. Hung, Y. H. (2003). Service Quality Evaluation of Service Quality Performance Matrix. *Total Quality Management & Business Excellence, 14*(1), 79-89.
24. Hung, Y.H., Huang, M.L. and Chen, K.S. (2003). Service quality evaluation by service quality performance matrix. *Total quality Management & Business Excellence*, 14(1), 79-89.
25. Jain, V. G. (2012). "Customer Perception on Service Quality in Banking Sector". With Special Reference to Indian Private Banks in Moradabad Region. *International Journal of Research in Finance and Marketing (IJRFM), 2*(2), 597-610.
26. Jyoti Agarwal (2012), Customer satisfaction in Indian Banking Services (A study in Aligarh District) International Journal of Computing and Business Research (IJCBR) ISSN (Online): 2229-6166 Volume 3, Issue 1, January 2012, pp. 1-14.
27. Kangis, P. and Voukelatos, V. (1997), "Private and Public Banks: A Comparison of Customer Expectations and Perceptions", *International Journal of Bank Marketing,* Vol. 15, No. 7, pp. 279-27.
28. Kotler, P. (2003). Marketing Management. NJ: Englewood Cliffs: Prentice-Hall.
29. Kumar et al (2009), "Determining the Relative Importance of Critical Factors in Delivering Service Quality of Banks: An Application of Dominance Analysis SERVQUAL Model, *Managing Service Quality,* 19 (2), pp. 211-228.
30. Kumar, M, K. F. (2010). Comparative Evaluation of Critical. *International, 27* (3), 351-377.
31. Lasser et al (2000), "Service Perspectives and Satisfaction in Private Banking", *Jouranl of Services Marketing,* Vol.14, No. 3, pp. 244-271.
32. Lewis, B. (1989). Quality in Service Sector - A Review. *Interntional Journal of Brand Marketing, 7*(5), 4 - 12.
33. Malhotra, M., and Arora, S. (1999), Customer Satisfaction – A Comparative Analysis of Public and Private Sector Banks, *Abhigyan*, Vol.17, No. 3, pp. 19-30.
34. Maya Basant Lohani, D. P. (2012, October). Assessment of Service Quality in Public and Private Sector Banks of India with Special Reference to Lucknow City. *International Journal of Scientific and Research Publications, 2*(10), 1- 7.
35. M.K. Rampal and S.L. Gupta, "Service Marketing–Concepts, Applications and Cases", Galgotia Publishing Company, New Delhi, 2010, pp. 289 - 291.
36. Mishra J.K. and Jain M. (2006-07). 'Constituent Dimensions of Customer Satisfaction: A Study of Nationalised and Private Banks'. Prajnan. 35(4). 390-398.

37. Mohamed Siddik and Dr M. Selvachandra (2011), A Study on Customer Satisfaction towards E-banking services of ICICI bank in Chennai City, IJEMR - September 2011-Vol. 1, Issue 4.
38. Mokhlis, S., M. N. (2010). Ethnicity and Choice Criteria in Retail. *International Journal of Business and, 5* (6), 258-270.
39. Mokhlis, S., S. H. (2009). Commercial Bank Selection. *European Journal of Economics, Finance and Administrative Sciences, 1* (16), 263-73.
40. Mylonakis, J. (2007). A Research Study of Customer Preferences in the Home. *International Research Journal of Finance and Economics* (10), 153-66,.
41. Newman, K., 2001. Interrogating SERVQUAL: a critical assessment of service quality measurement in a high street retail bank. *International Journal of Bank Marketing*, 19(3), pp. 126-139.
42. Olawale Fatoki, C. C. (2011). Factors Influencing the Choice of Commercial Banks by *International Journal of Business and Management, 6* (6), 66-76.
43. HYPERLINK "http://www.jstor.org/pss/1251430" \t "_blank" \o "A conceptual model of service quality and its implications for future research" Parasuraman, VA Zeitham and LL Berry, (1985), *"A conceptual model of service quality and its implications for future research" The Journal of Marketing*, 1985,
44. Puja Khatri and Yukti Ahuja (2008), Study of customer satisfaction in public sector and private sector banks of India, International Journal of Engineering and Management Sciences (I.J.E.M.S.), Vol. 1(1), pp. 42-51.
45. Ravichandran, K., Mani, B. T., Kumar, S.A. amd Prabhakarn, S. (2010), "Influence of Service Quality on Customer Satisfaction: Application of SERVQUAL Model, *International Journal of Business and Management,* Vol. 5, No. 4, pp. 117-124.
46. R.K. Uppal (2009), "Customer Service in Indian Commercial Banks: An Empirical Study", Asia Pacific Journal of Social Sciences, Vol. I, No. 1, Jan-June 2009. pp. 127-141.
47. Saima, H. A. (2008). An Empirical Analysis of the Determinants. *Pakistan, 46* (2), 147-155.
48. Santhiyavalli, D. M. (2011, September). Customer's perception of service quality of State Bank of India - A Factor Analysis. *International Journal of Management & Business Studies, 1*(3), 78-84.
49. Sharma, R. (2010). Bank Selection Criteria Employed by MBA Students in Delhi: An Empirical. *Journal of Business Studies, 1* (2), 56-69.
50. Siddique, M. N.-E.-A. (2012). Bank Selection Influencing Factors: A Study on Customer. *Asian Business Review, 1* (1), 80-87.
51. Soteriou, A.C. and Stavrinides, Y. (2000), "An Internal Customer Service Quality Data Envelopment Analysis Model for Bank Branches", *International Journal of Bank Marketing,* Vol. 18, No. 5, pp. 246-52.
52. Sureshchandar, G.S., Rajendran, C., Kamalanabhan, T.J. (2001), "Customer perceptions of service quality – a critique", *Total Quality Management*, Vol. 12, pp. 111-24.

53. Tahir and Abu Bakar, (2007), "Service Quality Gap and Customers' Satisfactions of Commercial Banks in Malaysia", International Review of Business Research Papers Vol. 3, No. 4, pp. 327-336.

54. Vijay, M. Kumbhar (2011), Factors Affecting on Customers' Satisfaction: An Empirical investigation of ATM Service, International Journal of Business Economics and Management Research, Volume 2, Issue 3 (March, 2011), pp. 144–156.

55. Vimi Jham and Kaleem Mohd Khan, (2008), Customer Satisfaction in the Indian Banking Sector–A Study, IIMB Management Review, Volume 20, Number 1, pp. 55-67.

56. Virparia, V. (2013). Study on Factors Affecting Customer. *Golden Research Thoughts*, *2* (8).

57. Wang, Y., H. and (2003). The Antecedents of Service Quality and Product Quality and their Influences on Bank Reputation: Evidence from Banking Industry in China. *Managing Service Quality, 13*(1), 72-83.

58. Wang.Y. Lo H and Huj, Y. (2003). The Antecedents of Service Quality and Product Quality and Their Influence on Bank Reputation: Evidence from Banking Industry in China. *Managing Service Quality,* 72-83.

59. W/mariam, G. (2011). *Bank Selection Decision: Factors.* Project Report for Master of Science in Accounting and Finance, Addis Ababa University, *Department of Accounting and Finance.*

60. Woodside et.al. (1989), Linking Service Quality, Customer Satisfaction and Behavioural Intension", Journal of Health Care Marketing, Vol. 9, No. 4, pp. 5-17.

61. Yavas et al, (1997), "Service Quality Assessment: A comparison of Turkish and German Bank Customers", *Cross Culture Management: An International Journal,* Vol.14, No. 2, pp. 161-168.

62. Zahari, W., Yusoff, W., and Ismail, M. (2008). FM-SERVQUAL: a new approach of service quality measurement framework in local authorities. *Journal of Corporate Real Estate*, 10(2), 130-144.

Websites

1. "http://www.sbh.com" www.sbh.com
2. "http://www.hdfcbank.com" www.hdfcbank.com
3. "http://www.nabard.org" www.nabard.org
4. "http://www.rbi.org.in" www.rbi.org.in
5. "http://www.sbhyd.com" www.sbhyd.com
6. HYPERLINK "http://tgbhyd.in" http://tgbhyd.in
7. "http://karimnagar.nic.in" http://karimnagar.nic.in

Annexure - I

Questionnaire for Customers Impact of Service Delivery by Banks in Rural Areas

-by ***E. Hari Prasad Sharma,***
Assoc. Professor in Management,
Vaageswari Group of Colleges, Karimnagar.

Dear Sir,

I, E. Hari Prasad, Ph.D., scholar at Dr. B. R. Ambedkar Open University, Hyderabad. I am conducting a survey on "Service Quality by Banks in Rural Areas", and I would like to know your opinion about the level of your expectations and perceptions of rural banking products and services in the Karimnagar District. It will be really helpful, if you can complete my 'service quality' questionnaire. There is no right or wrong answers; it is your views that are most important.

All data and information given by you will be kept at most confidential and utilised for academic purposes only and no names will be involved. Your co-operation is highly significant, as the results of this study will be used to develop new techniques in order to improve the rural banking products and services.

Thank you in advance for your time and consideration.

Section–A
Personal Information about Customers

1. Name of the Bank in you have a/c.
2. Place/Location of the Bank.
3. Gender of the Customer (Put Tick Mark in Appropriate Box)
   ☐ Male ☐ Female

4. What is your age?
   (a) 20 or less
   (b) 21-30
   (c) 31-40
   (d) 41-50
   (e) 51-60
   (f) 60 plus
5. What is your highest qualification?
   (a) Masters Degree
   (b) Graduation
   (c) Professional Degree (BE, B.Tech, MBA, B.Law)
   (d) Intermediate
   (e) S.S.C.
   (f) Less than S.S.C.
   (g) No Formal Education
6. What is your occupation?
   (a) Agriculture
   (b) Employee-Government/Private/Semi-government/Local Authority/Pvt. Sector
   (c) Profession – Business/Doctor/Lawyer/Consultant/Please Specify if others
   (d) Manual worker Retired
   (e) Housewife/ Househusband/ Student
   (f) Not employed other, specify..........................
   (g) Student
7. What is your gross annual income?
   (a) Less than ₹ 50,000
   (b) ₹ 50,001 to ₹ 1,00,000
   (c) ₹ 1,00,001 to ₹ 5,00,000
   (d) Above ₹ 5,00,000
8. What is your marital status? Married/Single
9. What banking services are you currently using?
   (a) Current Account
   (b) Savings Account
   (c) Investment Account

(d) Overdraft
(e) Personal Loan
(f) Debit card
(g) Credit card
(h) House Loan
(i) Mortgage Loan
(j) Other, please specify ....

10. How long have you been a customer of this bank?
    (a) Less than one year
    (b) One to three years
    (c) Three to Five years
    (d) More than Five years
11. How often do you visit your bank each month
    (a) One time or less
    (b) Two to Four times
    (c) Five to Ten times
    (d) More than Ten times
12. What purpose do you visit this bank frequently for?
    (a) Managing Saving a/c or Current a/c
    (b) Operating Loan a/c
    (c) Operate Safe Deposit Locker.
13. Please rank 1-11 to the following statements showing the reasons that influenced you to open account with this bank. (1 being most influencing factor)

Sl. No.	*Influencing Factors*	*Rank*
1	Place of the Bank Branch	
2	Banking Business Hours	
3	Employees Attitude/Behaviour	
4	Bank Advertisement in T.V.s/News Papers etc.	
5	Mobile Messages alerts	
6	References of friends/relatives	
7	Prompt Services of Bank	
8	Qualitative Services	
9	Value Added Services	
10	Less Transactions Cost.	
11	Govt. Benefit/Others	

Section–B
Services, Facilities and Amenities Provided by the Bank

1. Services

Please mention that the following services offered or not offered by the bank in which you are operating account. (Please put mark appropriate one)

Sl. No.	*Services*		*Offered*	*Not Offered*
	A. Accounts			
1	Saving Account			
2	Current Account			
3	Demat Account			
4	Safe Locker Facility			
5	Insurance Accounts			
	B. Loans			
6	Personal Loans			
7	House Loans			
8	Vehicle Loans			
8.1	Two Wheeler Loans			
8.2	Car Loan			
8.3	Commercial Vehicle Loan			
9	Agricultural Loans	Land Mortgage Loans		
		Seed Loans		
		Live Stock Loans		
		Farming Equipment Loans		
10	Education Loans			
11	Gold Loans			
12	Land Loans			
13	Mortgage Loans			
	C. Other Innovative Services			
14	Credit Card			
15	Debit Card (ATM Card)			
16	Smart Card			
17	Agri Card*			
18	Kisan Credit Card			
19	Internet Banking			
20	Tele Banking			
21	Mobile Banking			
22	Electronic Fund Transfer (EFT)			
	D. Others (Please Specify)			

2A. Service Encounters (Relationship between bank employees and customers). Please express the extent of to which you agree with the following statements about your relation with bank employees.

SA–Strongly Agree	A–Agree	N–Neutral	D–Disagree	SD–Strongly Disagree

Sl. No.	*Statements*	*SA*	*A*	*N*	*D*	*SD*
1	Front Office Employee (Receptionist) notices, welcomes and greets the customers.					
2	Receptionist asks customer May I Help You sir.					
3	Receptionist asks customer to be seated					
4	Required suggestion, help and cooperation are provided by the bank employees.					
5	Bank employees speak pleasantly with smiling face.					
6	Bank Employees are friendly with customers.					
7	Bank Employees are informative.					
8	It is easy to approach or meet Bank Manager or other superiors in the Bank.					
9	Bank Employees responds properly to the phone calls.					
10	Bank Employees shows reasonable interest in me as a customer.					
11	Bank Employees thanks me for transacting with them					
12	Bank employees handles any problems/interruptions efficiently.					
13	I enjoy myself dealing with the employees of this bank.					
14	I wish to continue my relationship with this bank for long.					

2B. Please specify the time taken by the bank to provide the needed service

Service Timings of Bank			
Sl. No.	*Service of Bank*	*Standard Time*	*Actual Time Taken*
1	Cash Receipt		
2	Cash Payment		
3	Issue of Draft		
4	Collection of Outstation Cheques		
5	Updating Pass Book		
6	Issue of Cheque Book	15	

3. Facilities and Amenities Provided by the Bank

In the success of banking, facilities and amenities provided by the bank to the customers play a vital role.

On the left hand side, IMPORTANCE of these services, and right hand side ACTUAL QUALITY of these services are given. Please rate these services provided by the bank.

Importance	*Score*	*Actual Quality*	*Score*
Very Important	5	Excellent	5
Important	4	Good	4
Some What Important	3	Fair	3
Not Very Important	2	Poor	2
Not at all Important	1	Very Poor	1

Please indicate the score (nos. assigned in the above table) against the statement at left and right sides of each statement.

Imporatnce	*Facilities and Ameneties*	*Actual Facility*
	Location of the Bank	
	Parking Facility	
	Information about working hours	
	Information about service timings	
	Availability of personal assistance/guidance	
	Display of identification boards at counters	
	May I Help You Counter	
	Proper Lighting	
	Information about available services and products	
	Electronic token number display and audio announcement system	
	Waiting Room/Place	
	ATM facility at the branch	
	Attractive Flooring	
	Drinking Water	
	A/C Facility	
	Dust Bins	
	Toilets Facility	
	Complaint and Suggestion Box	

Section–C
Customers' Quality Expectations

The present survey aims at taking your opinion about bank. Please show interest and spend few minutes of your valuable time to provide the extent to which you think bank should possess the following features. What we are interested in is a number that best shows your expectations about your bank offering banking services. Please put your ranking against the below expectations.

Sl. No.	Statements	Strongly Agree 5	Agree 4	Neutral 3	Disagree 2	Strongly Disagree 1
	A. TANGIBLES					
1	The Bank must possess the sophisticated and good looking infrastructure.					
2	Physical facilities at banks should be visual and attractive.					
3	Bank employees have to be in neat dress and appear dignified.					
4	Materials (statements or passbook) with bank should be visual and excellent.					
	B. RELIABILITY					
5	If the bank promises something, it will do.					
6	If customers have problems, the bank has to show sincere interest in solving them.					
7	The bank ought to perform the services at right time.					
8	The bank should provide service at the time it promises to do so.					
9	The Bank should keep accurate/error-free records.					
	C. RESPONSIVENESS					
10	Employees of the bank ought to inform customers exactly when service will be performed.					
11	The Bank employees ought to give excellent service to its customers					
12	The Bank employees must be willing to help the customers.					
13	The Bank employees should be always ready to respond to customers' requests.(x)					
	D. ASSURANCE					
14	The Bank employees should always try to infuse confidence in the customers.					
15	Customers (you) have to feel safe in transactions with the Bank's employees.					
16	The Bank employees always ought to be courteous and polite with customers.					
17	The Bank must possess employees have complete knowledge to answer queries of customers.					
	E. EMPATHY					
18	The Bank has to give individual attention to customers.					
19	The Bank operating hours must be convenient to all customers.					
20	Bank employees ought to understand the specific needs of their customers.					

Section–D
Customers' Perceived Quality

The following statements relate to your feelings about your bank (SBH/DGB/AB). Please show the interest and spend few minutes of your valuable time to provide the extent to which you think your bank should possess the following features which described in the statements. What we interested in is a number that best shows your perceptions about your bank offering banking services. Please put your ranking in respect of the below statements.

	Statements	Strongly Agree	Agree	Neutral	Disagree	Strongly Disagree
		5	4	3	2	1
	TANGIBLES					
1	My Bank has the sophisticated and good looking infrastructure.					
2	Physical facilities at my banks are visual and attractive.					
3	My Bank employees are in neat dress and appearing dignified.					
4	Materials (statements or passbook) with my bank are visual and excellent.					
	RELIABILTY					
5	If my bank promises something, it will certainly do.					
6	If customers have problems, my bank will show sincere interest in solving it.					
7	My bank performs the services at right time. As per time mentioned.					
8	My Bank provides service at the time it promises to do so.					
9	My Bank keeps accurate/error-free records.					
	RESPONSIVENESS					
10	Employees of my bank inform customers exactly when service will be performed.					
11	My Bank employees give excellent service to its customers					
12	My Bank employees are always willing to help customers.					
13	Bank employees always ready to respond to customers' requests.					
	ASSURANCE					
14	My Bank employees always try to instill confidence in customers.					
15	Customers (me) always feel safe in transactions with my bank's employees.					
16	My Bank employees always courteous and polite with customers.					
17	My Bank employees have complete knowledge to answer queries of customers.					
	EMPATHY					
18	My Bank gives individual attention to customers.					
19	My Bank operating hours is convenient to all the customers.					
20	Bank employees understand the specific needs of customers.					

Section–E
Overall Satisfaction of The Customer

1. The **overall service quality** of the **said** bank is (circle the number that best describes your feelings)

Very Good	*Good*	*Average*	*Poor*	*Very Poor*
5	4	3	2	1

2. The service quality of the said bank met my needs

Strongly Agree	*Agree*	*Neutral*	*Disagree*	*Strongly Disagree*
5	4	3	2	1

3. Please specify your grievances/complaints against the bank.
   1.______________________________
   2.______________________________
   3.______________________________
   4.______________________________
   5.______________________________

4. Please give your suggestions to improve the bank services.
   1.______________________________
   2.______________________________
   3.______________________________
   4.______________________________
   5.______________________________

5. Your **overall satisfaction** with the said bank (circle the number that best describes your feelings)

Very Satisfied	*Slightly satisfied*	*Neutral*	*Slightly unsatisfied*	*Very unsatisfied*
5	4	3	2	1

6. I would **recommend** the bank to my friends and relatives (Circle the number that best describes your feelings)

(Very High Probability)	*Probability*	*Neutral*	*Low Probability*	*(Very Low Probability)*
5	4	3	2	1

7. In future, I will **remain loyal** with the bank. (Circle the number that best describes your feelings)

(Very High Probability)	*Probability*	*Neutral*	*Low Probability*	*(Very Low Probability)*
5	4	3	2	1

Thanking You Very Much

(E. HARI PRASAD)

Index